World and Church

World and Church

EDWARD SCHILLEBEECKX

Translated by N. D. Smith

SHEED AND WARD · NEW YORK

© Sheed and Ward, Ltd. 1971

Originally published as *Wereld en Kerk,* Uitgeverij H. Nelissen
Bilthoven (Holland) , 1966

Nihil obstat: John M. T. Barton STD LSS *Censor*
Imprimatur: + Victor Guazzelli *Vicar General*
Westminister, 29 March 1971

Library of Congress Catalog Card Number: 78-103361

Standard Book Number: 8362-1351-3

Manufactured in the United States of America

CONTENTS

ABBREVIATIONS

AAS	*Acta Apostolicae Sedis*, Rome 1909–
Denz.	H. Denzinger, *Enchiridion Symbolorum, Definitionum, et Declarationum de Rebus Fidei et Morum*. Where two references are given, the first is to the new numbering of the 32nd and later editions and the second to the old numbering
Kath. Arch	*Katholiek Archief*
PG	*Patrologiae Cursus Completus, Series Graeca*, ed. J. P. Migne, Paris 1857–
PL	*Patrologiae Cursus Completus, Series Latina*, ed. J. P. Migne, Paris 1844–
RB	*Revue Biblique*, Paris 1892–
RSR	*Recherches de Science Religieuse*, Paris 1910–
I, II, III, IV Sent	Thomas Aquinas, *In Quattuor Sententiarum P. Lombardi Iibros*, I, II, III, IV
ST	Thomas Aquinas, *Summa Theologiae*
TT	*Tijdschrift voor Theologie*, Utrecht and Bruges, 1961–

World and Church

I

RELIGION AND THE WORLD: RENEWING THE FACE OF THE EARTH

A great deal has already been written, and arguments have long been conducted, about christian humanism, but it is doubtful whether man, despite his seeking, will ever pene-trate fully to the heart of this reality for the simple reason that he is here confronted, in the last resort, with a problem, the two terms of which merge into the mystery, on the one hand, of man's existence as spirit in the world and, on the other, of God's being God, the deeper mystery into which we have been allowed to enter through the mystery of Christ. Although it is, of course, impenetrable, a mystery does always have a nucleus of openness, of intelligibility—it always pre-sents itself to man's experience and reflection via conceptual, recognisable ideas which at least provide us with some perspective. In this way, we are able, within the mystery, to become more sharply conscious of its content, at least sufficiently conscious to be able to live from it. In this essay, I hope to make some contribution to our understanding of the mystery of christian humanism.

1. The challenge of the present situation ⟍
The polarity between christianity and the world is, in one form or another, as old as the christian religion itself. I am alluding here to the actual situation of the believing christian as man in the world. In its full proportions, this situation did not, however, become acutely problematical until our own times. Previously, the issue at stake was the relationship be-tween Greek philosophy and christian belief or the relation-ship between believing and knowing. Later, it was the rela-tionship between belief and positive science. Since the nineteenth century, however, the problem has become wider. The strong humanist reactions of Herder, Humboldt, Feuer-

bach, Stirner and Nietzsche confronted Catholics with all the aspects of humanism and made many of them reconsider them. But it was not until the twentieth century that the problem was forced on us as a whole, in all its dimensions, by marxist and existentialist humanism.

It is no longer a question of a serene Renaissance humanism in which the humanist was still a fine, broad-minded gentleman, the classical man of good taste. It is also no longer a question, at least not exclusively or above all, of a seething high tide of life, an exuberant, dionysiac joy in life and the world resulting from the triumphant discovery of the physical dignity of being man, as it was at the time when naked, gilded girls went marching through the city, simply because they were rejoicing in being alive, to meet the Emperor Charles v. The modern humanist is more profound, more integral, more serious. He is more matter of fact, sober and real. He wants to unearth an essential human dignity from the delicate situation that is called human existence and which he likes to call 'the human predicament'.

Both in marxist and in existentialist circles, this humanism is generally framed within a perspective without God, in which all supraterrestrial expectations are firmly excluded. As early as the nineteenth century, Feuerbach wrote: 'In all my writings, my aim is to call men to life—not theologians, but anthropologists. I want to make them love men instead of loving God. No more supraterrestrial expectations, but commitment to the terrestrial.'[1]

Nearer home, A. Vloemans wrote, only a few years ago:

The way out of our spiritual misery can be seen with some clarity...from the moment that it becomes clear that we, Western men, have given ourselves over for centuries to a delusion, the false idea of the Absolute and the Transcendent... We must break with that tradition. Man has believed for too long in the Other one, the Perfect one outside himself. The time has come for him to cease decorating the dead body of the Transcendent one with garlands of withered leaves and to turn at last to himself.[2]

[1] Ludwig Feuerbach, *Gesammelte Werke*, pt 8, p 29.
[2] A. Vloemans, *Integraal humanisme en de toekomst der cultuur*, 59.

2

The concrete realisation of this, for Marxist-Leninist human-ists, is what has been called *travaillisme*. This movement aims to give men the world as a sphere of work. Man realises him-self in work. This kind of humanism can no longer be in-different to the situation of injustice in which man lives. The human dignity of work in a material world, which man must, in justice to all, re-interpret and recast for the benefit of the whole human community, defines the very essence of marxist humanism—it is the humanism of 'man the producer' and of 'social man'. Work is understood in the economic sense in marxist thought: 'Communism, Marx has written in this sense, is the return of social man, that is, of man who has at last become human and it is a complete and conscious return with all the wealth of previous development. Communism thus coincides with humanism,'[3] and 'Communism is man's becoming conscious of this new humanism'.[4] This philosophy has resulted in a social mystique with a conscious and daring programme of engagement. Because of its supraterrestrial expectations, which would appear to close men's eyes to his urgent tasks in the service of a happy working community in this world, christianity has been branded as an essentially anti-humanist force.

Existentialism, on the other hand, looks for its humanism at the zero-point of the free will which itself decides what life is worth. Simone de Beauvoir has given a very neat summary of this attitude of mind:

> Existentialism does not condemn man to an incurable state of misery. If man is not naturally good, he is not naturally bad either. In the first place, he is nothing. It is his task to make himself good or bad, according to whether he accepts his free-dom or denies it.[5]

Generally speaking, existentialism also seeks to construct a non-theist humanism. As Sartre has said, 'God is a useless and

---

[3] H. Lefebvre, 'L'homme des révolutions politiques et sociales', *Pour un nouvel humanisme*, Neuchâtel 1949, 135.

[4] R. Garaudy, *Le communisme et la renaissance de la culture française*, Paris 1945, 60.

[5] Simone de Beauvoir, 'L'existentialisme et la sagesse des nations', *Les temps modernes* 3 (Dec. 1945), 398-9.

costly hypothesis and we aim to do away with it.'⁶ Elsewhere, Sartre has written:

> The passion of man is diametrically opposed to the passion of Christ since man destroys himself as man so that God may be born in him. But the idea of God is a contradiction and we ruin ourselves in vain. Man is a useless passion.[7]

Merleau-Ponty has expressed the problem in this way: 'Faith in God kills in us the sense of man and his historicity'.[8] For these thinkers, then, the problem of humanism is presented as: if there are no supraterrestrial expectations, what is the terrestrial, secular meaning of man? What makes human life open to life, what makes it worth being lived? The question is, as the existentialist A. Camus has formulated it clearly: 'Judging whether life is or is not worth the trouble of being lived.'[9] The existentialists take life on this side of the grave so seriously that they would rather seek refuge in suicide than go on living in a world that has no meaning within this world.

This existentialist and marxist humanism brings us, christians, face to face with the problem of christian humanism. We have, after all, to admit in all sincerity that history has shown that many Catholics have looked for an alibi in the 'supernatural' and 'supraterrestrial' in order to escape from the harsh terrestrial tasks of a secular plan of life and that, in this, they give evidence of a mistaken view of God's transcendence. They often leave the economic, political, social and scientific setting in order of human life in the world to the non-christians and wait themselves ... for the *parousia*, the end of time, in the meantime trying simply to earn their living.

---

⁶ J.-P. Sartre, *L'existentialisme est un humanisme*, Paris 1946, 34.

⁷ J.-P. Sartre, *L'être et le néant*, Paris 1943, 708: 'La passion de l'homme est inverse à celle du Christ, car l'homme se perd en tant qu'homme pour que Dieu naisse. Mais l'idée de Dieu est contradictoire et nous perdons en vain; l'homme est une passion inutile.'

⁸ Maurice Merleau-Ponty, *Sens et non-sens*, Paris 1948, especially p 191.

⁹ Albert Camus, *Le mythe de Sisyphe*, Paris 1943, 15: 'Juger que la vie vaut ou ne vaut pas la peine d'être vécue.'

The fact of marxist and existentialist tendencies in humanism confronts us with the problem in this acute form: have we, christians, living in and through grace and for the kingdom of God, also a terrestrial task in this world to fulfil? Ought we too—and perhaps we in the very first place, for even more compelling reasons than non-christians—to undertake the responsibility of setting the world in order? Or is christianity still to remain indifferent towards the process of humanisation in the world? Human and christian existence itself is therefore at stake—the whole man, believing in a life 'beyond the grave' and living in the world here and now.

I will try, then, to do as I have been asked to do and illuminate this problem from evangelical principles.

2. The biblical view of the world: the 'cosmos'

We use the word 'cosmos', world, in a very different sense from the Bible. Since the Greek translation of the Hebrew bible, the general Greek meaning of *kosmos*, the universe ('heaven and earth' is what appears in the original Hebrew), the good creator of which is believed to be God,[10] has entered the Old and New Testaments, in which *kosmos* is also used in the neutral sense of the earth or the world of men as such, without any religious qualification at all (as in Jn 13:1). In addition to these meanings, however, John and Paul especially used *kosmos* in a characteristically biblical sense which was essentially religious and, at the same time, fundamentally non-Greek and non-Roman. Their vision was neither cosmological nor metaphysical, but historical, i.e. in accordance with the history of salvation. In this context, then, *kosmos*, the world, means fallen mankind, not, however, as a static entity, like scholastic 'fallen nature', but as a historical, dynamic reality. *Kosmos* in John and Paul is the world of men under God's 'anger', in other words, humanity in its deepest foundation, the religious significance of which man cannot change himself. The reality of human existence as life in the world was here given the religious meaning of an existence opposed

[10] In the New Testament, for example: Acts 17:24; Jn 1:10; 1 Cor 3:22; Rom 1:20.

5

to salvation, the antipode of the kingdom of God. In John and Paul, everything belonging to this *kosmos*, its spirit and mentality,[11] its wisdom[12] and even its grief,[13] in a word, the whole of the kosmos itself,[14] is diametrically opposed to everything that comes to us from Christ. Whether sound elements worthy of man are present in this existence without salvation is a question which only arises incidentally and very exceptionally in the mind of Paul and never in the case of John.[15] I insist, moreover, that this view is purely *religious*, that is to say, it does not consider mankind in itself, but in its relationship to God which has been broken. But this relationship with God is not one relationship beside many other relationships—it penetrates all the others and gives them their deepest and ultimate meaning. As a result, a religious dislocation, via man's moral life, also causes a terrestrial catastrophe *within this world*. The religious is given a 'cosmic' resonance. The *fundamental situation* itself is infected, distorted, affected at its root and confused—'we were by nature children of wrath' (Eph 2:3). The very meaning of human existence is lost and then the fine aspects which are still to be found lose their real and ultimate, all-determining meaning. The whole cosmos is therefore, according to Paul, 'held accountable to God' (Rom 3:19)—it is subject to God's judgement.[16] John formulated this drastically: 'the whole world is in the power of the evil one' (1 Jn 5:19). It was evident to both John and Paul that the devil was the 'prince of this world' who was responsible for this situation without salvation.

[11] 1 Cor 2:12.
[12] 1 Cor 1:20–1; 3:19; 2:6ff; 2:14; 1:26.
[13] 2 Cor 7:10.
[14] 1 Jn 4:4f.
[15] Neither John nor Paul deny the goodness and the value of the world of creation as praised by the Old Testament. What they say, however, is that these values have been misused. The very fact that this misuse goes against the inner promptings of things themselves (see Rom 8:22; Phil 3:21) shows that they are not bad, but positively good. The New Testament, however, is not so much in the perspective of the optimistic Old Testament faith in creation as in that of the salvation of mankind, involved in sin, by Christ. The New Testament does not provide a systematic exposition of every aspect of the human predicament and my exposition of the New Testament concept of 'cosmos' is intended as no more than an introduction.
[16] Rom 3:6; 1 Cor 6:2; 1 Cor 11:32.

They were, however, both fully conscious of the other side of the coin. God nonetheless loved this world—'God so loved the world that he gave (us) his only Son', not 'to condemn the world', but to pronounce the liberating *absolvo* over it.[17] God had compassion on this world, which we have called a world 'without salvation'. He became the *sōtēr tou kosmou*,[18] the saviour of unredeemed mankind. He came to share our situation without salvation. Because of their situation without salvation, Paul used a very strong word and called men *douloi*, slaves or servants,[19] and said explicitly (in Phil 2:7) that the Word took precisely this form of a servant, that is, he entered a world where the evil one ruled. In the form of a servant, however, Christ broke this rule and gave a new meaning to the world and to being a 'servant'. This is so true that Paul could boldly assert that, had the prince of this world known that he was having the 'Lord of glory' crucified, he would have frustrated this plan (1 Cor 2:8), since this crucifixion marked the end of the rule of the evil one. But this wise divine plan of salvation eluded him (ibid).

Just as the first Adam was tempted by the devil and involved in the fall of the evil angels, so too did the evil one try, at the very beginning of Christ's public life, to lead the second Adam astray and establish his kingdom (Mk 1:12). But his plan failed: 'The light shone in the darkness, and the darkness was not able to take it in its grip.'[20] 'Since therefore the children share in flesh and blood, he himself likewise partook of the same nature, that through death he might destroy him who has the power of death, that is, the devil' (Heb 2:14). Christ's love overcame the situation without salvation: 'I have overcome the world' (Jn 16:33). The entry of God himself into this world brought meaning and sense into the world of men and the result of this redeeming entry of God into the world in the person of Jesus Christ went to the very root of

[17] Jn 3:16f; 12:47.
[18] Jn 4:42; 1 Jn 4:14; also 2 Cor 5:19; Rom 11:15.
[19] Rom 6:16, 17, 19, 20; 6:6; 15:21.
[20] This is a more correct translation perhaps of what John intended to say when he used the Greek word *katalambanein* in Jn 1:5. See also Jn 12:35.

7

human existence. In this context, Paul said explicitly: 'If anyone is in Christ, he is a new creation' (2 Cor 5: 17), meaning not only that man has acquired a new reality, grace, but also that the whole man has, as man in the world, been renewed in and through grace in Christ, in other words, that the mystery of Christ and our incorporation into this mystery through baptism marked the end of the 'cosmos' in the biblical sense of the word. 'By the cross of our Lord Jesus Christ,' Paul said, 'the world has been crucified to me, and I to the world' (Gal 6: 14). The believing, baptised man, the christian, thus lives concretely in a new world. The whole of his being man in this world is baptised and christianised. By Christ, the optimistic faith in creation is once again situated in its original sphere of life in which it can freely breathe. The world of creation is, in christians, as christians, withdrawn from the yoke of evil. As though it were a second day of creation, God pronounces his approval over mankind in Christ: 'He saw that it was good'. Paul said this explicitly: 'There is now no condemnation for those who are in Christ Jesus' (Rom 8: 1). The redeemed world ceases to be 'cosmos' and is now called the kingdom of God. 'Just as we have borne the image of the man of dust, we shall also bear the image of the man of heaven' (1 Cor 15: 49). Anyone who lives in Christ has, like Christ, overcome the world. 'For whatever is born of God overcomes the world,' said John (1 Jn 5: 4) and he added, 'Who is it that overcomes the world but he who believes that Jesus is the Son of God?' (1 Jn 5: 5).

This, then, is how the bible sees human existence, and this biblical view is not metaphysical, but ethical and religious. Outside of Christ, man's existence lacks ultimate meaning. In Christ, on the other hand, the whole of human existence has commenced a new life.[21] The whole of christian humanism is contained in this and it is in her growing awareness of this datum of faith that the church has become more sharply conscious, in this biblical view of life, of the real place of humanism within the mystery of Christ, just as understand-

21 I do not propose to discuss the question of pre-christian religious man here.

ing of the meaning of man's being in the world has grown
and matured in the human mind.

Having sketched out the biblical view of the 'cosmos', I
will now go on to give a broad outline at least of the content
of this increasingly conscious christian humanism within that
perspective.

3. An examination of the christian situation of man

A. *Christianity as the accomplishment of a deeper mystery in
developing human history*

What is absolutely new in christianity is, as we have already
seen, that God himself has entered the order of our life in this
world, or rather, the disorder of that life. Scripture proclaims
this exultantly again and again: 'He has appeared,' 'he has
revealed himself',[22] 'the light has appeared in the darkness'
(Jn 1:5). God has appeared among us in the form of men!
He, who, as far as he is concerned, does not form any part of
the structure of our world, but transcends it in creative freedom, has himself entered this structure as a fellow-creature.
He has become a man in the world. The immaculate, sinless
and holy one, who is raised far above sin in a transcendent
and sovereign way, has entered a world of sin in which he,
although remaining without sin, nonetheless became the victim of the sin of his fellow-men. Christ, the content of our
religiosity, forms a part of history—the son of a Jewish
mother, of David's lineage, born in Bethlehem, a little town
in Judea, and condemned to death under Pontius Pilate by
the machinations of an illegal judicial procedure. A man,
therefore, who appeared for a limited period of time in the
world and, like all men, disappeared again. Indisputably,
then, he was deeply caught up in the net of terrestrial events.

But—and this is what is new in this episode—a deeper
mystery was accomplished in this human history of Christ, a
mystery which was withdrawn from the temporal event
although it took place in that temporal event. God accom-

[22] Tit 3:4-5; 2 Tim 1:9-10; Mt 6:14; Jn 2:11; Rom 3:21; 16:26; Col 1:26;
Tit 1:3, etc.

plished an act of salvation in those terrestrial happenings of the man Jesus, because that man was at the same time God. All his human acts therefore took place in a perspective of salvation—they possessed more than simply historical volume. The appearance and the self-revelation of God in human history was called in the Old Covenant *mystērion*, a mystery. 'By mercifully entering the world, he has consecrated this world.'[23]

This biblical and patristic concept of mystery throws a surprising light on to the problem of humanism. It is not directly concerned with reconciling terrestrial and supraterrestrial expectations with each other, but it is concerned with showing a twofold perspective in the one evolving historical human event. The kingdom of God comes about in human history itself. In being in the world, in which man humanises himself by spiritualising the material world which he recasts for his own use—in this being in the world, a deeper mystery is also accomplished. It acquires its ultimate meaning of a reality which is richer in meaning—being in Christ. Being in the world naturally demands, of itself, humanism. That is to say, as an evolving being that comes into spiritual possession of himself and fully realises himself in all his dimensions in extending the world, man has the task in this world of humanising himself by humanising the world. Being in Christ—christianity—does not contradict this evolution and task. Being a christian is not one of many ways of being in the world. It is rather a dimension in depth which includes all the superficial dimensions of being in the world and not something added to them. A deeper life in God, in *Christ*, causes the whole of our being man to enter a new mystery. Being in the world is not the kingdom of God, but it is part of it. Included in this way in the mystery, setting in order and humanising life in this world becomes a hidden beginning of the eschatological redemption, which is also a redemption of the material, humanised world. The temporal task of regulating life on this earth is thus, via man's moral and religious life, drawn into the eternal framework beyond the limits of the purely temporal. This is the theological consequence of the

---

[23] Martyrology of the Dominican rite at Christmas vigil.

dogma of the creation in connection with the dogma of the redemption and of the resurrection of the body and the birth of the 'new heaven and the new earth' of which scripture speaks. It is in this sense that humanism, definitive humanism, shows, in being in the world, the other side of the coin of our 'being in Christ' and thus an essential life of redemption. The hidden growth of the redemption of all human values thus forms a part of the mystery which, thanks to our 'being in Christ', is accomplished in the process of humanisation of man's cultural task. The terrestrial is therefore not simply a route to the eternal. Anyone who is in Christ is perpetuating the terrestrial and making it into the heavenly social environment. Just as our spiritual life in Christ will only be a completely 'spiritual' life eschatologically—it is, in other words, a life towards which we are already growing now—so too is the new heaven and the new earth nothing other than the future eschatological event that we are already preparing now in our christian work of humanisation. It is not only man's soul that is redeemed—the soul exists only as incarnate subjectivity and insofar as it is connected, in and through corporeality, with the whole of the material world and with other people. The whole has to be redeemed. Otherwise, our redemption, which is after all a religious redemption, is unauthentic and unsound and not a redemption of *people*.

The deepest basis of this definitive humanism which is defiant of time is consequently situated in our 'being in Christ', our sacramental entry into Christ's saving history. It is in this way that a deeper mystery is accomplished in human history, a mystery which gives history a more embracing and a definitive meaning. Outside the mystery of Christ, humanism has no lasting meaning. Within the mystery of Christ, however, it becomes an aspect of our redemption in action: 'thou renewest the face of the earth!'

B. *Tensions between salvation and absence of salvation in man's history on earth*

The assertion that the task of the christian community is the hidden beginning of heavenly humanism would, however, seem to be contradicted by the apparent facts of human history. After twenty centuries of christian life, it is hardly possible to be more than moderately enthusiastic about its humanity in a world that lives under the constant threat of another world war when it has still not recovered from the terrible effects of the last. I should like to draw attention to the two immediate causes of this conflict in order to indicate, if possible, its deeper bases.

1. Being in the world, whether it is thought of in the context of being in Christ or not, is, in itself and by reason of its own constitution and structure, a 'being in situation'. Man is a seeking, groping being who does not follow his own course unerringly because of an infallible natural impulse. He freely chooses his own course in life and, as a being who is both free and temporal, he is naturally unstable and inconstant, with the result that this freedom has to reorientate itself again and again in a permanent state of tension. Risk and fiasco are essentially bound up with the human situation, whether this has or has not entered the new world of Christ. The possibility of conflict is therefore essentially present in our being man—our being in Christ does not change this in any way.

2. This constitutional character of our being in the world is not repudiated by our being included in a deeper, christian dimension of life. Man's condition of being in the world means that it is possible for him to plunge into a situation without salvation, into disaster. Even though this ancient religious situation without salvation has been, in principle, overcome by Christ's death on the cross and his resurrection, its material and sociological consequences continue to weigh heavily on and to be actively felt in the new christian order of life. This was taught explicitly by the Council of Trent and history has made us experience it personally. Sin especially remains in the world, a malignant cancerous tumour that is constantly spreading. The old and the new worlds exist side by side and intermingled, as the parable of the wheat and the tares tells us. Thus, when we look back at human history, we

always perceive two fundamental tendencies in it—an up-
ward, constructive movement and a downward, destructive
movement, and these two movements are intermingled. This
intertwining of the old world and the new, heavenly world
can lead to the factual human situation, which is the result of
these two tendencies, growing above men's heads so that the
small community of saints on earth, together with all men of
good will, is not equal to such a situation and mankind is
thereby drawn into catastrophe. Both individually and col-
lectively, the harmony between mankind and grace will
therefore always come about in painful conflicts and at the
same time any new humanising achievement will be per-
verted into a new, refined, dehumanising factor. Atomic
power, for example, is one of the mightiest accomplishments
of the whole process of humanisation, at least in the technical
sphere, and of man's control of his environment, but it is also,
in the hands of sinful and loveless men, at the same time a
destructive, satanic weapon.

Various factors, then, work together to produce conflict—
the very nature of our being in the world which is not ex-
propriated by our being in Christ, the sinful weakness of those
who have nonetheless entered Christ's saving history, that is,
christians themselves and all men of good will and finally
mankind which keeps outside the mystery of Christ. The
ancient cosmos still exists for those who do not accept Christ
and, as Paul said (1 Cor 7:31), christians live among such
people. Christians are those who have been chosen 'out of the
world' (Jn 15:19). Christ leaves them 'in this world' (Jn
17:11; 13:1; 1 Jn 4:17), just as he himself lived 'in the
world' (Jn 9:5), but they no longer belong to that world
without salvation. There is, however, always a danger that
this world will attract them and John warns christians of this:
'Do not love the world or the things in the world' (1 Jn 2:15).

An even deeper reason for this conflict is to be found in the
fact that Christ's saving history, the source of man's redemption in the world, is not yet complete. Our factual redemption
has not yet become evident and visible: 'It does not yet appear
what we shall be' (1 Jn 3:2). The ultimate fact of redemption

which has not yet taken place will be inaugurated by a final historical event—Christ's *parousia* or triumphant return. If man's chance of salvation and that of his humanism as well is to be found in the mystery of Christ, then, as long as the final event of this mystery has not become a reality, our redemption will continue to be incomplete. 'In this hope we are saved' (Rom 8 : 24). Humanism too is always a humanism on the way, a humanism that is eschatologically stretched.

The christian's task in society, then, is a beginning, an active commitment to this heavenly humanism. This initial commitment, however, is always influenced, as we have seen, by various factors which result in conflict, factors such as man's very situation of being in the world which in itself implies risk, the constant threat of sinfulness in the christians who undertake this task of humanisation and their being involved in a world in which the 'mystery of evil' is always active. This means that the mystical beginning of this heavenly humanism is always, like christian life as a whole, a constantly repeated relative fiasco. It is, in other words, a humanism which is brought about laboriously in conflict and friction, with the consequence that every new contribution to humanism always contains the possibility of new conflict. 'Inch by inch we will penetrate again the world which was taken away from us by sin so as to give it back to you as we received it from you on the first day, ordered and holy. Do not measure out that time for us, Lord.'[24] Humanity is therefore more the work of man's penetrating more deeply and fervently into the love of God than a question of purely technical and social progress. Catholic novelists, such as Bernanos, Graham Greene, Stefan Andres, Carlo Coccioli and Gertrud von le Fort, therefore prefer to portray the infamous, the disrupted and the rootless members of society, the outcasts from a safe 'humanist' pattern of life, and to show them as saints in whom God's grace triumphs. They may do this with a one-sided emphasis, but we can still hear God's voice in these novels.

[24] Georges Bernanos, *Sous le soleil de Satan*, Paris 1926, 362.

C. *The tension between the aspect of mystery and the historical aspect of human history*

The real problem of the humanist plan, brought about by our waiting for the *parousia* and the continued effect of the ancient situation without salvation, in other words, by the antagonism between good and evil in human development, has its basis, however, in an even deeper reality. This is the fundamental tension between the historical aspect of this upwards and downwards movement in history and the aspect of mystery that is accomplished within it. God's entry into human history, his grace in other words, does not cancel out man's history on earth—on the contrary, by entering history God himself becomes, in and for historical man, the most intimate content of man's existence, not in any sense the competitor with man's historical growth. On the other hand, he does not become lost in or disappear into this history, which continues to let glimpses of an eternal background shine through. It is clear therefore that it is not the historical aspect of human history, but the divine aspect of mystery that is accomplished within this history which is the 'one thing necessary' that gives the historical its deepest meaning. We cannot oppose God to this terrestrial growth, but on the other hand we cannot identify this terrestrial mystery with the supernatural mystery. God, despite his deep intimacy with us in history, is completely different, and this imposes on us, in the coming about of the kingdom of God, the fundamental duty of self-dispossession, which is merely the other side of the coin of our loving dedication to God's greater value. This renunciation of ourselves and of human history, which does not find its ultimate meaning in itself, is therefore the fundamental, real and not simply platonic act of self-emptying which bears up the whole of our being in Christ. The bible thus contrasts the impulse of the fallen angel who did not empty himself and pulled the first man down with him in his fall—'You will be like God' (Gen 3:5)—with the second Adam, who did not regard equality with God as plunder—'a thing to be grasped' (Phil 2:6)—but renounced it and

15

accepted self-emptying (ibid) as the point of departure for and the permanent basis of his historical existence in the world. We are therefore faced, because of the very fact that history is not simply history but a revelation of God in which Christ moreover accomplishes an even deeper mystery, with the possibility in principle and the necessity of being able to and having to risk and renounce everything for the 'pearl of great value', the kingdom of grace.

4. Humanism of the redemption

The realisation of this possibility and necessity is directly based in the movement upwards and downwards of human history, insofar as a deeper mystery is accomplished in this history by Christ. Because of God's entry into the world, this accomplishment applies to every historical event, including the historical fact of the relative failure of humanism and its constantly recurring situation of conflict. In and through the constructive humanist endeavours and the destructive anti-humane tendencies of mankind, Christ accomplishes a deeper mystery. Man's 'being in situation' and the after-effects of the earlier situation without salvation are re-interpreted into a means of salvation—into the characteristically christian sphere of experience of 'being and living in Christ', which must be built on self-emptying as a function of union with God. The anti-humane factors and the relative failure of humanism are incorporated in Christ by God's transcendent guidance of the world into the plan of redemption and directed from within towards the eschatological, definitive humanism in which the human community of saints on earth will be completed. The conflict itself, which I have discussed above, thus acquires a deeper meaning. It becomes an offering and comes under the vivifying shadow of Christ's cross. This at the same time means that the humanising and spiritualising process of the world and of humanity does not take place in the last resort according to high-handed human plans, but is directed by the imperceptible but firm hand of God the Father which, by Christ in the power of the Holy Spirit, accomplishes the entire terrestrial and superhuman mystery of salvation. It may seem fantastic to say that man's technical control of the world may in the end bring about the final downfall of the world, but, in view of the twofold tendency in human development, this fantasy is probably sober reality. This catastrophe will certainly be a divine intervention, but it will not take place without the introduction of terrestrial causes—either the normal course of natural forces or free human misuse of man's increasing control of these forces. But, whatever concrete course it takes, it is certain that God will accomplish the last great mystery in this final catastrophe which will herald Christ's return. Conflict and fiasco are therefore always a 'passover' for those who live in Christ, a way through to heavenly humanism. It is not God's love which gives this painful aspect to terrestrial humanism, but the divided, torn world itself. God's love remains true to itself, is consistent in its effect and penetrates everything, including this division in the world, which thereby acquires an aspect of salvation which it does not have in itself. Later, when human sinfulness is judged by Christ's *parousia* and the parable of the wheat and the tares is fulfilled, God's love will appear in its true form, without the dramatic character that human sinfulness and failure gave it before.

It is clear, then, that the definitive meaning of humanism, insofar as it is the other side of the coin and the reaction, in man in this world, of the grace of the resurrection, is also conditioned by the grace of the cross. Terrestrial humanism, as the beginning of heavenly humanism, is consequently, through its christian character, essentially a humanism of the redemption—a struggle, like that between Jacob and the angel of God in Genesis. Jacob won his case, but was lamed. He was nonetheless blessed (Gen 32: 24–31).

We may therefore conclude that christian humanism is a laboriously won fruit of the mystery of the grace of the passion in historical, humanising and developing mankind. That is the *mystērion* of christian humanism which, in its deepest essence, merges before our eyes into the mystery of the God-man Jesus Christ, the broken man who, in and through his being broken, became the saviour of the *kosmos* (1 Jn 4: 14;

Jn 4 : 42). The risen, triumphant Christ therefore bears the stigmata of the drama of his redemption! When Christ—the 'hope and centre of all times', as a liturgical hymn says on the feast of Christ the King—appears, it will 'become public' (1 Jn 3 : 2) what a wealth, both supraterrestrial and terrestrial, 'being and living in Christ' contains. God himself will then give us the 'new earth' and the 'new heaven'. It will be the last, lasting and eternally young mystery which he will accomplish in mankind in the world.

2
HUMBLE HUMANISM

1. Humanism and humility

Humility cannot be found in non-Christian writings, in the Epicureans, the Stoics, the Manichees or the Platonists. Even though excellent moral and disciplinary guidance may be found in the writings of these schools and elsewhere, humility will not be found there. The way of humility has a different starting-point—it comes from Christ.[1]

This problem was often debated fiercely in the Middle Ages. But what most interests us today is not how the medieval scholastics critically interpreted the text—this is something that we ought not to expect from them—but their personal position on the problem of humanism, which was to a great extent posed for them in the form of the question as to whether the pagan *magnanimitas*, nobility of soul, ought to be included in christianity and whether *humilitas*, humility, was characteristic of a distinctively christian attitude towards life. Bonaventure[2] defended, with undisguised violence, the exclusively christian nature of humility and saved magnanimity as being an integral confirmation of humility itself which magnanimously scorned the world and itself—*contemptus mundi, contemptus sui*—for the basic reason that man is simply nothing, created from nothing and reborn from the nothingness of sin by grace. In this way, he eliminated man's natural awareness of himself. Albert[3] and Thomas,[4] on the

[1] St Augustine, *Enarr. in Ps. XXXI* 18 (*PL*, 36, 270): 'Haec aqua (see the context) in nullis alienigenarum libris est, non in epicureis, non in stoicis, non in manichaeis, non in platonicis. Ubicumque etiam inveniuntur optima praecepta morum et disciplinae, humilitas tamen ista non invenitur. Via humilitatis huius aliunde manat: a Christo venit.'

[2] *Quaestio de Humilitate*, a. 1; Quaracchi edition, pt 5, pp 122–3.

[3] *In IV Ethic.*, Tract. II, cap. 2: 'Qualiter magnanimitas sit virtus'; Vivès edition, pt 7, pp 296–8.

[4] *In III Sent.*, d. 33, q. 2, a. 1, sol. 4, ad 3; Moos edition, pp 1050–1; see also his entire treatise *de magnanimitate* (II–II, q. 129) and *de humilitate* (II–II, q. 161).

other hand, accepted, in addition to magnanimous humility, also natural magnanimity which included not pride, but humility, with the result that they did not see any specifically christian, virtuous attitude in humility, viewed generally.

The controversy within medieval humanism simply provides us with the opportunity of approaching the problem of humanism from the point of view of christian humility. First of all, however, I will briefly outline the special aspect of humility as revealed to us in the Old and New Testaments.

In the Old Testament,[5] humble man was originally poor man, in the material, economic and social sense. Humility and poverty were practically identical. The humble were the poor who were oppressed by the ruling class. There were two possible attitudes towards this social misery—it could be accepted in gentle resignation or it could be opposed in bitter revolt. Resignation and gentleness came gradually to form the moral background to the concept of 'social humility' and both were represented in Hebrew by one word, the corresponding Latin words being *humilis et mitis* (*corde*), that is, humility (poverty) and gentleness. It was in this way that the religious ideal of humility and poverty came about. God was experienced as the only way out in all cases of misery. To be poor or to be humble became a religious attitude—it was 'good to be humiliated and poor'. Humility was thus *a definite attitude towards* God. Finally, the concept of humility and poverty came, in the last books of the Old Testament, to be completely dissociated from its original social and economic context and humility, whether one was rich or poor, oppressed or not, was an inward religious attitude, the religious sense of one's own impotence and need of God's intervention, bestowing grace.

Christ brought the message of salvation to the poor and humble: 'The poor have good news preached to them' (Mt 11 : 2–5). It was to those who felt a deep need for God and who confessed their own moral impotence that Christ brought the glad tidings. The rich—those who, in their self-satisfaction,

---

[5] See A. Causse, *Les Pauvres d'Israël. Prophètes, Psalmistes, Messianistes*, Strasbourg 1922; J. Loeb, 'La littérature des Pauvres dans la Bible', *Revue des Etudes Juives*, Paris 1890–2.

had no need of God—were ignored. In the words of the Magnificat, God 'sends them empty away'—he gives them a wide berth, leaving them in the emptiness of their being full of themselves. He looks lovingly, however, at the 'poor'—he looked down in grace at Mary's humility and, because of her need of God, her 'humility', it was given to her to be full of grace and to be filled with God.

Christ therefore began his beatitudes with 'Blessed are the poor',[6] that is, blessed are those who are inspired by religious need of God.

The Greek attitude to life seemed to be diametrically opposed to this christian humility. The Hellenic magnanimity, the great-hearted confirmation of man's dignity, despite the menacing anger of the gods and of nature, in other words, of fate, which spread suffering, pain and death, appeared to be the antithesis of christian humility. Even though this pre-christian nobility of soul[7] changed a great deal in appearance throughout Greek thought, as can be readily ascertained from an examination of aristotelian, epicurean, stoic and neo-platonic magnanimity, for example, the basic Hellenic features remained—man is alone in an incongruously alien and irrational situation, but he nonetheless asserts, in full aware-ness of himself, his own human dignity, his own beauty. The wise epicurean magnanimous man laughs at fatality, but without the luxury of a calm 'knowing' smile. The aristotelian magnanimous man may deliver man from capricious fortune,

[6] Mt 5:1-4. The addition 'in spirit' (cf Lk 6:20) to 'poor' in the Greek and the Latin translations indicates the religious significance of the Hebrew 'poor'. See M. J. Lagrange, *Commentaire sur Saint Matthieu*, Paris 1947[8], 82. The gentleness contained in 'poverty' was expressed in another beatitude in the translation; both, however, constitute the one beatitude of the humble. See Lagrange, op. cit., 83.

[7] See Th. Deman, *Le Témoignage d'Aristote sur Socrate*, Paris 1942; Ch. Moeller, *Sagesse grecque et paradoxe chrétien*, Tournai and Paris 1948; A. Festugière, *L'Enfant d'Agrigente*, Paris 1941; idem, *La sainteté*, Paris 1942; idem, *L'Idéal religieux des Grecs et l'Evangile*, Paris 1932; D. Amand, *Fatalisme et liberté dans l'antiquité grecque*, Louvain 1945; E. Bréhier, *Du sage antique au citoyen moderne*, Paris 1921; Chrysippe (Les grands Philo-sophes), Paris 1910; A. Brémond, *Rationalisme et religion* (Archives de Philosophie, Vol. XI, cahier IV), Paris 1935; M.-J. Lagrange, 'La philosophie religieuse d'Epictète et le christianisme', *RB* 9 (1912), 5-21.

make him assert his autonomy in the terrestrial sphere and call upon him, the elite man at least, to realise on his own authority his human beauty and greatness, but he does not understand the mild mercy of God. God does not come closer to him and does not concern himself with the human predicament. The stoic magnanimous man may transform, as if by magic, the oppressive *Moira*, Fate, into goodness and affirm his own greatness of soul by resigning himself with serenity to the inevitable and adjusting himself to the divine order of the world. The pain that he suffers in so doing is borne magnanimously, but love is not admitted into the suffering human heart, only the coldness of a rigid and blind legality. Plotinus' magnanimous man is detached from the world and lets the rays of the good and the beautiful shine over his soul, but he, like all the others in this tradition, knows nothing of the *agapē* that comes down from a good God who has taken part in the historical drama of love with man.

This pagan attitude was not one of positive pride—it was rather the absence of christian humility.[8] When the Greek came into contact with christian humility, however, he was often filled with scorn and contempt. Celsus, for example, bitterly attacked christian self-emptying.[9] Origen admitted that christians did sometimes invite scorn by their foolish and ignoble humility and he tried therefore to reconcile the good aspect of magnanimity with christian humility.[10] As John Chrysostom declared, there was no genuine humility without humane nobility of soul.[11]

Thus the problem of self-awareness and awareness of God was presented in clear terms. In a current formula in the

[8] We should, however, never lose sight of the great difference between the pagan world before Christ and that which followed Christ. 'Ancient civilisation, especially that of the Greeks, was infinitely less dangerous to the christian, if at all, than post-christian civilisation' (Ch. Moeller, *Sagesse*, 318). 'Classical paganism . . . was expectant. Every pagan must be judged according to the welcome that he gives to the good news' (A. Brémond, *Rationalisme*, 26).

[9] See Origen, *Contra Celsum* VI, 15 and II, 62–6. See also K. Holl, *Urchristentum und Religionsgeschichte*, Gütersloh 1925, 19ff.

[10] *Contra Celsum* VI, 15.

[11] *Homilia in Joann.* LXXI, 2.

middle ages, humility was defined as a sense of one's own nothingness—*sensus propriae vacuitatis*. Thomas stands out as the one great figure who had the courage to go in a different direction from his contemporaries and to reconcile man's sense of God with his awareness of himself. I will now try to approach the problem of christian humanism from the point of view of christian humility.

2. Humble humanism as man's sense of being a creature

Humility is not a diminution or a denial of human values, pusillanimity or smallness of soul, or a compulsive denigration as evil of something which man regards, in his heart, as nonetheless inwardly valuable and precious to him. True humility presupposes a loyal acceptance of human greatness, but it regards this precisely as a *creaturely* value. Humility does not consist of a denial, but of a *confrontation*[12] between divine and human values, in which the humanly beautiful and civilised is accepted as God's gift. Humility includes experience and awareness of self, but awareness of ourselves as God's gift. The sensitive point of humility is to be found in the delicate attitude of the humanist who, while being aware of his own value, keeps his gaze fixed on God.[13] Humility is man's sense of being a creature, the *religious respect* which man has when he accepts something that is naturally valuable.[14] Awareness of being a creature is thus the basis of humble humanism. Christianity is the vehicle of this central saving dogma of God's good creative power which conceived in love a beautiful plan of the world, which numbers the sun, the moon and the stars, creates the history of the world and buttresses and creatively supports man's ascent in civilisation towards community-building love in justice. Simply from the point of view of the creation, the christian humanist is con-

[12] See Thomas, *ST* II–II, q. 161, a. 1, ad 5; I, q. 104, a. 1. This brings us again face to face with the biblical concept of humility.

[13] Thomas, *ST* II–II, q. 161, a. 2, ad 3: 'Humilitas praecipue videtur importare subiectionem hominis ad Deum'.

[14] See *ST* II–II, q. 161, a. 4, ob. 1 et ad 1; II–II, q. 161, a. 2, ad 3; a. 1, ob. 4 et ad 4, etc.

scious, in deep humility, of the religious dimension in depth
of his humanism. Trust in himself, *habere spem in ipso*, the
tense spring of Hellenic humanism, is introduced by the christian humanist into the reverent and dedicated atmosphere of
his sense of God and of being a creature—*habere spem in
ipso, tamen sub Deo*, reliance on himself, but on himself as
God's gift, as the humanist Thomas said.[15] The christian
humanist thus accomplishes his task in society in humility
and in humble awareness of himself.

The idea of creation is thus the basis both of the humility
of the humanist and of the humanism of the humble christian. Humanism must be humble, religious, in order to be
fully itself. Humility acts as the norm for christian humanism, because it leads and directs this humanism, as a human
participation in God, towards God's glory, which must radiate
from this humanism. The christian knows, and the philosopher must realise, that God, the loving creator who dis-
tributes values, is inwardly concerned with human progress,
of which he, the creator, is the great inspirer and promoter
and in which we, the creatures, are the humble collaborators.
This humility does not paralyse the courageous action of the
christian humanist whose aim is to build up a technical,
economic, socio-political and artistic world order in which
the human community of persons can prosper in love and
justice, and vital moral and religious action is promoted. It
simply covers all this activity with ardent reciprocal love for
and gratitude to the creator of so much that is beautiful. The
Old Testament hymn of the religious people of nature,
'Praise the Lord, all you works of the Lord ... praise the
Lord, you sun, moon and stars', is sung endlessly by the christian humanist, who completes it, making it a mighty 'Praise
the Lord, you art, science and culture ... praise the Lord,
you just and community-building love'!

3. Humble humanism which confesses sin

'A humanism which did not take into account suffering, sin
and death, which did not place them *in the centre of its view*

[15] *ST* II–II, q. 128, a. 1, ad 2.

24

of the world, would be radically incomplete.'[16] The history of man and our own experience of life does, after all, teach us that this social task, directed towards the ultimate ideal of a moral and religious community of persons, is always threatening to fail and does in fact partly fail again and again. Sin flourishes in the heart of every human being. Human society 'lives in a state of mortal sin'. The 'prince of this world' who gains support through *uncontrolled* human passion brings about, in addition to this humble humanism, an anti-humanist power. Just as creation develops towards a community-building love as a distinctively human glorification of God, so too does the power of evil grow at the same time. Sin is like a malignant growth which is constantly trying to break down *charis*, gratuitous love. 'A kind of anti-grace ... permeates nature (and) lives in it.'[17] The ideal of creation peculiar to humble humanism implies a hard struggle against sin and its consequences. 'When the wars came', Guardini has said, 'they seemed to be natural disasters and they were this as well, but they were the enormous eruptions of the accumulation of evil in millions of hearts, in the terrible abysses of mankind.'[18] Humble humanism has to take the reality of sin into account. Human freedom, that sovereign gift of creation, is also the centre from which humanism is threatened with death. In blasphemous language, but one which sharply depicts the risk involved in human freedom, Jouhandeau has written in a disturbing book:

> It has always been possible for man to make the risk of the world fail. ... Where I am, there too is my free will and where my free will is, there too is absolute and eternal hell in power ... I carry within me the power, if not the right, to counterbalance God... God revealed himself in sin itself when he allowed me to sin eternally ... all the greatness of God and man

[16] Ch. Moeller, *Sagesse*, 19.
[17] Vladimir Lossky, *Essai sur la Théologie mystique de L'Eglise d'Orient*, Paris 1944, 128.
[18] R. Guardini, *The Lord's Prayer*, London 1958.

is in that gift in which he gave me the power to hate him for ever.[19]

It is certain that, in the kingdom of good and the kingdom of evil, heaven and hell already have their beginning here on earth—the sense of God and humanism, the loss of God and anti-humanism. *Man* is the commencement of those warring powers. The first task of any genuine humanism, in which full justice is done to all that is distinctively human, is therefore the struggle against sin—evil—through which the great anti-humanist power has to be eliminated. The humanist himself has first of all to strike his breast in penance and confess his guilt. If he is a sober realist, he will not believe in a naturally moral aristocracy: '(The petition of the Our Father, "forgive us our trespasses") exhorts us not to elevate ourselves above the mass of men with an aristocracy of conscience, but to take our place honestly in the common human responsibility (for sin)'.[20] The humble humanist confesses that there is in fact only an aristocracy of grace which illuminates the feeble conscience and gives it strength. Contemporary existentialist writers have made the fallacious idea of the naturally moral hero go up in smoke and have depicted man's tendency towards sin, the 'fatality' of *free* sin, in colours which inevitably remind the christian of the dogma of original sin.

This, then, is another reason why the genuine humanist should be humble. The Catholic doctrine of 'healing grace' clearly illuminates this. Is it not true that sin is the greatest danger with which humanism is threatened, because it crushes its very heart—its humility and sense of being a creature—and deprives the social task of humanism of its moral and religious dimension and therefore makes humanism recede in an ebb *in regione dissimilitudinis* instead of rising in a tide? Is it not also true that sin is the great possibility for every human being who is caught up in the great catastrophe of sin and who contributes himself to its ever-increasing power? In view of this situation, the humanist is bound to

[19] *Algèbres des valeurs morales*, Paris 1935: I have quoted freely from the whole passage, pp 213–29.
[20] R. Guardini, *The Lord's Prayer.*

ask God, in all humility, for the help of his healing grace if he sincerely wishes to achieve his legitimate social task on earth. It is only in humbly receiving God's grace that humanism can ever be itself and be humanism in the fullest sense. Humanism that is left entirely to itself can only be a destructive obstacle to the ultimate success of this social task.

4. Humble humanism which consents to the absolute greater value of the gift of salvation

God's loving initiative, his act of love in creating man, is only one aspect of his one great plan of salvation directed towards the *deification* of created man. He did not correct his work of creation by conferring grace. The creation itself was the first evidence of God's saving love. Creation is thus, together with its acme, humble humanism or humanism as the conscious glorification of God, inwardly directed towards the life of grace. This means that the humanist task in society, man's audacious commitment to establishing a socially, economically and politically well ordered community in which science and art, love and justice can prevail, is not simply a demand of creation, but also a commission which has been imposed upon us by the life of grace itself. Humanism thus becomes a part of our saving task. If, moreover, the supernatural gift of salvation is intimately connected with the religious dimension in depth of the humanism of creation which, of its very nature, possesses a powerful tendency towards God, then it follows that supernatural deification can also be accepted in the very name of humble humanism.

Man's acceptance of the gift of salvation also means that an even deeper humility is imprinted on what is already a humble humanism. Man's consent to grace, that is, to God as God, to God's inner wealth, includes his humble confession of God's absolute greater value, greater than his work of creation, in other words, than humanism. Humanism remains a work of creation, but grace is deification, by which creatural non-being participates in God's interiority. In this participation in grace, humanism is taken up and drawn into the *kingdom of the mystery*, in which the divine possibility absolutely transcends all human possibilities, with the result that human-ism, in joyous surrender and inner readiness to sacrifice, lays itself open to the mystery's unsuspected tasks of love. It is here that humility, humanism's being 'of God' and 'for God', cele-brates its supreme triumph: 'I will be a father to you, and you shall be my sons and daughters'.[21] This humility is the basis of the most audacious human pride—the pride of the child of God, being proud of God!

5. Humble humanism which accepts the grace of the passion

It was not God's creative love that brought evil into the world: 'For thou lovest all things that exist, and hast loathing for none of the things which thou hast made, for thou wouldst not have made anything, if thou hadst hated it' (Wis 11:24). Evil is simply the destructive work of human freedom. 'The whole world is in the power of the evil one' (1 Jn 5:19). Even Christ's death on the cross was the work of free human sin.

But God made an oasis in the world of evil. 'And I will say to Not my people, "You are my people".'[22] 'For thou wast slain and by thy blood didst ransom men for God from every tribe and tongue and people and nation, and thou hast made them a kingdom and priests to our God, and they shall reign on earth' (Rev 5:9–10). God chose from this evil world a holy people of rulers, his church. 'Christ loved his church and gave himself up for her, that he might sanctify her, having cleansed her by the washing of water with the word, that he might present the church to himself in splendour, without spot or wrinkle ...' (Eph 5:25–7). The gift of salvation is in fact a redeeming grace which delivers men from evil. The relative failure of good as well as the triumph of evil are transformed by the love of God's creation and salvation into an instrument of grace. That is the ultimate strength of the goodness of God's creation, which is not checkmated by the risk involved in human freedom. The wave of misery which was poured out over the world by sinfulness became the re-

[21] 2 Cor 6:18: cf 2 Sam 7:14; Is 43:6; Jer 31:9.
[22] Hos 2:23; cf Rom 9:25 and 1 Pet 2:10.

28

demptive means of salvation. It was not by virtue of itself, but through God's plan of salvation in sending Christ into the world to experience the human predicament and to give a new face to suffering, misery and death by taking away their 'stimulus', sin—'Behold the Lamb, who takes away the sin of the world'—that humanism acquired its definitive attribute, which has been held up to scorn by Celsus and all those spiritually related to him throughout the ages—the humility of Christ's death on the cross. Christ, as Paul has said, did not want to cling to the glory of the absolute and perfect value of God, which would have poured itself out over his human face in accordance with the inner law of the receiving of a human nature into a divine person. On the contrary, he emptied himself,[23] extinguished his glory, as the fathers of the church added, and, what is more, 'humbled himself . . . unto death, even death on a cross'. In this act, the power of evil was transformed into transcendent power to save. The murder of Christ by men was, for Christ himself, at the same time a loving and humble surrender to the Father. The triumph of evil over Christ and the failure of his life heralded the definitive triumph of Christ. This humility was the way to exaltation and glorification (Phil 2 : 8–9).

It is through the saving significance of the relative failure of the power of good within God's plan that christian humanism acquires its deepest character of humility. The New Testament therefore coined a Greek word, unknown to the Greeks, to express this *new christian situation*: humility, *tapeinophrosynē*. Like Christ, the church goes on her way, through the relative failures of her task of creation and salvation, towards her glorification: 'Until the end of this age, the church will continue her pilgrimage amid the persecutions of the (power of the evil) world and the consolations of God'.[24]

The christian humanist will always have to experience, in a real sense and in fact, inner detachment from society by

---

[23] Phil 2 : 6–11. See P. Joüon, 'Notes philologiques sur quelques versets de l'Epître aux Philippiens', *RSR* 28 (1938), 223–32. See also Heb 12 : 2.

[24] Augustine, *De Civitate Dei* XVIII, 51: 'Usque in huius saeculi finem inter persecutiones mundi et consolationes Dei peregrinando procurrit Ecclesia.'

reason of the absolute greater value of the gift of salvation in *humility*,—because of the sin brought about by the power of evil and also because of God's saving power which has transformed this evil power, against which man was not proof, into an instrument of salvation. He knows that terrestrial humanism is an unfinished symphony with unavoidable (relative) fiascos. And he realises that his humanism is a struggle similar to Jacob's with the angel of God—Jacob won his case, but he was lame afterwards (Gen 31 : 24–31).

6. Humanism as the 'new creation'

This humble humanism which accepts the grace of the cross certainly introduces sacrifice into the very heart of humanism, but it does not retard or paralyse its audacious intention in any way. On the contrary, the lack of a genuine—humanist—social system is one of the real causes of the growth of the power of evil, of which that lack was already the consequence. The life of grace itself, the kingdom of good, the grace of the passion—this spurs us on to pursue the aims of humanism with determination. Pope Pius XII warned us against supernaturalism, which automatically expects salvation to come from holiness, and has urged Catholic laypeople to accept responsibility in political and social life and, even though the situation may threaten to become intolerable, not to give way to defeatism. Through sin, the world became chaos again, through Christ it must be recreated into cosmos—that is the biblical view of the recreation of everything in Christ, as it has been worked out by Irenaeus in particular.[25] It is in this struggle to set the world in order again, the struggle of the 'new creation', that sacrifice has a central place. Christ crucified is, after all, the principle of the new creation: 'The Son of God was crucified for everything, because he has imprinted the sign of the cross on all things' (Irenaeus). The

[25] See also A. d'Alès, 'La doctrine de la Récapitulation en saint Irénée', *RSR* 6 (1916), 185–211; E. Scharf, *Recapitulatio Mundi. Der Recapitulationsbegriff des heiligen Irenäus und seine Anwendung auf die Körperwelt* (*Freiburger Theologische Studien* 60), Freiburg i. Br. 1941.

grace of the cross is, however, essentially a grace of the resurrection.

Thus christian humanism is basically a moral and religious undertaking in christian humility and christian magnanimity. The church must 'harvest' the whole cosmos. 'The glorious Church, without spot or wrinkle, is the ultimate end to which we are led by the grace of Christ's passion', as that great humanist, Thomas, declared.[26] The wonderful hymn of creation of the three young men, in which the creator is praised for the 'creation of heaven and earth and of the people of Israel', is continued without ceasing by the redeemed church of Christ, which sings her hymn of creation to the glory of 'God, the creator of heaven and earth and of the church'[27]— the cosmos and the church experienced by men as the conscious glorification of God! Only the humble, the 'poor in spirit', will be permitted to experience the triumph of humanist christianity when the community of men on earth has reached completion as the community of saints.

[26] Thomas, *ST*, III. q. 8, a. 3, ad 2: 'Esse Ecclesiam gloriosam, non habentem maculam neque rugam, est *ultimus finis* ad quem perducimur per passionem Christi'.

[27] Cf Hermas, *Visions*, 1,3.

3
PRIEST AND LAYMAN IN A SECULAR WORLD

1. Anonymous christianity

I find it difficult to imagine that a sincere militant communist atheist possesses not one shred of authentically theist faith, just as Paul believed that the Athenians were 'very religious' and told them so (Acts 17:22). I do not believe in the absence of religion from the working-class world, although I do believe in its having fallen away from the church. Wherever there is some sense of justice, truth and above all genuine brotherhood, there is God too. Anonymous religion can take hidden forms. Wherever, despite complete rejection of the church and even moral degradation, sincerely objective values are accepted, to the point where people are prepared to fight for them, there is a latent but genuinely religious life. God has many names—the fathers of the church even called him 'the one with many names'. We would indeed be guilty of injustice were we to say that the working classes are without any spark of authentic religious sense, when, on the other hand, we make every effort to look for genuine religious elements in the pre-christian pagan world and in fact find them there. In the words of the Acts of the Apostles, 'God does not leave himself without witness.'[1] His grace seeks out all men.

I have no need to enlarge on the doctrine of *fides implicita*, in the sense of anonymous faith, here, despite its importance. But the truth of this doctrine seems to me to provide one of the clearest lines of guidance in the orientation of our apostolate.

This apostolate among the workers outside the church is therefore the task of bringing 'pagans' to *explicit* faith, that is

[1] Acts 14:16–17. See also Acts 17:27 and in fact the whole of the introduction to and the speech in the Areopagus, Acts 17:22–30.

to say, of bringing Christ to them, and the task of igniting the smouldering element of anonymous religion in them from the inside with the redeeming appearance of Christ and, from that point, the task of bringing them to the church and her sacraments, 'that they know (in the biblical sense) thee the only true God, and Jesus Christ whom thou hast sent' (Jn 17: 3). Christ and his church, the visible appearances of God's saving love, are not known—that is why these people's hidden faith in God is so hesitant, anonymous, degenerate and fragmentary. Only Christ can do away with the anonymity of God. The saving fact of the redeeming Christ, continued in the sacramental church, is the *christian* revelation which expresses the distinctively christian religious aspect of salvation within the generally supernatural, preparatory revelation of the 'God of salvation' that is vaguely perceived by all men. The problem of 'dechristianisation' should be understood in the strictly etymological sense of the word, that is, as a falling away from *Christ,* with the result that man's theist, anonymously supernatural faith in the 'God of salvation' is weakened and almost disappears behind life itself, in which it nonetheless frequently betrays its presence in an uncomprehended and mutilated form. This anonymous faith in God can be purified in the light of the fact of Christ and perfected so that it becomes an explicit and consistent confession of faith in God. The terrible floods in the Netherlands in 1953 called forth a very deep sense of the brotherhood and togetherness of man and great generosity throughout the world. This was living proof not only that human sentiment was still noble, but also, at a deeper level, that many people were conscious of an anonymously religious feeling of brotherhood in which men's hands were extended to God's grace. Grace simply cannot be regarded as the private property of practising christians. There still remains a large tract of missionary territory to be christianised in the depths of every christian and the pentecostal fire of the *church* smoulders in the heart of every 'pagan'!

The framework of our apostolate is therefore: 'What you worship as unknown, this I proclaim to you' (Acts 17: 23). I

believe that this also applies even to the lowest levels of the
working class and that this can constitute the greatest testimony of the apostolic presence of a 'worker-priest' in a
working-class environment outside the church. In other
words, the anonymity of the workers' latent faith in God
can be made open and explicit by the priest's explicitly living
in such a way that love and the sense of justice and of truth
lose their anonymity in the visible figure of a christian who
embodies this love, justice and truth. It also means that this
active presence of the priest only establishes the first contact
and that his work of showing the religious sense of love must
be supplemented by the work of another priest who does not
do manual work, but who gives an explicit christian content
and meaning to the visible anonymity. The christian faith
will give the true content to the clarified religious sense of
loving brotherhood, togetherness and justice.

The deepest meaning of the apostolate is always an *ad-
mirabile commercium*, a 'wonderful interchange'. The church
as the people of God is a community of faith and love which
looks forward in expectation to the *parousia*. It is a community of grace and this grace is, of its very nature, expansive
and apostolic, a grace directed towards others,[2] a 'fraternal
grace'.[3] In connection with the article of faith that refers to
the 'holy, Catholic and apostolic Church', Aquinas made a
striking allusion to the missionary and radiating apostolic
character of the most intimate and personal grace: 'Everyone
who is himself addressed by God in grace must be at the
service of his neighbour.'[4] Just as Christ was the visible
appearance of God's invisible love, so too is the sacramental
church the visible appearance of this inward community of
grace.[5] This visible church, the exteriorisation by means of
which the interior life of grace is at the same time constituted
into deeper interiority, contains two functional apostolic

[2] Thomas, *In I Sent.*, d. 16, q. 1, a. 2, ad 1: 'Gratia tendens in alios.'
[3] *ST*, II–II. q. 14, a. 2, c. and ad 4: 'Gratia fraterna'.
[4] *Expos. in Symb. Apost.*, in *Opusc. Theol.* II, ed. Marietti 1954, n. 975,
p 212.
[5] *ST*. III, q. 60, a. 5, ad 1: 'Expressior significatio gratiae Christi.'

activities—the priestly or hierarchical activity and the characteristically lay activity, both as the visible sign of the apostolic impulse of the church's inner life of grace. In other words, the church's apostolate has two aspects—on the one hand, the interior effect of the grace of the Holy Spirit and, on the other, the two exterior functions of this interior effect of grace, the priestly hierarchy and the laity. The priest and the baptised layman are therefore the two essential functions of the church which make the supernatural presence visible in this world—the 'sign set up for the people'.

The different apostolic functions of the priest and the layman are one and the same in that they both essentially establish contact between holiness and sin. God's becoming man, the presence on earth of the God-man Christ, was essentially an entry into a sinful, weak world—God, Love, made contact with sin. Christ died from that contact. But this was the great apostolic mystery of the redemption—unholiness apparently triumphed in contact with holiness, but in reality the very opposite took place, for 'through death he destroyed death'. This encounter between holiness and sin resulted in the defeat of sin and in redemption and sanctification, deification and transformation from sin to holiness. Anyone who, though stained with sin, touched in faith the hem of Christ's garment, was at once healed. Zacchaeus was a sinner, but redemption entered his house and his heart together with Christ, the holy one. The Holy Catholic church is the same in her holy and sanctifying, lay and hierarchical functions. The church comes into contact with sin—that is her vocation. But this contact is also, for anyone who comes forward to meet the church in faith, healing, sanctifying and redeeming. Contact alone with the church should be a *grace* for men.

It is on this that we base the whole apostolate of the visible church with her two functional apostolic activities—the priestly activity and the lay activity, both of which must be fundamentally an active presence of the community of grace of the church on earth.

2. A re-examination of the priestly apostolate

A. *Primary functions of the priestly apostolate*

The priest is, by definition, the 'steward of the mysteries of God' (1 Cor 4: 1), the *oikonomos* of the mysteries of Christ. In St Paul the text refers only to the fact that priests are the heralds, preachers and proclaimers of the mystery of Christ. But as early as the fourth century, the scope of the Pauline text was extended by the church fathers to include within the work of Christ's salvation not only the historical act of Christ's redemption, but also the celebration of this mystery, that is, the sacraments in which the mysteries of Christ remain accessible to us, men of all times, *in mysterio*. In the patristic period, then, the task of the priest, as the 'minister of the mysteries of God', consisted of preaching and liturgy— he was the minister of the word and sacrament (Augustine). Preaching and the sacramental apostolate remain the essential task of the priest. These two functions are therefore mentioned explicitly in the preface to the ordination of the presbyterate: 'So that the number of priests may be sufficient for the *offering* and the manifold celebration of the mysteries ... ; thou hast added *teachers of the faith* in order to be helped by them in the proclamation of the word throughout the whole earth.' We are not free to hold a different view from this if revelation, continued in the living tradition of the church, teaches us to see the priestly apostolate in this way.

The proclamation of the word and the ministry of the sacraments are, moreover, not separate activities—they are essentially related to one another. Just as the revelation of the word analyses, throws more light on and shows in greater detail the revelation of reality itself, so too does the proclamation of the word illuminate and explain more fully the sacramental presence of this revelation of reality and invite men to enter personally into this reality.

1. THE MINISTRY OF THE WORD

In the apostolate of the priest we should always remember that preaching is a *paradosis*, a tradition. We proclaim the christian faith—our preaching is a delivering of the Good News. As priests, we are only invested with authority to proclaim God, who appeared in Christ and lives in the church, together with the moral and religious consequences of this in the lives of men. We bear witness to the living God, to Christ. We should use no eloquence except in the ardour of our testimony. As Verlaine correctly said, 'take eloquence and wring its neck'. Our function in the *paradosis* is simply one of service and bearing witness.

There is a great need for adaptation in preaching. It is only by preaching the living God that we will strike home. And let us thank God for it! Our present age is crying out for the simple bread of religious truth—the redeeming presence of Christ and his new law. The church will be able to catch on again if we preach the visible coming of God and if we give men one single vision of the christian plan of salvation. People cannot live from a hundred separate truths, but they can live from one single idea and, for us, that idea is the fact of Christ. Think of the political leaders and their propaganda —they do not present people with intellectual expositions of various ideas, they put forward one basic vision, one idea which is constantly cropping up in the various themes. Think of Augustine and his preaching to his people in *De catechizandis rudibus*, telling them that the mystery of Christ was the great history of salvation of a people in which the listener himself was personally involved. It is clear that he made his mark and that we do not with our preaching from manuals. Two and four make six—this arouses no emotions. But two days' paid holiday plus four days' paid holiday make six days' paid holiday—that is a meaningful addition sum! This is, after all, the whole task of the proclamation of the word—to preach inductively. People must be personally addressed by *their* God, we must speak to them about their God in their lives. Two conditions are presupposed in this:

a. I have said that we do not preach in our own name, but that we hand on the Good News. But this message is not something that is alien to us. The 'teaching' church is also the 'learning' church. We are not only teachers, we are also, first and foremost, *believers*. In preaching because it is our task to preach, we are expressing our own deepest experience. Our *paradosis* is a piece of our personal life: 'I believed, and so I spoke' (2 Cor 4:13). Lacordaire called the preacher 'a man who takes his soul and throws it into the soul of his listeners'. That is why Paul said, whenever he was speaking about the *paradosis* that he communicated in his preaching, he gave himself with it: 'We were ready to share with you not only the gospel of God but also our own selves' (1 Thess 2:8). The living God whom we preach is also *our* God, whom we are really only handing on—we are passing on the God who has become all in all for us preachers to men, 'being affectionately desirous of you' (ibid). It is precisely this personal aspect of experience which will bestow originality on our preaching the truths of faith and will call forth the only preaching that is really 'inspired'. All the rest is 'trickery', and this no longer has any effect on people who hear so many far better examples of clever, eloquent trickery on the radio and in the cinema that their hearing is deadened by it and their minds are saturated and stupefied by it.

b. In addition to this objectively oriented element of experience, there must also be what I shall call the 'element of social experience'. As a believer, I accept the whole plan of salvation as the reality which effectively concerns the whole of mankind. It is a question of our God and the listener is therefore personally involved. If we bring the word of salvation to men, then, we have to take care that men really can hear this as an *answer*. A preacher who is not humanly and socially (at least in affective interest and, in our own times, perhaps also really and in fact) involved in the needs, the miseries and the problems of these people will not, in his proclamation of the word, be able to preach the mystery of Christ as the making public of the word of salvation to specific actual men. To do this, we must have a sound knowledge both of people and of the *paradosis*, and not only a conceptual knowledge, but also a real and experiential knowledge. The great transformation takes place in preaching—putting contemporary man in contact with the supratemporal mystery of salvation. The preacher who cannot play on those two keyboards of eternity and temporality will never touch the strings in the depths of the souls of his listeners, but will just be throwing eternal truths at random in the church like bricks that may land on the heads of his 'dear brethren', or else he will stay caught up in superficialities and not preach the living God. To be both God's and men's, with one's eyes fixed on their relationship with God—that is the fundamental condition of good preaching.

Adaptation in the apostolate has therefore, in the first place, to be concerned with the manner and the content of our stale preaching. Mgr Dupanloup once complained ironically 'Every Sunday, there are thirty thousand sermons in France...and the people *still* believe!'

We should not, however, lose sight of the sacramental significance of preaching in all this—the deeper mystery that is brought about by the power of the Holy Spirit in man's bearing witness through preaching. In the words of Augustine,

> See what a great mystery is accomplished here: the sound of our words strikes your ears, the Teacher, however, is in you... The external instructions are an aid, an invitation to devotion. But the one who teaches your hearts has his throne in heaven.[6]

While we are preaching, the Holy Spirit is at work in the hearts of those who are listening by addressing them inwardly. Without our preaching this inward speaking is lost to men in the noise of life—the preacher is the radar, tracking it and bringing it explicitly to men's consciousness. As Sertillanges once wrote, preaching is 'revealing souls to themselves'. We elaborate what the Holy Spirit says inwardly to men. The priest has therefore to hear, in the sounding board of his heart, both men's questions and the Holy Spirit's answer to

[6] Augustine, *In I Epist. Joan.* III, 13 (*PL*, 35, 2004–5): 'Iam hic videte magnum sacramentum: sonus verborum nostrorum aures percutit, magister intus est . . . Magisteria forinsecus, adiutoria quaedam sunt et admonitiones. Cathedram in coelo habet qui corda docet.'

these questions and to elaborate this answer as a word of salvation and express it as a word of grace in his preaching—as the redeeming word, the Good News. That is preaching—'the word of faith which we preach' (Rom 10:8). (Woe therefore to the priest who improvises—unless the circumstances are beyond his control—and fills up a quarter of an hour with a hit or miss sermon. He does not know what is God's! [Mt 16:23].) In good preaching, dogma and moral teaching are fused into a single connected whole. What people need from us is, if I may put it in this way, that we should, independently of scholastic treatises, preach the 'triune God', the God who 'creates and governs', the 'Word made flesh', the sacraments of the church and the 'last things' and that we should also, from these starting-points, go on to preach christian ethics as a life of grace, of uncalculating love, ardent hope and surrender in faith, a God-centred life, something that is more than the ten commandments and yet always forges ahead in individual, family and social life here on earth. If we can link all this inductively with the facts of human life and with concrete human problems, we shall inevitably make people sit up and listen with interest. We must show men the way to the depths of God, but this way goes towards God through the depths of man himself! If we are in touch with life and have a fundamental view of the history of salvation from which the life of the living God is discernible and in which every human being is personally involved, we shall preach effectively.

Pure preaching therefore demands not only constant contact with the living God in prayer and human experience, but also the sustained practice of going back to theological sources. We must again and again reactivate our theological understanding so that we can continue to treat dogma in a free yet orthodox manner. Theology enables us to transpose, to rethink in intelligible language what is inwardly experienced, but ultimately cannot be communicated, in the life of faith as participation in the faith of the church. Then we shall be able to impart to people the reality of what faith is, without using scholastic terms that are incomprehensible to most of the faithful. The church is bound to confess in all humility that scholastic theology is to blame for the wretchedness of so many sermons. Theology is, of course, the science of the word of salvation that we have to preach. The fact is that all priests find out that it is in fact not true, probably, I feel, because they are not really familiar with scripture, the fathers and the real Thomas Aquinas. The word of salvation is not patristics or scholasticism, nor is it even holy scripture— these are all only witnesses. No, the word of salvation is the living God himself, the God of our own times, our God who is eternal and yet visibly realised his definitive plan of salvation in Jesus Christ and accomplishes it in us in the sacraments of the church. In our preaching, we must above all be bold. Our respect for the dogma of faith, for the ineffable mystery of God and his plan of salvation, will give us, if we really take our theological studies to heart, a safe 'illative sense' and at the same time the firm certainty that God has revealed his plan of salvation for us, people of today. I agree that he revealed it too for people at the time of the apostles, but the apostles had to tackle that problem in their own times. Certainly I agree that God's plan is also revealed for people in a hundred years' time—but future priests will just have to tackle that task. We are the heralds of the reality of revelation for contemporary man. For us, God has revealed himself to people living in the next street, in the great city and in the 'missions'. Every dogma has a saving value for these people which we have to make clear to them. And if many people feel no deep need in their lives for the dogma of salvation, then we must try to make them long for it, that is, we must unleash that longing in them. If we fail, then we must go on preaching the message of salvation in season and out of season until they learn that, *at least for us*, christian faith is our happiness, our salvation and our hope and that we can bear witness to our happiness and our redemption. It is not human life that gives value and meaning to dogma—it is dogma itself that brings this value and meaning with it. It gives an *answer*, even when there is no conscious question. 'Behold, the days are coming, says the Lord God, when I will send a famine on the land; not a famine of bread, nor a thirst for water, but of hearing the words of the Lord' (Amos 8:11).

What I have said here about 'preaching' should not, of course, be applied only to sermons, but should be taken in the broadest sense, with reference to instruction, catechising, house visits, spiritual guidance, conferences and retreats and ordinary contacts between priests and laypeople.

'Unless the Lord builds the house, those who build it labour in vain' (Ps 127:1). And the Lord is not God in his heaven, but God in our hearts. Our motto has always been, is now and should continue to be *contemplata aliis tradere*.

2. THE SACRAMENTAL APOSTOLATE AND THE PRIEST AS A 'PERSONAL SACRAMENT'

I have dealt elsewhere[7] with the important problem of strict sacramentality and shall confine my attention here to the general and constant sacramental appearance of the priest. The apostolate and thus the 'apostolicity' of the priest as priest is distinctive in that it is he who has the task of realising, throughout the history of the church, the actual connection linking men with Christ's mysteries, his historical acts of redemption. The priest's primary function is thus mediatory and all the other work that he may undertake must be geared to this function. It is only by being directed towards this end that his other work will gain its distinctively priestly and religious significance. The priest is not a redeemer. There is only one redeemer, mediator and apostle (in the sense of one who is sent) and that is Christ, who, by the sacrifice of the cross, offered his body—that is, himself, together with his mystical body, which is potentially the whole of mankind—in complete self-emptying and in total dedication to the Father. The bond between Christ's body and his mystical body is the sacramental reality—the eucharist and, dependent on this, the other six sacraments—and the priest is, by virtue of his ordination, essentially the minister of this bond. He must always be fully conscious of this fact, that he is in this way in

---

[7] *Sacramentele heilseconomie*, Bilthoven 1952; an abridged version of this work is translated as *Christ the Sacrament*, London and New York 1963.

the fullest sense a priest and that his kerygmatic apostolate and all his other pastoral duties flow from this and must also flow into it. He will then also be conscious of the fact that it is Christ who redeems men and not he and that his function is one of service to men and not one of playing the little dictator over them. He will therefore not be intent on trying to tie people to himself, but will play the modest role of servant between God and men. The art of being a priest is that of 'attaching people to his person by *detaching them from his ego* and by leading them to the only master who is interior', as Jean Guitton once said, so strikingly, in a different context.[8] God included priests above all as human assistants in man's personal ascent to God. The inner, divine teaching and supporting effect of God on the one hand and, on the other, the outward, human, priestly help of the priest as the human version of what God inwardly suggests are the two constitutive elements of the priestly apostolate. I can perhaps best define the priest's helping task with regard to the inner, spiritual life of men in the following way: (1) the priest is the silent, *reverent witness* of the work of the Holy Spirit in the lives of the people entrusted to him; (2) he is the *critical authority* of the reactions and the interpretations that people themselves give of the effect of the Holy Spirit in their lives and (3) he is also someone who makes explicit the unnoticed, hidden guidance of the Holy Spirit. The priest is therefore outside the sphere of his people's intimate, inner spiritual life and association with their Saviour, but from outside he does nonetheless have contact with this inward reality. He has a purely preparatory and episodic function especially in the theological life of the people entrusted to him. He has to teach these people to *believe* concretely, to *hope* concretely and to be the human version of Christ's saving *love* in their concrete environment. At the same time, he has also, in addition to giving objective guidance in this way, to take into account the concrete psychological and social possibilities of his people.

[8] J. Guitton, *Lumen Vitae* 5 (1950), 160.

All the activities that the priest undertakes in his pastoral care must be personal acts of love, first of all his properly sacramental acts. As the minister of the sacraments—a personal sacrament—the priest is, so to speak, the first to receive the grace that God intends for the other people and he has to transform this grace in his heart and adapt it to specific people. If it is true that the sacrament is invalid without the intention of the minister of the sacrament, then it is also true that a sacrament which is not just valid but also priestly and apostolic must be an act of prayer and of apostolic love on the part of the priest himself. 'Do you not know that those who are employed in the service of the temple get their food from the temple, and those who serve at the altar share in the sacrificial offerings?' (1 Cor 9: 13). This applies not only to the material needs of the priest, but also, and indeed in the first place, to his religious needs—his personal involvement in the stream of grace that comes from the altar. The sacramental life of the minister of the sacrament must be the very heart of his sacramental apostolate. Christ's apostolate was of its very nature sacramental—he transformed into human acts what he had seen, loved and experienced in the Father. As a man, he sensed what was human and as God he sensed what was divine, after first having personally and sacramentally realised it in himself—in his very becoming human, which was not simply an event that took place at his conception, but was a continuous task throughout his entire life on earth, since he went on transforming the fullness of his high priestly grace into constantly new human acts. His entire appearance was one long drawn out administration of sacraments, a making visible and a giving of divine realities.

The sacramental appearance of the priest must be like this. Our humanity is the 'matter' and our divine life is the 'form' and our human, powerless approach to men thus becomes an epiphany of God, a translation of divine goodness into human goodness. It is only then that we priests will be not just valid, but also apostolic sacraments. Every priest who appears in the home of a believing family is a valid sacrament, but his appearance is fully apostolically fruitful, especially in the case of non-believers, only if it is not an 'empty' sign, but a transformation, a human version of God's merciful desire to save men. This also means that it is not really a question of us, but that we are simply a sacramental sign, a way through, people who point, from ourselves, towards the other, Christ himself, who is to come, and do so in such a way that this pointing out becomes a sign, in our priestly appearance. The authentic, real sacraments that we administer will then be simply the culmination of our entire sacramental and priestly appearance. That is why the formulae used in the rite of ordination do not provide any sublime theological reflections about the activities of the priest as proceeding from his ordination, but they do repeatedly admonish him that these sacramental acts should at the same time be 'acts of grace', that is, acts of prayer. The administration of the sacraments (in the strict sense), even though these may be valid apart from the priest's personal religious attitude, is only a personal and apostolic act if the administration becomes an act of faith, hope and love as intercession for the person to whom the sacrament is dispensed. It is only then that the priest's sacramental apostolate is fully an 'act of character and grace' and Thomas did not hesitate to call the sacramental grace of such an apostolic sacrament greater than that of a careless, unprayerful administration of the sacraments. In this connection, it should be noted that, despite their apparent 'modernism', certain contemporary methods in the apostolate are nonetheless entirely in keeping with the deepest meaning of the sacramental apostolate. We are redeemed by Christ's sacrifice, in which the sacrifice of all mankind was virtually contained. Through the sacraments, and especially the eucharist, we must involve ourselves existentially in this sacrifice, so that the meaning of our sacrifice and the real sacrifices that we make in our day-to-day lives also form part of the *ratio sacrificii* of the mass. Christ offered *his and our* sacrifice on the cross, with the result that our suffering, and especially our act of dying, in principle participate *suo modo* (*mysterioso*) in the 'objective redemption'. Through our involvement in the sacrifice of the mass, 'Christ's sacrifice and ours', accomplished by Christ on the cross, also becomes really and personally *our own*. The priest accomplishes the celebration of this mystery, that of 'Christ's sacrifice and ours' on the cross, in a sacramental manner, but he must also, as a believer, together with the other believers, involve the sacrifice of his own life in a personal manner in this sacramental act. In this way, 'Christ's sacrifice and ours' on the cross will become *our* sacrifice of 'Christ and ourselves.' The priest's grace, the grace that is derived from the apostolic accomplishment of his ordination as priest, will therefore sustain the apostolic priest in the sacrifice of his life as a priest to the people entrusted to him. An extreme attempt, like that made by the worker-priests, who have left everything and become everything for their people, seems, then, to me to have been prompted by a profound understanding of the objective and the subjective form of christian sacramentality and especially of the sacramental sacrifice of the cross, and it bears witness to their pure vision that we are redeemed only by *sacrifice*. It seems to me to be profoundly Pauline and, although we do not all need to put this particular solution into practice, their attitude of priestly sacrifice still makes us feel ashamed because we are far too much 'valid sacraments' and far too little sacrificing and fruitful sacraments.

B. *Pastoral work among the working class*

Faced with an isolated world of working-class people who are completely cut off from all priestly influence, it is all very well to talk about the essential functions of the priest, his kerygmatic and sacramental apostolate. It is also easy enough to talk about 'man who is religious by nature'. Using different language, of course, we talk in the pulpit about man's 'existential need of God', and that is real. But, in the slums behind the church that is calling for God, people are calling out for so many basic and more lowly needs to be satisfied that they are hardly conscious of the higher needs. Any sudden religious need or question that is occasioned by some chance contact is quickly swallowed up by the pattern of life in the back street and the general environment of the mass. The atmosphere of the district in which the people live and of the factories in which they work is the active regulator here. This means that our proclamation of the word and our sacramental apostolate will be a hopeless task if secondary, but nonetheless urgently needed modern forms of the apostolate are not actively developed. It becomes, in the long run, impossible to preserve an open attitude towards the sacramental preaching of the priest in an environment of misery and oppressive and deafening manual work, in an uncertain, disconnected sphere of life in which so many different kinds of propaganda exert an influence and in the midst of nervous exhaustion and promiscuity. In addition, there is also that feeling of half-conscious revolt against the propertied classes, which these people consider the representatives of spiritual and moral values as well, so that their bitterness is also directed towards the religious and moral values themselves and towards the church. It would, of course, be fundamentally wrong to maintain that the hierarchy and the Catholic laity did not make their voices heard in social matters even before the publication of Marx's *Communist Manifesto* and did not put their convictions into practice. All the same, it is a fact that this constructive Catholic protest did not become a powerful and dynamic movement until very late and that socialism had become a dynamic force long before we had created an equally powerful working class movement. It is true—there was an abundance of church documents, but they did not evoke an effective response in the *collective reaction* of Catholics until very late. We must have the courage to assert both the one and the other, not, as is fashionable nowadays, in a spirit of morbid self-accusation, but in a spirit of humble realism.

Grace and the priestly and apostolic offer of grace are not just suspended in the air—they are concerned with people who are to live as christians. Grace deifies real man, who needs human fellowship in the world to live humanly. Supernatural life certainly touches a dimension in depth, but it is not a separate life alongside or above the sphere of human fellowship and life in the world. Unhealthiness in these basic structures normally has an inevitable influence on the religious life.

This being in the world and personal interactions between men thus form the necessary environment for man's becoming a person and, in this case, for the worker's becoming a person. Since the subject that is receptive to grace is not simply an abstract 'human nature', but the human person in a living community, it follows automatically that the priestly apostolate must take these anthropological structures into account. If the worker is passively involved, partly because of inhuman conditions of work in his contact with this world, in the rhythm of a mass-psychology in which intersubjectivity loses its personal character, then it follows that his religious experience, which must, of its very nature, be the free adoption of an attitude towards God, will be made extremely difficult. It is therefore urgently necessary for this situation to be put on a sound basis and for the worker to be helped towards becoming a person again if his life is to become directly open to the Good News. The very structure of human life itself therefore calls for various methods which will make the kerygmatic and sacramental apostolate of the priest practically possible.

Bad conditions in the system of work will thus necessitate all kinds of structural reforms. The social and psychological laws of intersubjectivity will have to be expertly worked out in a personal perspective—the influence of public opinion, especially that exerted through the modern technical means of the press, radio, cinema, television and so on, but also that brought about by personal love-contacts in ordinary, everyday I–thou encounters. All this will require a great deal of research. The causes of the falling away from the church will have to be investigated and the possibilities of re-establishing contact between the working-class masses and the church in the most favourable way will have to be studied, so that a feeling of good will at least may grow among the workers towards the ecclesiastical organ of the Good News, which can then be proclaimed to them. All this, including the purely technical solutions to the problem, must remain an expression of apostolic love.

To maintain that these methods are too human and deny

the gratuitous transcendence of the effect of grace is to misunderstand the existential manner in which 'supernature' is interwoven with 'nature'. It is, of course, true that, because of its transcendence, the life of grace itself can be experienced in any environmental conditions and even in an inhibited, distorted and morbid psychology. Actual social poverty can become a voluntary poverty as the expression of an extreme experience of God. But one cannot expect a whole mass of people to do this, especially if the entire rhythm of life makes a free choice of attitude very difficult. An inhuman situation is not the normal or the most favourable one for the unfolding of grace. But even more important than this, it is the highest task of any human person to involve himself existentially, as a *free*, *personal* being, in Christ's sacramental plan of salvation. From this point of view, then, we are also bound, for the benefit of the worker's personal life of grace, to work so as to set his personal essence free, so that he may become a person.

I will show later how these tasks come primarily within the domain of the layman and not the priest. But, as it is a fact that the layman has only just become conscious of his *christian* vocation in this world in this matter and is consequently lagging behind here, it seems to me that the apostolic priest is obviously bound to perform a certain amount of supplementary work in this sphere himself, as far as he is able. I do not mean, of course, that the study of the relationship between secular problems and christianity is simply supplementary work—this certainly forms part of our priestly task. But I do mean that all kinds of organisational work are occasioned in connection with the concrete solution to such problems and that this material and organisational activity often takes up far too much of the priest's time and prevents him from fulfilling his specifically priestly mission.

It is a fact that one of the most important aspects of our modern age is the emancipation of the workers and that this movement began originally not with intellectuals and ideologists, but in the very heart of the working class itself. It was only then that ideologists became aware of this ferment and gave it an ideological framework, thus making the movement all the more powerful. Our realisation of this is of importance to us—it shows that we have to work in a twofold direction in our apostolate among the workers. We have to act directly with the workers themselves and we have, at the same time, to act with the intellectual elite. In my opinion, it is wrong to imagine that we can solve the problem simply by influencing the intellectuals, for they have certainly *given form* to the workers' sense of justice, but they emphatically did not give rise to this sense of justice. The formation of an intellectual elite must always be accompanied by a direct influencing of the workers themselves, although we should not, on the other hand, underestimate the influence exerted by the intellectuals.

The non-christian working-class movement has, moreover, become such a closely knit, dynamic force that present-day society has been divided into two quite separate blocks—the world of the workers, which has, with the passage of time, moved farther and farther away from the church, and the so-called 'capitalist' world, in which the workers include the church, probably wrongly in principle, but unfortunately rightly in fact and historically speaking. Thus we have a situation which is completely different from the apostolic situation of the middle ages, when the church was at one with community life on earth. The leaders of the non-christian working-class movement have consequently developed a sense of justice with regard to the things of this world which is often legitimate in this respect, but which is at the same time opposed to religion and the church, with the result that the church has frequently felt constrained to pronounce excommunications. The workers as a whole are not really capable of making a clear distinction between so-called political action, of which they accuse the church, and a purely religious act with a directly religious object, religious motives and religious means. Under these circumstances, it has not been difficult for their leaders to widen the gulf between christianity and the world still farther.

It would, however, be wrong, in my opinion, to attribute alienation from the church exclusively to industrialisation. Although it is most marked in the industrial areas, this 'silent apostasy from faith' is also taking place in the country districts as yet untouched by industry. What is more, it is not only confined to catholicism—it is also happening in protestantism and in the other churches and, according to reports, even in islam and the religions of the Far East. It is, in fact, a world phenomenon. It is not even confined to the church communities. It is a universal social phenomenon and is, in a word, a break with the tradition of the past. The transformations that are taking place in the entire social system and a certain 'conversion to the authentic' on the part of mankind as a whole are such that the 'older forms', both within the church and outside it, have come to be felt as a rigid and oppressive burden. The falling away from the church is therefore not, in the psychological and real sense, *ipso facto* a falling away from religion. Indeed, the very opposite would sometimes appear to be the case—several recent works indicate a certain awakening, outside the church, of man's sense of the religious. Those elements in the church communities which have become incarnate in this world appear as too worldly and, what is more, to be too closely linked to a civilisation that is crumbling while a new civilisation is on the point of breaking through. The renewal is spontaneously opposed to patterns in the church which are so closely bound up with a dying civilisation. Criticism of the church undoubtedly includes a great deal of prejudice and a lack of humble acceptance of the church's involvement with the world. It is also generally levelled at the hierarchical church exclusively, and the anonymous, simple, but deep holiness of so many christian mothers and other believers who, after all, also belong to the church, is quite overlooked. But, on the other hand, there is so often a germ of truth in many of these criticisms. How does the church appear in fact to the workers? What strikes them in particular about the church? Not so much her religious strength as all kinds of para-religious forms and activities in which the church has been forced by adverse times and circumstances to seek refuge. For the worker, then, the church signifies all kinds of social and political positions of power which he feels to be contrary to his own interests. He does not meet the church concretely in her real religious sphere, but in her terrestrial sphere as a worldly power. In other words, he is not faced with her essential sacramental and religious appearance, but with her non-essential terrestrial appearance. In practice, the real church is often hidden in these appearances—as the religious sacrament of love, she is frequently concealed behind positions of worldly power. Although it is possible to say, on the one hand, that this is an inevitable necessity, it is also clear, on the other hand, that a certain break with the traditional church does not always necessarily mean dechristianisation. It may also be a symptom of man's desire for a renewal of the church and his need for evangelical revival. What has been the reaction on the part of the priestly apostolate to the mass of the workers who have moved away from the church, since, shall I say, the turn of the century? We are bound to admit that it has often been an attitude which has emphasised this isolation. Catholics have tended to confine themselves more and more within their enclave and their priests have tended to let the ninety-nine lost sheep go and to devote their energies to the task of watching over and keeping the one faithful sheep safe. Their attention has almost exclusively been taken up with those who continued faithfully to go to church and all kinds of organisations have been set up to preserve for them a christian framework of life which they no longer found in their normal working environment—the parish cinema, the parish theatre, confraternities and so on.

On the one hand, however, we should not denigrate the apostolic activities within the church of the so-called 'catholic institutions' that have been in vogue since the beginning of the century. On the contrary—they have been a great blessing to the church, not only in the negative sense, by preventing an even greater falling away from the church, but also in the positive sense, by educating those who have remained faithful to the church to become more personal and responsible christians. Furthermore, the christian apostolic emancipation of the laity, which, in a later section of this chapter, I shall call one of the greatest possibilities of the present apostolic situation, would not have been so conscious and so vital without them. On the other hand, however, we are bound to place on record that this traditional pastoral care has been based on an attitude of defence against increasing alienation from the church. There has been a lack of that missionary fervour which is so essential to christianity in any period of history and the message of christianity has not been taken to those who no longer acknowledge it or who, in their ignorance, have misunderstood it. Confronted with the failure of the traditional methods of pastoral care on the one hand and the risky element involved in modern pastoral methods on the other, an apostolic eschatological tendency has arisen in many circles, especially since the second world war. The present revival of the idea of *parousia* is not exclusively attributable to the revival of scriptural and patristic studies—the modern apostolic necessity has a great deal to do with it. This can be traced quite concretely in the case of Germany where, at the time of the Catholic Centre Party, there was no mention, in christian, spiritual and theological writings, of this eschatological tendency, whereas, from the moment that the external position of power of the German church was broken, all kinds of eschatological publications saw the light of day. The same tendency is discernible in France—it is clear, for example, from the *Préliminaires* of *Dieu-Vivant* how the spiritual situation impelled men towards eschatologism. In any case, the attempts of the modern apostolate to bring about what has been called an 'incarnation' will have to take into account the eschatological tendency which is essential to christianity and which correctly affirms in all clarity the church's transcendence over the world and all man's apostolic efforts. If, however, eschatologism acts as a brake on the necessary element of incarnation in the apostolate, then it can hardly be regarded as an authentically christian expectation of the *parousia*. The very opposite is true—Paul himself said that persistent apostolic activity, culminating in the preaching of salvation, must be the great precursor of Christ's second coming in glory.

In contrast to the traditional care of souls and the too one-sided eschatological tendency, we now have the modern pastoral care first formulated in 1943 by such priests as Godin and Daniel, later elaborated in the books of Michonneau, Chéry, Boulard, Loew, Lebret and others and then to some extent sanctioned in France by the letters sent round by Cardinal Suhard, which were really a strong official encouragement of the attempts of many apostolic priests that were viewed so critically and so sceptically. They too were firmly convinced that the church would never pass away, that she was built on an imperishable rock and that she would pass through all crises as through a crisis of growth. The present moment, the contemporary situation of the church, is never the central point in the life of the church. It would therefore not be because of their exceptional efforts that the church would not pass away—that would be a challenge to grace. On the other hand, however, they were clearly aware that we, priests living *now*, have a task to fulfil in the world of today, that we are, at this particular time, responsible for people and that we therefore have, in the meantime, to take the Good News to all men now, so that it reaches them effectively and can be understood by them. The fact that the church is imperishable is undoubtedly an enormous truth, but in the meantime the fact that this imperishable church is not reaching many people is just as enormous! The church is, after all, not only imperishable—she is also an imperishable *organ of salvation*, and this means that she must *never cease* to bring salvation to people. If she does, she is failing in her essential vocation.

This insight leads us to make the just assertion that, if ninety per cent of people are outside the church, ninety per cent of our pastoral care must be directed towards these people, without neglecting those who still go to church. This principle, sensibly and discreetly applied, seems to me to be indisputably a primitive christian principle. The church is essentially missionary. She places catholicising love at a higher level than the defensive instinct. This is why the pioneers of modern pastoral work are looking outside the para-religious institutions for contacts with the dechristianised masses. They are sharply aware of the fact that the church is the vehicle of a catholicising invitation to love and they want this charity to be apparent without the harness of the church's positions of worldly power. They are not in any way neglecting those who have remained faithful to the church, but they are absolutely convinced that the apostolate among those who still go to church should not only aim to deepen the inner christian life of these people and to make it more personal, but also try to impart to them a missionary enthusiasm. This requires a revival of liturgical and sacramental life in the parishes at a deeper level and probably also a revaluation of its outward forms. Without going into concrete details here, I will simply refer to the missionary character of the *Directoire pour la pastorale des sacrements à l'usage du clergé, adopté par l'assemblée plénière de l'Episcopat pour tous les diocèses de France,*[9] in which the French episcopate, guided by preliminary theological study, made extremely helpful and suggestive innovations in the parish liturgy a few years ago.

This is the general direction taken by the official *Directoire*.

1. The administration of the sacraments should at the same time have a kerygmatic significance. There must be a proclamation of the word, setting out the meaning of the sacramental event. The prayers themselves, in the case of a baptism, for example, are therefore to be said in the language of the people.

2. The administration of the sacraments should also be accompanied by training of the conscience and of the theologal sense of the people.[10] An end should be made to routine sacramentalism and ritualism and to the hidden superstitious tendencies which so often accompany such ritualism in the minds of many believers.

3. In their administration, the sacraments should inspire Christians with a sense of community and of individual apostolic responsibility.

A baptism, a funeral or a marriage would thus become

---

[9] Published by the Union des Oeuvres Catholiques in the series *Questions pastorales*, no. 5. Paris (n.d.).

[10] For the meaning of 'theologal', see *Christ the Sacrament*, 16.

authentic acts of the parish community of believers in which
the sacraments would be really experienced, as they were in
the Roman christian period, as a *sacramentum-iuramentum*,
an involvement in life, penetrating deeply into so-called profane life and into all the encounters and dealings that take
place in this world between christians and non-christians. In
this way, the sacrament becomes an integral sacrament of the
faith of the church, a testimony to faith on the part of the
whole believing community, which the individual then carries
with him in his personal life of testimony out into the world.
We have therefore to emphasise more strongly the theologal
religious commitment of the sacramental life and not simply
be content to administer valid sacraments, to regulate marriages 'juridically' and so on, without making sure that the
inner religious commitment of the recipient of the sacrament
is changed. Perhaps the most striking characteristic of this
Directoire, then, is the genuine concern of its authors for
various categories of people who are outside the classical
rubrics of ecclesiastical law (unbelievers, heretics, schismatics,
apostates and public sinners), but who have been placed outside the framework of this law by the present situation in the
world. These include, for example, people who are not practising Catholics, but who ask to receive a sacrament such as
that of marriage, people who are excluded from the sacraments because of their way of life, those who do not go to
church, but who want their children to be baptised, non-
practising Catholics who still make their Easter duties and so
on. In their *Directoire*, the French bishops do not repudiate
such people, but, on the other hand, they insist that there is
no quick solution to their problem. What is required in all
these cases is a gradual, pastoral formation of the conscience.
Any other course of action would endanger the very principles
of the church, because people would then inevitably be reinforced in their impression that the sacraments are a kind of
formality, like the work of a notary, a town clerk or other
public official, in which formal difficulties often arise, but in
such a way that they always remain a pure question of
formality. This kills the power of sacramental christianity to

win souls. Christians can so easily and so often be regarded by those who think differently as people who marry in church and go to mass on Sundays, but who, in the rest of their lives, think, feel, behave and live just like non-christians. This kind of christian life leaves the others cold—it does not shock or disturb them. Sincere non-christian militants are quite indifferent to this sort of christianity—they feel that it is simply not worth while to become a christian for a way of life that is not an active commitment to life.

In the case of such dechristianised people, it seems to me that it is more useful—however delicate a task it may be—to build up temporarily on an ignorance that cannot be overcome and to form the conscience first, rather than to seek refuge immediately in an uncritical administration of the sacraments. In this connection, one of the measures outlined in the *Directoire* is very instructive. If there is, for example, haste in the case of a marriage when one of the parties is 'dechristianised', that is, he was born of baptised parents, but is not baptised himself and is a 'pagan', there should be no rapid catechising followed by baptism. On the contrary, the priest should not baptise the person, but ask for a dispensation on grounds of the *disparitas cultus,* instruct him in the christian faith for several months and form his conscience and only then administer baptism. It is only in this way that formalism can be prevented in christianity and the christian lay community can exert a missionary influence on dechristianised people. It is only in this way that christianity will again be made conscious of itself as a personal, all-embracing task in life. It will then, of itself, become apostolic and win souls, not by chasing after them, but by the personal testimony of the lives of christians themselves. The testimony of christian charity and of a fully sacramental christian life is essentially *doctrinal,* even though it is implicit. It is a proclamation of the truth of God's love for men, a testimony of the truth that is accomplished in the witness in and through his christian association with love. We tend far too much to think that preaching is only doctrinal when it communicates concepts. This is not so. Our active christian life,

57

borne up by experiential knowledge, can also be a genuine communication of dogma.

In connection with the reactivation of liturgical sacramental life, modern conditions also require a longer period of catechumenate. There is even a need to return, without resorting to archaic forms and methods, to some extent to the original catechumenate which flourished especially in the third, fourth and fifth centuries. This was, of course, a catechumenate for adult converts from the pagan world and is thus analogous with the modern situation. Their instruction lasted for three whole years. Towards the end of the third year, as Easter was approaching, the various initiations that now take two minutes to perform during the ceremony of baptism were carried out over a period of time. This intensive dogmatic and moral course of instruction closed with the catechumen's solemn confession of faith, which was consciously accepted as a life commitment. This was followed, during Holy Week, by a detailed kerygmatic clarification of the sacraments of initiation that the catechumen was to receive at Easter itself. The most noteworthy characteristics of this ancient catechumenate, then, are the gradual nature of the whole of this christian initiation and the involvement of the catechumens in the liturgy.

Later on, the situation changed. Children were baptised immediately after they were born and the whole of their education as christians was post-baptismal, taking the form of a spontaneous adaptation to an environment that had been completely christianised, simply by living in it. As they grew up, they breathed in the air of christianity. When they reached the age of discretion, they went to church with their parents and once again automatically assimilated the liturgical and sacramental catechesis.

A further change took place in the modern world. Protestantism made it necessary for a *vademecum* of orthodox doctrine to be compiled—the catechism. Since the Reformation, then, christian instruction has been conceptually doctrinal and quite independent of the liturgy. There were no serious disadvantages in this during the sixteenth and seventeenth centuries as the whole environment was still christian and instruction through the catechism was simply a perfection of what the children had been absorbing for a long time at home and in the community around them. But, since the laicisation and the dechristianisation of the environment that took place especially in the nineteenth and twentieth centuries, the situation has again become quite different. The catechism no longer has any point of contact either with the church's liturgical and sacramental life or with the concrete problems of life which are felt, psychologically, to be real. The catechism consists of abstract doctrinal affirmations which are no longer based on what children have already learnt to practise in concrete at home, since the family environment is already dechristianised.

This has led to many different adaptations in the field of modern pastoral work. We can certainly derive a number of suggestions from the ancient form of the catechumenate adapted to the modern situation. There is, after all, no sense in beginning, in a dechristianised working-class environment, by building a church and then enticing people to it, possibly via the church hall where films are shown, if they do not understand the meaning of going to church. We must be bold enough to draw the consequences from their ignorance which cannot be overcome, with the result that our whole apostolic effort will have to be directed towards making going to church and all its consequences the culmination of a long period of preparation and initiation. It should be much easier to communicate to dechristianised people the meaning of belonging to the church as an inner need of awakened faith if faith in the redeeming fact of Christ has first been aroused in them. This demands, of course, a patient gradual approach, but it will produce better results than bluntly insisting on ecclesiastical laws. These laws are certainly not to be neglected, but they demand a certain preliminary formation of conscience; otherwise, at least in the present situation, whenever these laws are not kept, a situation of sinful 'bad faith' or ignorance may arise. The fact that the priest goes on pointing out that baptised but dechristianised people are bound to hear mass

on Sundays does not, *ipso facto*, do away with the psychological condition of ignorance that cannot be overcome! But,
if these people are really addressed personally by the fact of
Christ and the event of Christ has really aroused their interest,
they should once again begin to understand, from this point
of departure, the meaning of the church as the sacramental
extension of Christ and thus also move from ignorance to
'knowledge' with regard to the church's commandments and
the obligation to fulfil them. This method can often seem to
be delicate and hazardous and it can also give rise to intricate
'problems of conscience' for the priest, but this only indicates
the importance of a thorough theological knowledge accompanied by a clear insight into the complexity of the human
psyche. These 'dechristianised' people who have already been
inwardly seized by the person of Christ may, for the time
being, not keep the commandments of the church, but their
priest can regard them as already won over and they may
already be helping him actively in his apostolate. This may
well occasion surprise, scepticism and even disapproval among
some of his colleagues, those who place too much value on the
number of confessions, communions and properly conducted
marriages in their parishes and too little on the religious
background and the existential experience of these essential
acts of the church.

It is, of course, true that, for believing christians, the church
points directly to Christ. But for the great mass of people who
have been brought up to be against or indifferent to the
church, the church is the priest who lives among them, does
good, shows love, tells them about Christ and only from that
point refers them back to the 'great' church. It is therefore
only gradually that the church will appear to these people in
her purely religious form. The converts, gathered round their
'worker-priest', will probably view that great church distrust-
fully for a while, the great parish church that is not their own.
This, however, seems to me to be of secondary importance—
we should not do violence to the psyche of these people. If
their own district priest, whom they trust completely, makes
contact with the great parish church and if the parish priest

of this middle-class church makes friendly visits to their priest and to them, their antipathy may gradually be overcome. There is also no reason why bigger districts at least should not be raised to the status of parishes.

There has been a good deal of controversy concerning the territorial structure of the parish as a hindrance to pastoral work. Many people have advocated a change in the law of the church so that the pastoral care of christian communities can be given a natural basis rather than be forced, as it is now, within the pattern of a definite territory. Under the present territorial principle, people who do not form a naturally connected community are grouped together for the purposes of one single pastoral task. This system completely ignores the natural community as a basis for common apostolic action. The reformers are urging that various more homogeneous groups of people who need their own special pastoral care should form a parish and be entrusted to a priest.

On the one hand, it is obvious that the territorial principle, despite its many inconveniences, is still the best solution if we wish to avoid creating a 'class' church. On the other hand, however, this territorial principle could certainly be applied more elastically. In many cases, a working-class district, a seamen's quarter and other closely knit communities could be raised to the level of parishes. The formation of parishes from existing communities in this way would certainly be a more favourable basis for instruction and for the whole of parochial pastoral work. An improvement could be made too in the selection of parish priests. Under the present territorial system of dividing parishes, a 'middle-class' parish priest tends to neglect one part of his parish, while a 'working-class' priest tends to overlook another part. The territorial division would certainly seem to be the most practical in country districts, although this principle has its difficulties in the towns and cities. Yet I can hardly envisage a situation in which we had 'parishes of retail tradesmen' or 'parishes of office employees'. This principle strikes me as too unchristian. It is calculated too strictly on a basis of differentiated natural groupings and these groupings should in fact be brought together by the christian community. In my opinion, it is only obvious that this principle should be applied, and practical to apply it when there are, as I have already said, naturally clearly marked and enclosed groups of people who have just been brought back again to christianity, so as to overcome inevitable difficulties in the relationship between such groups and the parish which is completely alien to them and in which they would not feel at ease. To oblige people like this to go to a dignified 'posh' mass on Sundays in the middle-class parish church would be like making them go to a reception in a splendid salon, where they would be afraid to move an inch. Education of these workers towards a popular culture of their own should help to bridge these gaps gradually. Generally speaking, the canonical principle of the parish *territorium* may still, despite all its shortcomings, be regarded as the best and we should look for the solution only in a greater number of parishes. We shall have accomplished a great deal already if we manage to distinguish, in the minds of the workers, between what is *essential* in christianity and what are simply incidental historical aspects of 'incarnation'. The workers should not, in their renewed christianity, imitate in any sense the way of life and habits of middle-class christians. We must not make christian practice more difficult for them by imposing on them purely transitory, traditional elements, habits and customs which they may not like or easily accept. These include, for example, collections of money during mass, special devotions which are alien to them, class differences in the case of nuptial masses or funerals, the celebration of mass in the morning instead of in the evening, which would suit them better, and so on. We must, then, be careful to avoid giving them the impression that there is a separate supernatural life alongside the natural life. The christian, however, does not lead a double life—he leads one life with an effectively, transcendentally deepened theological horizon.

On the other hand, however, there still remains the very real problem of pastoral work among workers who do not live together in one district. Contact with these dechristianised people on the part of the priest seems to me to be almost completely excluded at present. I can therefore understand very well that, in the absence of soundly trained christian workers, laymen who will bear witness, apostolic priests come forward with the wish to take over this task for the time being. And, of course, a priest must be among the people. But he must be among them as a priest, that is, formally and as a mediator between God and men. This priestly being among the people can, however, take on different, divergent forms in accordance with differing historical situations. The fact that some priests are nowadays employing exceptional means because of the great gulf separating the mass of working-class people from the church seems to me to have been inspired by a great trust in the grace that calls all men. Let us briefly consider two of these exceptional means that are concretely put into practice. Firstly, the priest goes and lives as a priest in his own working-class home in a working-class district that is alienated from the church, but he does this in order to work directly *as a priest* and to do charitable work. Not only can one have nothing at all against this—it also seems to me to be completely priestly. Secondly, the priest goes and works as an ordinary worker in a factory among other workers. This method is, in my opinion, 'para-priestly'. It is far more a method that should be reserved for a period of transition, during which christian lay workers are not able to play a decisive part in the factory as witnesses and for so long as the isolation of the working-class world remains a factual datum. It is temporary, supplementary work. The lack of understanding with regard to this method, which can certainly create complications and moral problems for the priest concerned, seems to me to have been occasioned by a certain intellectualism. Surely our ideas have become utterly saturated with the middle-class outlook if we regard it as perfectly normal—and we usually do!—for a priest to spend the whole of his time absorbed in astronomy, entomology or some similar scholarly pursuit and yet as beneath the dignity of the priesthood for a priest to do manual work and, what is more, to do it with a directly apostolic intention—in order to show forth the christian idea of life in a working-class environment, not only by telling people how they ought to live by the relatively easy method of preaching to them, but by actively giving them a living example of the christian way of life in hard reality. It is easy enough to agree with the mocking comment of the worker who said, 'I didn't think you became a priest in order to rivet bolts all day long.' But the answer to this is just as pungent: 'I didn't think I became a priest in order to play football with the boys or show Queen Fabiola on the screen of the parish cinema!' As the Abbé Godin has said so pertinently:

> What will make these people 'believe in' priests?...His chastity? They cannot believe in it or, if they do, they regard the celibate priest as an abnormal man without human desires. His obedience? But they obey too, and their obedience is harder. His goodness? Is that enough? No, it is purely nega- tive—these simple people will not, in only a few encounters, clearly notice the goodness of the priest as different from that of tactful politeness and affability. After all, the registrar whom they have just left after seeing him to get married, for example, was affable, eager to please and dutifully polite, so was the jeweller and the furniture salesman...Well, then? The priest's *affirmation of a life of poverty*. Educated people who could earn a lot of money—they must believe in it to live like that.[11]

That was the apostolic method of the poor man Dominic! We should always be open-minded towards apostolic methods which may perhaps not appeal to us personally, but which some people are inspired by charity to put into practice, and to do so without any romantic feelings. Even though all con- tact with the church has been broken, there is still the com- mon basis of shared humanity and human brotherhood. Of course, the church is not a church of workers, any more than she is a church of respectable citizens or middle-class people, nobles or peasant farmers. She is the church of *all people*. But because she is at the moment the church of many people with the exception of the workers, this special pastoral care of the workers is quite legitimate. 'Christianity must spread. It must enter the pagan environment and bring into it the light of Christ. But if it is to be active anywhere, it must at least be

11 P. Glorieux, *Un homme providentiel: l'abbé Godin*, Paris (n.d.), p 72.

there *aliquo modo*. It is, however, in the world of the workers *nullo modo*.'[12] The conclusions are obvious—abandoning the apostolate in those environments would mean betraying our mission, while we should look for contacts in those environments where they are possible and where they create an atmosphere of trust. Surely missionaries in the Congo are also to a very great extent 'worker-priests', although for a different reason? Structural reforms alone will not automatically make these dechristianised people into christians, especially if they know what a big part socialists (and communists) also play in demanding such reforms. We should not forget that, although Catholics also have their own progressive social programme now, the workers still look on the marxists as their saviours and no gradually implemented plan for social improvement will ever make them change their minds. The most urgent need here is for personal contact in human, helping love. The principle of a small group of three priests living together in a working-class district seems to me to be excellent—one worker-priest, one priest to do the priest's work and to visit people in their homes and one priest to receive people. This idea of a differentiated function within the small community of priests is the ideal solution.

This does not in any sense mean that most 'priests of the workers' must become 'worker-priests'. God preserve us—we should have cause to complain of the quality of their work! No, this apostolate above all calls for exceptional moral and religious strength and balance. The worker-priests' method came to be viewed in France with a certain amount of suspicion because a number of dubious men with restless temperaments, studying in the seminaries or later working in various dioceses, joined the ranks of the worker-priests out of a spirit of adventure. As soon as a lack of balance or romanticism creeps into this type of work, it is better to keep away from it. I would refer here to only one ecclesiological 'foundation' of the worker-priest movement. If we regard the church *in fieri*, then priests are the organ of Christ called into being

[12] P. Glorieux, *Un homme providentiel*, 286.

by him in order to found and to *form* the community of the church (the foundation of the church by Christ began with the establishment of the *hierarchy*). The priestly hierarchy, guided by the episcopate, makes the community of the church come into being. The ordinary priest is the one who is *sent* by the episcopate—it is he who plants the church in pagan environments or to whom a definite flock is entrusted for his pastoral care. We are now confronted with the fact that the world of the working classes is outside the church—it is not simply 'dechristianised', but is becoming, with the passage of time, more and more pagan. It is unbaptised. The whole problem of the apostolate here is therefore one of establishing the church anew. The priest himself is essentially called to do this. But—because of various situations that have in fact developed, every formally priestly contact is in practice impossible. The worker-priest's form of penetration is therefore nothing but an application of his priestly mission to found the church. But let us be quite clear—there is no question of any 'dogmatic' or 'theological' foundation of the worker-priest's apostolate here. What we have here is the intervention of a *minor rationis* which is, however, simply the concrete assessment of a factual situation—the acceptance of facts leading, on the basis of the priest's mandate to establish the church, to this particular form of penetration, that of the worker-priest. It is, in a word, a bold *conclusion* from the combination of human experience and priestly mission. In view of the fact that the priest is the one sent by the episcopate, this manner of 'planting' the church should also meet with the approval of the worker-priest's superiors. Others, however, have made a different assessment of the facts and this should give the worker-priests a sense of humble realism and a broad-minded approach wherever differences of opinion arise. This, however, should never be allowed to give rise to the sterile situation in which each side accuses the other of heresy.

3. The revival of the lay apostolate

The church, as the community of inward grace, is essentially expansive, conquering and missionary and, as I have already said, the two fundamental functional activities in the visible, sacramental appearance of that community of grace are represented by the laity and the hierarchy. This means, then, that we priests should not expect everything from our apostolate, which is only a differentiated organ alongside and in co-operation with the apostolate of the laity. The success of our priestly apostolate is therefore dependent on its being co-ordinated with the activity of the laity. The great event of our own times—the 'voice of God'—is, in my opinion, without doubt the fact that the priestly hierarchy is gradually freeing itself from its former too worldly commitments and concentrating all its efforts on its own *religious* mission and that the Catholic laity is at the same time becoming fully conscious of its own distinctive vocation within the world and is making its christian life incarnate in this vocation, while still continuing to regard striving towards holiness as the sole necessity. It is unfortunately true to say that, in the past, priests have tended too much to misjudge the specific task of the laity and have at the most used lay people as a help in their own priestly, pastoral work. They have also tended to look down on the laity—as was expressly acknowledged by a papal bull in the middle ages. There has been no conscious recognition of the laity as a functional apostolic activity of the community of the church—it has simply been regarded as the object of the church's care. The strength but also the basic weakness of Catholic Action, when it first began, was undoubtedly the introduction of the laity simply as a help in the hierarchical apostolate. This basic error was, however, remedied by Pius XII when he enlarged Catholic Action and even more when he gave canonical sanction to the Secular Institutes and thus bestowed open recognition on the distinctively lay status.

We must, however, first of all establish precisely what a 'lay' person is. In the history of the church, the lay state has been defined as distinct from the monastic state and also as distinct from the priestly hierarchy. Since the recent papal pronouncements on the Secular Institutes, however, the concept 'lay' has become both more difficult to define and at the

same time more strictly defined—the lay Catholic is the baptised person who does not belong to the priestly hierarchy,
but who either fulfils a secular task *in the world* (and does this
either in the light of the general aspiration towards christian
perfection or as a 'religious' in the broadest sense of the word
who aspires to the state of perfection in the strict sense) or
who does this, not in the world, but in a monastery, as a lay-
brother or sister or one who does not take priestly orders. We
are principally concerned here with the laity in the first sense
and in its double category.

A. *The 'professed' laity in the world*

In addition to the general holiness which applies to all
christians, Christ also gave us the inspiration for radical holiness, practised by carrying out effectively the evangelical
counsels as perfection in love. Two aspects should be distinguished in this state of perfection. Firstly, there is the inward life project, in other words, a striving towards perfection
in love by effectively carrying out the evangelical counsels, a
practice which is inwardly sanctioned by an authentic way of
life, a fundamental commitment which will ensure that it is
continued. This is, as it were, the mystical aspect of the state
of perfection, its divine essence instituted by Christ. Secondly,
there is the juridical or canonical aspect of the state of perfection. This is a definite and concrete way of life led by certain
christians with the *official* confirmation of the hierarchy of the
church that the so-called moral state of perfection is in fact
realised in this way of life. This juridical aspect, then, is the
church's official and canonical recognition of a definite way of
life as a real striving towards perfection in love in accordance
with the evangelical counsels and intended as an effective
commitment. This juridical aspect does not therefore bring
about the state of perfection, as has recently been claimed in
some quarters, but it does ratify it, as it were, *ex officio* and at
the same time makes it subject to certain juridical conditions,
namely, communal life (at least in the Latin church) and the
taking of vows in the canonical (varying) sense.

Until 1947, Rome only recognised this state of perfection

in the case of monastics and of non-monastics who lived in broad outline in accordance with the monastic state, that is, communities of priests who did not take public vows. Since the apostolic constitution, *Provida Mater*,[13] and the documents relating to this constitution,[14] however, the state of perfection has been extended to include not only those leading strictly monastic lives, but also lay people who fulfil their secular task in the world. This means therefore that the evangelical state of perfection is open to various gradations and that the historical forms of realising the state of perfection may, in other words, differ 'almost fundamentally'. Lay people living in the world—manual workers, lawyers, doctors, office workers and so on—can thus, simply as lay people in their secular environment in the world, fully practise the essential part of the religious life[15] by joining a Secular Institute. This seems to me to be an enormous extension with unsuspected possibilities for the apostolate.[16] According to article 1 of the *Lex peculiaris saeculariorum institutorum*, the aim of these Secular Institutes (which have existed for a long time, but were not in principle recognised as a 'state of perfection' until 1947) is defined as follows: 'they are societies of religious or laypeople, the members of which observe the evangelical counsels *in the world* with the aim of attaining christian perfection and of carrying out the apostolate in the full sense of the word'. This state of perfection, then, is not a flight from the world, but a commitment within the world on the part of the christian layman to be, in and through his secular professional or working life, practised in true perfection in love, a christian fermentation for his fellow-workers or colleagues. It is therefore not a question of Catholic Action in the official sense, that is, direct help in the apostolate of the hierarchy, but of *typically lay life in the world*, as a worker, a lawyer or a docker, which is not excluded from the strict state

---

[13] Issued on 2 February 1947; see *AAS* 30 (1947), 114–24.

[14] Motu Proprio, *Primo feliciter*, 12 March 1948 and the instruction **Cum Sanctissimus**, 19 March 1948; see *AAS* 40 (1948), 283–6 and 293–7.

[15] 'Substantia vitae religiosae': see the instruction *Cum Sanctissimus*, *AAS* 40 (1948), 293.

[16] See *AAS* 39 (1947), 120ff.

of perfection of the 'religious life'. These christians are thus lay people who may or may not live in a community, but who work in a secular environment as separate people in the world. All that they must have, however, is a lasting bond with the Institute, which must have one central house where the superiors reside and where the members can be accommodated when they are ill, in old age and so on.

It must above all be emphasised that these 'religious' and 'professed' lay people occupy an exceptional position in the general sphere of lay spirituality. Such lay people might be the providential link between the workers who were alienated from the church and the priest. If these institutes had been more widely spread (and they are already more widespread than many people imagine), there would have been no need for the question of the worker-priests ever to have arisen. Workers, members of a lay Secular Institute, are the concrete realisation of what has now to be done by the worker-priests in the absence of such lay people. They are genuine workers who are professed religious, 'worker-religious', not because of a transitory measure, but by virtue of their vocation, on the basis of their bringing, within their secular lay office, evangelical perfection in love, realised in a living person, as a leaven among unbelieving lay people. One Italian bishop even went so far as to take a worker of this kind from a Secular Institute, keep him with him for two years, give him a summary but sound theological training and then ordain him. Afterwards, this man resumed working as a worker—not as a 'worker-priest', but as a 'priest-worker'. The results in the factory where this 'religious' is working have apparently been astonishing.

The deep meaning of this new movement to which Rome has given its sanction is to establish an apostolate of presence and, what is more, an apostolate of 'professed' presence in the world through lay people who will go to the limits of magnanimity and who will, in their external appearance (by celibacy, real working-class poverty and insecurity, and so on), will bear witness to the fact that they are possessed by Christ. Several of the older monastic orders in Germany already have a Secular Institute which forms, so to speak, a loose fourth category in addition to the classical categories (fathers, brothers and lay-brothers). The characteristic feature of the older monastic orders, their withdrawal from the world, is given its *inward* radical life pattern in these institutes and, moreover, its visible externalisation in the vows of poverty, chastity and obedience.

In my opinion, these Secular Institutes, in which the lay member *remains fully lay*, offer enormous possibilities in the apostolate. Their members are the shock troops of the apostolate and they fully embody in their lay lives Cesbron's definition of the worker-priests in *Saints Go to Hell*: 'to be the representatives among unbelievers of religious unrest'. In my opinion, too, these workers will be more readily and more easily accepted by dechristianised workers than priests who lay aside their real work as priests for the time being purely in order to practise the apostolate of presence. Even those who do not believe prefer, I think, to see a priest performing his *own* function.

B. *The (married) laity in the world*

Even lay people who do not come within any so-called canonically recognised state of perfection and therefore normally marry have a special apostolic function in and through their lay membership of the church and they have this function not primarily as helpers in the apostolate of the priests, but in and through their lay task in the world in the perspective of a christian inspiration. In the first place, it is they who should be doing, among other things, much of the social work that is now done by priests. They are responsible for the humane ordering of society as the basis of the life of grace. That is their vocation. The priest himself builds on the basis of their work in order to undertake the religious intention apostolically.[17] Our aim in religion can never be to build up a well regulated community here on earth. The aim of religion transcends this. But the special task of the laity is to regulate

[17] I have analysed the task of the laity *within* the church herself in volume IV of 'Theological Soundings', *Mission of the Church*.

life here on earth and to do this *autonomously*, that is, not as
tools of the priestly hierarchy, but as full lay people.

The laity thus has a very important part to play in social,
political and economic life and both the working class and
the intellectual leadership have to share in building up an
environment that is receptive to grace. Laymen who are
competent in this sphere must be responsible for the structural reforms of society—the hierarchical church cannot
make any positive contributions to this task. The church
certainly has a social inspiration, but she is in no way
competent to apply this inspiration to concrete situations.
This is the task of the laity. But it is not simply a question of
'applying' the church's social inspiration—this lay task always
demands a human evaluation of concrete facts. What is more,
the church has, in herself, no mission to judge this lay task.
Given the church's social inspiration, the laity thus has a
creative function to fulfil. The church, for example, accepts
the need for a state authority, but this does not mean that she
judges which is the best concrete form for the state to assume
in this or that particular situation. This comes within the lay
sphere of competence and it is for lay people to assess the
situation autonomously, to apply whatever concrete measures
are necessary and to be personally responsible for their actions.
The 'church's social teaching' is therefore a rather ambiguous
concept, especially if the concrete measures that are applied
after a personal evaluation of the concrete facts are simply regarded as having been 'taken from the social encyclicals'
when a different evaluation of the facts might have led to
a very different application of the same principles of the
church's social teaching. The 'church's social teaching' and
'particular solutions in this world' are thus radically different
and it is the legitimate task of a responsible laity to form
the link between the two. (This does not mean that it is
not *possible* for the ecclesiastical authority, *if need be*, to dis-
approve of a solution arrived at by laymen and good in itself,
if the church as a whole requires this disapproval.) In itself,
however, the assessment of particular facts in this world comes
within the sphere of competence, not of the hierarchy of the

church, but of the christian lay community. The hierarchy itself does not build up any secular social institutions—it is the laity which does this. We should be seriously misjudging the distinctively lay vocation within the church if we were to deny this lay responsibility and thus compel the church herself, in her administrative capacity, to find concrete solutions to worldly matters in which she is not competent to act. The layman alone has the obligation to form his own free, autonomous opinion in the social, political and economic sphere in the light of the christian faith and sound social philosophy. The church is therefore committed to the temporal, terrestrial task of ordering life in this world *through her laity* and, in view of the fact that 'terrestrial facts' are constantly evolving, the Catholic laity will have an unceasing, autonomous creative function in this sphere, especially in a time such as our own. It is therefore quite possible for Catholic lay people, without misjudging the church's so-called social teaching, to arrive at very different solutions because they make differing assessments of the concrete facts of the situation. The hierarchy must allow her laity complete freedom in this. It is only then that the basis of the reproach of 'clericalism', which is not always entirely groundless, will to a great extent be removed.

Apart from the leading function of the lay intellectual in the social, political and economic sphere, the worker also has his own distinctively lay task. And, in my opinion, we priests must, in addition to stressing the duty of these christian workers to bear integral apostolic witness to their faith, emphasising the importance of the commandment to love, the value, in a word, of their theological lives, also provide them with a 'theology' of work. We have to illuminate the human meaning of their terrestrial task in the ordering of a world which is receptive to grace and which consists of people who work in the light of grace.

In a word, the Catholic worker must be made conscious of the fact that his work is not only a means of earning a livelihood, but also a factor of the whole process of making men free and humanising them. Work—*ratio et manus,* as the ancients called it—is, after all, the bond which links men in a human manner with the world. The humanisation of mankind is to a great extent accomplished thanks to man's contact through work in and with the world—it is through this that man collaborates in the process of creation as God's helper, working with him. It is also through individual and collective sinfulness on the part of men and the inhumane conditions of work that have been brought about by this sinfulness that work can also have an alienating and depersonalising effect. Work must therefore, like every human value, not only be 'baptised'—it must also be accompanied by humane conditions. It is a fact that this christian idea of work (and therefore also the *right* to work) can unleash an enormous dynamism. There can be no doubt that the Young Christian Workers' movement was given a great stimulus by the consciousness of its members of the christian and humanising value of work. Production could thus be regarded as a contribution to the raising of the human person in the community and as collaboration in a spirit of solidarity in the task of ordering life in the world in the awareness that the worker was playing a part, by doing something not neutral and incidental, but essential, in making people receptive to the coming of the kingdom of God. This sense of playing an active part in a communal enterprise, not by ascetic exercise in addition to one's already arduous work, but in and through one's work itself, brings the virtue of surrender to maturity, even though the part played by each individual may perhaps seem to be unimportant. This can develop into a hidden mysticism in the heart of the noisy factory, a mysticism which need not take second place to the surrender of the contemplative monk or the apostolic priest, who constantly experiences a sense of apparent uselessness with regard to his priestly labours, but who, in divine surrender, does not give it up.

It is, of course, true that progressive methods in the apostolate, especially as practised in certain countries, are often viewed with scepticism. This is partly attributable to the fact that the people who are associated with these new forms of the apostolate do not always have well-balanced personalities and partly to the fact that pioneering is always accompanied by blunders. This should help to teach us that these new forms require priests who are not only better trained in dogmatics and in moral theology, but whose consciences are also well above average *in inventiveness and in creativeness,* who are morally mature, have sober and balanced personalities without any trace of fickle romanticism and are capable of dealing resourcefully with the dogmatic fact of salvation in contact with differing human experience and above all who lead a life of prayer in self-emptying and humility. What really counts is the gentle strength of a sound and holy personality which, as love, does not seek itself (1 Cor 13:5).

On the other hand, however, the element of risk involved in these new situations should not cause a candidate for the priesthood to fail in his apostolic mission to bring God to those places where men need him most and have him least purely out of fear. Tutiorism—the choice of the safer course —and considerations of safety can often lead to excessive caution instead of being a healthy and at the same time daring prudence. After all, God is 'also' there! It goes without saying that these new methods will claim their victims. But surely the older methods also had *their* victims? The risk is to be found less in the oldness or the newness of the methods of penetration than in the 'old man' whom we always carry with us together with our finest idealism. According to Pastor Hermas's image, the church will always resemble a poor old woman in whom Christ's glory, through new crucifixions, is again and again breaking through, modestly but triumphantly. The victory has already been achieved! 'Be of good cheer, I have overcome the world' (Jn 16:33).

Our religious sense of God must be decisive here and give us the courage to do what purely human considerations of caution would dissuade us from doing. Is it then permissible for lay people, outside the experience of the monastic life, to have to live in such situations and to live in them as christians, while we monks, after years of training, lack the courage to do so? In that case, we are demanding a great deal of these people, and very little of ourselves. All this only points to the fact that our superiors have a great responsibility to choose only well balanced people for these pioneering forms of the apostolate.

What must be regarded as a special reason for rejoicing is the firm will of these priests to approach the mass of people who are alienated from the church in a purely religious and purely priestly spirit. It is quite certain that the church is an incarnate reality which penetrates all the dimensions of human life and is not simply a suprastructure on top of a terrestrial community. This aspect of the church legalises every form of human penetration. But above all we must have the courage to proclaim the pure word of salvation, first by the act of loving contact and then, and at the same time, by the sacrament of preaching in its pure christian sense. Otherwise the workers will always be shy of the priestly appearance which calls to mind too much the things of this world and is too little a pure invitation to the God of love, who was so human in his love for the poor that he came to them in the flesh *as a man*. Another cause for rejoicing is the theological insight that the community of the church as such is the real, active, apostolic organ and that this organ is not only the church's priests, not only the parish, but every living member of the church. The priestly apostolate alone cannot solve the problem. The Catholic laity is more conscious than ever before of its irreplaceable apostolic task and it will be able to take over a great deal of the priest's work which is really the work of the laity, thus freeing him and giving him the opportunity to be a *priest*.

4
'THE SORROW OF THE EXPERIENCE OF GOD'S CONCEALMENT'[1]

During the reign of Philip II of Spain, a plan to make the two rivers, Tajo and Manzanares, navigable and thus to provide greater economic opportunities for certain isolated groups of the population was submitted to the governors. The government commission rejected the suggestion. It was freely admitted that the situation of these groups of the population was unsatisfactory and indeed intolerable. But the plan was rejected on these grounds—'if it had been the will of God that these rivers should be navigable, he would have made them so with a single word, as in the past: let there be light. It would be a presumptuous infringement of the rights of Providence for human hands to venture to improve what God for unfathomable reasons has left unfinished'.[2]

This fact indicates a distinctive attitude of mind. Although it now belongs to the past, this attitude still survives in many different and less tangible forms among us today. We have heard so much in recent years about the present-day 'absence of God' that we have all accepted it uncritically as a massive reality. It is, of course, clear that God is absent in places where we previously had urgent need of him because of our shortcomings as men in the world. Then we forced him to be present. What had, however, escaped man's notice at that time was that this presence lacked all the gratuity, the aspect of grace which characterises all genuine presence, with the consequence that man has now become blind to the distinction between absence and concealment, to God's unsuspected, deep presence as it is felt in our contemporary, more real experi-

<hr />

[1] The title is a quotation from Dr K. H. Miskotte, *Als de Goden zwijgen. Over de zin van het Oude Testament*, Haarlem 1965, 205. English translation *When the Gods are Silent*, London 1967, New York 1968.

[2] Quoted in M. Landmann, *Problematik. Nichtwissen und Wissenverlangen im philosophischen Bewusstsein*, Göttingen 1949, 55 n 13.

ence of human solidarity. Never before in history has God's presence in the world been so intimate and so tangibly real as now, in our own time, yet we do nothing but proclaim his absence everywhere, as though God were not really and most significantly present precisely at a time when impartial commitment to our fellow-men, service to others, is becoming a fundamental project in life and an effective force. Surely this is precisely what is happening in our own time—it is the central event of grace in post-war world history. God has consequently come infinitely more close to us now than he was in the past. Our repeated references to God's absence only serve to reveal how powerfully the older attitude of mind, which caused men to regard God as a 'long stop' or a God who 'intervened', still continues to have an unconscious effect on our views and values.

1. The correlation of our image of man and the world with our image of God

As long ago as the second century, Justin wrote: 'We Christians are called *atheoi* and, it is true, we are "godless" if what is meant by the word "God" is all kinds of pseudo-gods'.[3] Simply saying the word God does not in itself imply a religious sense, nor does not saying it imply the absence of religion or atheism. The word 'God' caresses man's lips far less now than it did in the past. This is a fact. But it is important to understand what this silence means. This modern phenomenon has been called *secularisation*, but this term is open to many different interpretations. It is up to us to evaluate the precise significance of the event which is taking place in our midst and which we are ourselves bringing about, and not immediately to call something that may in fact be a completely different event religious or irreligious—for example, a change in man's attitude towards his world.

After all, analysed in its primary and direct significance, so-called secularisation is not relevant in the religious sense.

---

[3] Justin, *Apologia* I, 6 (*PG* 6, 336): 'Inde et (nos christiani) athei appelamur; atque atheos quidem nos esse confitemur, si de opinatis eiusmodi dii agatur. Secus vero, si de verissimo illo Deo . . .'

Primarily and originally, this phenomenon is simply a basic change in man's attitude towards the 'world'. In the past, nature was experienced by man as the reality which transcended him. Feeling either lost or secure, he was situated in this immense nature with its mysterious forces. It inspired him with reverence and awe. At the same time, it was also the gentle mother. That was why religious man was able to experience nature simply as numinous—ancient man experienced God's anger or his blessing in the thunder and lightning, in the tempest and in the blowing of the wind. It was in this that the Jews experienced their history of salvation. Nature was the direct reflection of Yahweh's *kabhodh*, his glory and lustre. The fact that man's work has today become entirely scientific and technical means that he no longer experiences nature in this sense in the world in which he lives, but in the sense of a nature transformed by himself into a world of man.[4] The world in which man lives now has the lustre—or lack of lustre—of man himself who has made it. The natural world, which in the past was directly experienced as divine and numinous and which brilliantly displayed the *vestigia Dei* to man, has now been 'degraded' by the increasingly scientific and technical work of modern society to the level of raw building material in the hands of creative man. The world of today is nature insofar as it bears the *vestigia hominis*, the traces, not of God, but of *man*. From being divinised nature, it has become the work of man's hands. The world now points to man. Even raw nature, the thunder and lightning, the tempest and the wind, makes modern man think at once of the technical resistance offered by the dykes and the efficiency of the lightning conductors

[4] An immense number of books and articles have been written on this subject. I would mention only three general works: H. Schelsky, *Der Mensch in der wissenschaftlichen Zivilisation*, Stuttgart 1961; H. Freyer, *Theorie des gegenwärtigen Zeitalters*, Stuttgart 1958; R. Kwant, *De ontmoeting van wetenschap en arbeid*, Utrecht 1958; and the following written in the context of theology: J. Moltmann, *Theology of Hope*, London 1967; J. B. Metz, 'Die Zukunft des Glaubens in einer hominisierten Welt', *Weltverständnis im Glauben*, Mainz 1965, 45–62 and 'Welterfahrung und Glaubenserfahrung heute', *Kontexte (Süddeutsche Rundfunkserie)* 1 (1965), 17–26; K. Rahner, 'The man of today and Religion', *Theological Investigations* 6, London and Baltimore (Md) 1969, 3–20.

that he has made himself. And even though man has really only just begun to conquer nature, he no longer lives in a nature by which he feels overwhelmed or in which he feels secure and at home. He lives in a world that has been planned and produced by him and in which even raw nature has its special place in civilised society as a 'nature reserve'. As a conqueror, man goes out to meet nature and forces it to its knees by means of technical supremacy. The modern Prometheus really seizes fire from the sky. Nature no longer makes man think of the immense battle of a God against Leviathan, a battle in which primordial chaos was forced to become an ordered cosmos. The world in which we live today makes us think of man who himself overcomes Leviathan. The psalms, in which God's power is praised because of the glory of the sun, the moon and the stars, are today dying away on men's lips. Stones, trees and plants are no longer sacral places for him, in which God reveals himself. Direct, enthusiastic experience of the 'works of thy hands' has now become a similarly direct experience of the audacity of the 'works of *man's* hands', which is still only in its initial stages. Interpreted philosophically, this implies the degradation of nature from being the *subject* to being the *object* of man's control. Man has, for his part, discovered his own being as a subject. This change from cosmocentrism to anthropocentrism means that the once *theophanous* world has now become a *hominised* world, in the positive or the negative sense.

The original datum that we discover if we analyse the Copernican revolution of our contemporary experience of life is not, in the first place, a religious (or irreligious) event, but simply a change in man's relationship with the world. As such, it is a purely profane event that is concerned with this world—it is a changed experience of the world and of his own existence. The world is no longer simply 'nature', but an entirety of relationships on man's part with the terrestrial forms of his existence. In confrontation with this world, man is discovered as the subject, the demiurge of his terrestrial form of existence.

Many people experience this new interpretation of the

world and of man directly as a crisis in their religious life. We can say and are indeed bound to say that they should not, but, if we say this, we are misjudging the religious relevance of this event, which is not, as we have seen, the original datum, but a natural consequence of this datum. From the point of view of religious sociology, a certain correlation between the change in our image of man and the world and the *movement away from the church* at least is an exactly definable fact. This does not, however, provide us with any indication of the really correlative factors. The fact that French sociologists have established that there is a constant relationship between going to church every week and the possession of a bathroom at home does not point to any causal influence of the bathroom on regular church-going. It simply reveals that the practice of religion in France has been reduced by all kinds of historical, social and economic factors to the fairly well-off middle class. This is also true of our problem—the relatively constant relationship between the movement away from the church and man's new understanding of himself does not yet show the really correlative poles. What is clear is that man's new experience of his own existence, with its desacralising tendency as the expression of its *hominising* element, gives rise to the temptation to call God a 'useless hypothesis'.

The ascertainment of this sociological fact suggests that there is a correlation between our image of man and the world and our image of God. This correlation is indeed present, theologically as well. After all, long before he begins to reflect, man experiences his existence in this world. This existence in the world is at the same time a thinking existence and therefore also, however sketchily, an understanding of self and a world-view, in inseparable unity. Being with *himself* in human solidarity *in* this world is, moreover, the only door which gives man access to reality in its totality, since man cannot have at his disposal, in addition to his human existential experience, any other mysterious source of knowledge and consciousness of realities, including that of the God of creation or of revelation. There is no knowledge possible of realities of which no experience whatever is given. Since all human knowledge is based on perception, being consciously man in the world is man's only access to explicit consciousness here and now of all other possible realities. I cannot therefore discover God either, unless he makes himself known to me *in this world* as the creator of this world or by manifesting himself in grace and in the history of salvation *in this world* as the world of men. How could a divine revelation which was outside man's experience be heard—how, in other words, could it be a *revelation* to man?

My being with myself in human solidarity in this world is then, of its very nature, the focal point within which God too becomes visible to me as the creator and the bringer of grace and, what is more, I can only speak about the God of my salvation with the profane words, images and concepts derived from my interpretation of myself and my world-view. (The christian faith and the bible do not contain a single concept which does not have a profane, human content as well.) If this is so, then it is clear that any change in man's understanding of himself and of his world will, of its very nature, have repercussions on his image of God and on the whole of his relationship with God. The change in man's experience of the world as numinous nature to his experience of nature as inconsiderable but real building material for creative human freedom also has, by definition, a religious relevance. This can be misinterpreted and the new world-view can simply be experienced as the necessary casting out of all thought of God. Viewed critically, however, man's new world-view only means the casting out of the *old* image of God and the *old* forms of religion which were based on this—a becoming unreal of the empirical form in which the church appears. The true theological interpretation of and the directly raised response to the phenomenon of secularisation is therefore not disbelief or the secularisation of religion itself, but first and foremost a refusal to regard God as a factor *within this world*, the corner-stone of our universe, and a refusal to experience nature directly as *numinous*. Anyone who believes now in God the creator knows that, precisely on the basis of the divine transcendence of this act of creation,

God can only be present in the manner of absence, that he cannot be present as creatures are present for me and that he can therefore only be present as the experienced horizon of *creatural* presence. Although this new existential experience does also give rise to an atheistic understanding of self, it is not in itself a denial of faith, but a removal from religion and the church of those elements which religion had appropriated in a process of sacralisation and had, in so doing, withdrawn from their original *worldly* profanity.

This desacralisation of the world does not mean, however, that God becomes *unreal*. It does mean that the so-called cosmological proofs of the existence of God become unreal, that God becomes unreal for modern man insofar as he is presented and preached in a cosmocentric image of man and the world. In this sense, it is more difficult for modern man still to see God in the world. He can no longer experience God, with Paul and the writers of the Wisdom literature, as *phaneron*, as becoming as it were directly visible in the cosmos. In the older image of nature, it was virtually meaningless for man to deny the existence of God. His being in overwhelming, uncanny and yet at the same time mild nature —his immediate evidence of life—would have been made completely absurd by it. But, in the framework of his contemporary world-view, man in the world preserves his profane values, even if he denies God. We may not underestimate this situation. Behind all the forms of contemporary atheism, there is a real *experience*, undoubtedly not of God's non-existence, but certainly of facts that can be recognised historically. A life without religion—I am not saying a life without God (that is not dependent on us ourselves)—does not make man immoral, more stupid or less human or personal.[5] From the secular point of view, religion certainly does seem almost useless—it appears to yield no material result. Even without propaganda, it is here that atheism spontaneously attracts recruits. Atheists themselves therefore tend to regard history as an inevitable movement towards increas-

[5] J. M. le Blond, 'The Contemporary Status of Atheism', *International Philosophical Quarterly* 5 (1965), 37–55.

ing universal atheism. Christians are bound to make a distinction here. They readily admit and even welcome the fact that history is inevitably moving towards increasing desacralisation of the secular sphere, but on the other hand they continue to regard atheism as an ideological interpretation of historical facts which also retain their full value and meaning in a theistic and christian perspective and do not require an atheistic interpretation in order to be meaningful.

In the meantime, it is quite clear that a certain obscuring of God is undoubtedly the consequence of man's new understanding of himself and of the world. For the believer, there is basically in this an intensified sense of God's being as something incomprehensible, unimaginable and entirely transcendental, something which cannot be beheld and which is 'not of the world'. God has been deprived of his image and consequently it is now more difficult directly to understand man himself as God's 'image'. It is therefore possible for this situation to give rise increasingly to an atheistic explanation of existence, a phenomenon which, because of its present-day *social* dimension, makes clear and distinctly reveals what is possibly preying on the less accessible and obscure individual faith of all of us. The possibility of atheism (in all its forms) is essentially linked, on the one hand, with increasing secularity and thus with God's 'lack of standing' in this world and, on the other, with the freedom of meaningful human existence. God cannot deny himself, that is, he cannot deny his transcendence over the world. He cannot therefore make his existence compellingly evident and manifest to human knowledge, not even in the human appearance of Jesus Christ.

For the believer, however, secularisation is an urgent call to experience authentic christianity in a new way and in new forms. This does not mean that ancient or medieval christians, living in a numinous world, experienced christianity in a less authentically christian way. What it does mean is that christian authenticity itself passes through a history and that contemporary authenticity of christianity requires a critical attitude, not towards the ancient and medieval forms of re-

religion which, because of their evident social context at the time, were then authentic at least for people of that time, but towards the persistent clinging to patterns and forms which cannot have any *contemporary* social setting for modern christians and are consequently alien to life. Our new existential experience thus implies criticism of forms of religious experience which are derived from an earlier image of man and the world and *therefore* also from an outdated image of God. As the churches also have, institutionally, a communal aspect in which the religious attitude of their members is given a fixed form, it is obvious that the earlier religious attitude acquired, in the churches above all, a form that was, from the sociological point of view, hardly a supple one. It is consequently understandable that the process of secularisation displays a correlation with the movement away from the churches. From the theological point of view, this does not mean, however, that belief and active adherence to the church are in themselves in conflict with man's new understanding of himself, but it does mean, of course, that they are in conflict with the outdated forms given to belief in the church. The movement away from the church as a statistical datum of sociology therefore tells us, in itself, nothing about unbelief or non-christianity. From the theological point of view, however, it is undoubtedly a protest against the earlier forms of the church which modern man can no longer experience as a living reality and therefore, for modern religious man, a demand for the *aggiornamento* of the church herself.

But even this theological interpretation requires a more subtle shading, because, in religious experience, man's basic religious and christian intention cannot be adequately distinguished from the church's or from explicit forms of expression of this intention. Although these two aspects are not identical, they are nonetheless, in experience, intimately one. One never experiences the basic implicit religious intention unless it is contained within images which represent it and express it and which at the same time have a place in the valid image of man and the world. Criticism of the outdated

forms in which the church appears which expresses itself in
the movement away from the church therefore also bears
within itself the possibility that even the basic religious or
christian intention may become problematical, certainly
insofar as it is explicit. In this respect too, secularisation
which is to be welcomed from the point of view of faith is
not only a temptation to further movement away from the
church, but also to abandon religion. It provides a new possibility of an atheistic or at least, with regard to God, of a
really agnostic understanding of self in this world.

Thus, however much we, as christians, may welcome secularisation, not only as people who are carried along by the
current, but also as people who are urging it onwards, we
must at the same time have the courage honestly to admit
that secularisation does in fact make it more difficult for
modern man to go on believing or to remain a christian and
above all to do this within the context of the church. The
christian faith will only be able to provide the modern world
with solid guidance again when a new type of christianity has
emerged and the church has revealed her essential core in
renewed modern forms that are no longer alien to man's contemporary experience of the world and of his own existence,
and has included this contemporary human experience in her
understanding of what the church should be and at the same
time transcends it in hope.

Secularisation, the change from a deified nature to a
humanised world, is not a kind of necessary evil forced on
believing man as it were from outside, a situation that he has
somehow, as well or as badly as possible, to sort out himself.
It is rather an inner consequence of yahwism and of christianity and therefore also an inner aspect of the historical
evolution of christianity itself. I do not therefore wish to
make a direct appeal to the fact that this secularisation,
originating in the west with its christian history, will be
irresistibly bound to spread to the whole of the world, thus
constituting an almost fatal challenge to the oriental and
African religions especially. The christian confession of creation by a transcendent God is at the same time the funda-

mental affirmation of the secularity of reality—by definition, man in the world is, by virtue of this dogma of creation, *non-divine*, the one who is confined within specific limits. Their yahwistic faith in creation led the Israelites, unlike their neighbours, to regard the sun, the moon and the stars not as deified, numinous or sublime phenomena, but simply as ordinary lamps in the service of human day and night. It is only in history that all the implications of this fundamental desacralisation of the world are revealed. The modern process of secularisation, which began in a world the history of which had been christian (Russia and the west), has only *gradually* disclosed these implications in man's many-sided understanding of the world.

We can see this process of desacralisation taking place in the whole history of christianity.[6] What is more, we can see it taking place not only outside conscious christian reflection, but also when theologians or the magisterium of the church explicitly oppose it in conscious reflection. This inner tendency is also given in christianity insofar as christians believe in God as the *creator* and hope for a 'new world' as a definite possibility and as God's promise. This tendency may be checked, but ultimately nothing can hold it back. Thus we are able to see faith as reflection—theology—not only casting off the earlier numinous cosmology in the course of history, but also giving encouragement and free scope (though not always without conflict) to, for example, the autonomous practice of psychology, sociology and medicine—fields of knowledge which at one time always had a numinous co-efficient. Indeed, we have even seen, in our own times, theology disowning ethics and recognising this as something that is autonomously accessible to man as a being in the world with his fellow-men. Western man takes to himself what is legitimately his and this tendency is confirmed by theology, faith reflecting about itself, in the light of its own insights

---

[6] Secularisation and atheism in non-western countries, such as India, are also influenced by the west. On the other hand, these movements also derive their strength, especially in India, from certain inner tendencies that are present in the native religions.

into faith—even though this theological confirmation may sometimes come a little late.

2. 'I, God, am your salvation'

But, over and against this process of desacralisation, over and against contemporary secularisation, which is penetrating all kinds of human sectors of life and is indeed increasingly penetrating *all* these sectors, a new vision is also emerging. I should like to call this a *tendency towards sanctification*. We are, I believe, beginning to discover a new religious dimension in our being human in the world which is different from the religious dimension that was present in the earlier numinous view of nature. This is not simply because the chilliness of the modern process of secularisation has simultaneously brought about a remarkable resurgence in contemporary humanity of all kinds of pentecostal movements. It is also not only because the whole of our rationalised society has been developing too rapidly for modern man and threatening to overwhelm him, with the result that it has given rise to a new irrationality, thus causing man to look for new places where he can feel secure. (This is an event which requires as much interpretation as the fact itself of secularisation without security.) It is, as I have indicated, because of the dimension in depth of our christian confession of faith that this new vision has come about. Leaving things in their profanity and confirming them in this profanity, the modern believer knows that God has given man in the world a full, unconditional and absolute 'yes'. Many names were ascribed to Ptah, the supreme god of the ancient Egyptians, though this god did not disclose his true name and thus remained inaccessible to man. The God of the Jewish and Christian revelation, on the other hand, did make his real name known: *'eh^eyeh '^aser 'eh^eyeh* (Ex 3 : 14), translated in the Vulgate as *sum qui sum*, 'I am who am'. But this really means: 'I am your partner in covenant', or 'I am with you', in *all* circumstances.[7] The revealed 'name of God' is a divine, absolute 'yes'

---

[7] See Th. C. Vriezen, ''Ehje 'aser 'ehje', *Festschrift für A. Bertholet*, Tübingen 1950, 409-512, together with M. Reisel, *Observations on 'Ehyeh*

given to man and his world. What God is we shall notice and experience in his acts. The absolute freedom that is God, the one who is transcendent over the world and who does not need the world in order to be God has nonetheless spoken to man in the world. He has even made known as his deepest being, his proper name, I am the eternal lover of man, for man I am the future, absolute future: Yahweh, the lover man of man, is our salvation, that is, *yēšú'a*, Jesus. The humane element belongs to God's absolute being, which is absolute gratuity and freedom. It is indeed so gratuitous and free that his breaking out towards man is in no sense a completion of his being God, a *need* on the part of his being in order to achieve completion, and is therefore not pantheism. It is the absolutely free expression and manifestation of what he essentially is in inner completion. This is, then, the direct opposite of the self-satisfied pagan and hellenistic view of God.

The revealed name of God, *'eheyeh 'ašer 'eheyeh*, makes us realise in faith that the religious attitude to life is not only originally directed towards God, but also, equally originally, orientated towards man and the world and that this orientation also takes place under the coefficient of a constantly new future expectation for man and the world. Religion is not an attitude towards 'God', but an attitude towards the *totality* of reality, since religion is precisely a relationship with the living God who is the *ground of being* of all reality and the promise for man in the world. That is why religion is also originally a 'yes' given to one's fellow-man in the world. It is for this reason too that the unconditional 'yes', affirmative to the very end, that we give to man is also, at least implicitly, but certainly really, a *religious* event. This faith in God, as the Promise for man, also gives rise to a new hope for the world. Coming to himself in his going out towards the world, man cannot achieve his proper authenticity unless this world is also included in man's absolute future, which is purely grace of God. The history of the world itself is therefore sub-

---

'aser 'Ehyeh (Exod 3:14), Assen (Holland) 1957; M. Allard, 'Note sur la formule 'Ehyeh 'aser 'Ehyeh', *RSR* 45 (1957), 79–86. See also the essay by A. Deisler, cited below, p 93 n 8.

ject to the efficacy of God's promise and the christian view of
man thus also implies a secular eschatology.

All this is not rooted in man's 'being' insofar as this is seen
in the light of his understanding of himself and his view of
the world and thus in the light of his meaningful existence in
this world, but in the absolute freedom of God, who is his
own being and of whom revelation tells us that he has shown
himself to be a lover of men and that he will continue to love
men. This, of course, has repercussions on man's real being
that is only accessible to faith—as such man is in the world
with his fellow-men, finding security with God as man's
future, a security which is therefore in the sign of hope.
Man's acceptance of God's name is his living human answer
to the revelation of God as the promise and therefore, in this,
his answer to God's 'yes' given to man in the world. This is
why his saying 'yes' to man to the very end is intrinsically a
religious act. We are thus able to understand why the Catholic
tradition, despite its factual inconsistencies, nonetheless sees,
on the basis of the bible, a love which is directed equally to
God and to man in the world in *agapē* or charity, and
therefore calls this unconditional fellow-humanity a *theologal*
or divine virtue, a religious and not simply an ethical attitude.
But, because being man is not simply a communion of purely
inner subjects, christianity does not only imply 'fellow-
humanity'—it also equally implies social, economic and
political commitment. Commitment to the world thus forms
a part of the christian's theologal mode of existence. If care
for one's fellow-man in his concrete situation is, within the
framework of the new image of man and the world, the moti-
vation of all man's conquest of nature and all his construction
of an organised way of life within this world, then it is clear
that secularisation, insofar as this is a true humanisation of
the world or an unconditional commitment to the building of
a world fit for human beings to live in based on a radical
commitment to one's fellow-man, is not identical with the
coming of the kingdom of God, but that it certainly forms a
truly religious element of this future kingdom. This element,
however, merges into the mystery of the absolute future of

our being men which only God will give us in grace and which we *interiorise* by means of the active commitment of our hope. For, if the identity between the historical and the risen Christ inwardly links the history of the world with the *eschaton* by virtue of the transcendent act in which the Father raised the dead Jesus to be the Christ, then, for us believers, christian *hope* will link the *eschaton* with our terrestrial life in this world and this terrestrial life with the *esçhaton*.

3. The church, the sacrament of the world

This inner structure of religiosity, as man's living attitude towards the totality of reality and, in this, towards God, who is present everywhere wherever man says 'yes' unconditionally to his fellow-men, is explicitly and completely revealed precisely as a *religious* structure in the church. What grace, the *'eh^eyeh '^a^ser 'eh^eyeh*, is already bringing about wherever mankind in the world is encountered appears in the church as in a sacrament. In this connection, I should like to quote one of the most fortunate passages in the Second Vatican Council's *Dogmatic Constitution on the Church, Lumen Gentium*: 'In Christ, the Church is as the sacrament, that is, the sign and the instrument, of intimate union with God and of the unity of the whole human race' (n 1). The church is the 'sacrament of the world'. I personally think that this confession of faith is one of the most charismatically inspired texts of the council. This text is also all the more important in that it is again quoted in full—as though its consequences were spontaneously discerned—in the *Pastoral Constitution on the Church in the Modern World* (n 42). The church is the realising sign—the sacrament—of the mutual unity or *communio* of the whole of mankind, in and through her union with the living God. She is the community among men by virtue of their communion with God, the life or the living one. In this universal communion, the church fulfils a sacramental task, that is to say, she is the effective sign of this communion. She is the effective sign not on her own account, but because of the unity, peace and justice of God among men —the church is only an 'instrument' of God's unifying acts of salvation in this world and thus bound to service. At the same time, she is also the *sign*, because this mediatory realisation by the church is accomplished in a sign, that is to say, the church is the momentous visible form or meaningful presence in this world of an already accomplished communion of men—or a communion that accomplishes itself in *metanoia*—in and through their explicit community with God in Christ. In this way, the church is already the meaningful presence of salvation among us and, viewed in this way, she also has a value in herself, but only in orientation towards her mission in the world. This is because the sign and the mediatory realisation form a single whole. As a sacrament, the church has the task of making historically visible and present what is already implicitly active in the whole community of men, but is still looking for an explicit, concrete form. In other words, the church is the realisation of community among men, because she is herself *community*—the people of God and therefore the community of brothers. It is in this way that she is 'the sign set up among the people'.

The church, the form in which the 'being sanctified' of this world (as a profane reality) by the 'yes' spoken by the living God is shown explicitly, is therefore also the inward aspect of the history of this world sanctified by God's unconditional 'yes' because in it a fellow-man appeared (Jesus, the Christ) who is personally God's 'yes' or *amen* (2 Cor 1:20). Put in another way, in profane history, the sanctification of the world is concretely revealed at its source in a secularly explicit form—the fellow-man Jesus Christ, the Son of God, in whom the holiness of this world is completely triumphant over the sinfulness of the world or the world's saying 'no' to God. There is, then, an inner dynamism in the world of men which develops historically, is sanctified by 'God's name' and is again and again included within God's grace of forgiveness, so that this holiness can be explicitly experienced—in the church's confession of Jesus, the Christ, in whom God's 'yes' spoken to man in the world has not only personally appeared, but has also personally and humanly been assented to. A rejection of Jesus (against better judgement) therefore affects the world itself—it is at the same time saying 'no' to the world and to man. But an 'inspired' commitment to one's fellow-man, even if one does not explicitly know Jesus, is still a saving, implicit assent to and a longing for Jesus and his community-founding church. The deepest mystery of what is being accomplished in the way of grace in the profane world—by virtue of God's unknown and therefore unnamed Name—is *named* or proclaimed *by name* in and through the 'church of Christ' in testimony confessed *de facto* by acts. Thus membership of the church is bound at the same time to imply a hoping and militant impatience to change the face of the world out of love of man.[8] This is also why unconditional commitment to oppressed, suffering and tormented man is equally the church's presence and, for those who are not members of the church, the anonymous name for a true faith in salvation as the resurrection of man even including his corporeal life in the world.

All these implications of man's being in the world are named by their explicit proper name in the church's proclamation of the word. It is precisely this faith in eschatological salvation which makes the human spirit progressive in this world. It should not be thought of in this way, for example—that everything has already been accomplished in the event of Christ and that Christ's *parousia* will simply *make known* universally what has already been accomplished in a concealed manner. This would mean that our history on this earth was in itself an almost meaningless sequel played after the revelation that closed with Jesus. Christ is the completed promise, but he is still the *promise* to make all things new. We believers tend too much to give the impression that we simply *interpret* our being men in history differently from non-believers and we seem to forget that we have, by virtue of

[8] A. Deisler, 'Die Bundespartnerschaft des Menschen mit Gott als Hinwendung zur Welt und zum Mitmenschen', *Weltverständnis im Glauben*, 203–23; see also chapters 5 and 6 below. See also J. Moltmann, *Theology of Hope*, 225: 'The promise of the resurrection of the dead leads at once to love for the true life of the whole imperilled and impaired creation.' H. J. Schultz' *Konversion zur Welt* (Stundenbuch 42), Hamburg 1964, is, in my opinion, suggestive, but without sufficient light and shade.

God's promise, to *change* the world, to make it new. The christian faith, confidence in God as the promise, can never resign itself to the 'established order' or the present situation. It must always fight for still more justice, peace and unconditional love. Do our christian politicians and advocates of social reform think, I wonder, of *this* christian imperative?

It may, then, have become more difficult for modern man to discover God's presence in the world, but increasing sensitivity to the opportunities in life of one's fellow-man, whoever he may be, and the growing indignation about all forms of discrimination and degradation, stemming from a radical 'yes' to one's fellow-man, are unmistakable signs of an anonymous confession of *God's* 'yes' to man, a glorifying of God's name. Even in our atheistic world, then, God is for this reason probably closer to us than ever before. Our *unconditional* commitment to our fellow-man is, as Hans Urs von Balthasar has said, '*anamnesis* of the act of God in Christ and the practical recapitulation of the christian teaching about God, Christ, the church, Mary and even the sacraments'.[9] Elsewhere, I have called this unconditional commitment a true *votum Ecclesiae Christi*, an objective orientation towards the church.[10] The merciful Samaritan serves as an example for the christian.

But even this intensified presence of God contains, perhaps even more strongly than God's absence in nature, the supreme temptation of complete secularisation—van Buren's *The Secular Meaning of the Gospel*. It is here that we come to the very core of the present-day religious problem, which I cannot, unfortunately, discuss further, at least not here. I can, however, say that this supreme crisis is a human consequence of God's being God. God has become, because of his absolute inner self-evidence, the most problematical and defenceless being for the ambivalent being that man in the world is. God cannot give evidence of his presence unless he does this in a

[9] H. Urs von Balthasar, 'Gott begegnen in der heutigen Welt', *Weltverständnis im Glauben*, 20. See also his book, *Love Alone. The Way of Revelation*, London 1968.
[10] See pp 131–3 below.

kenotic act of self-emptying in which he must introduce the creatural between himself and us as the (ambivalent) sign of his presence. Whoever sees God with impure eyes dies of it— blessed are the pure in heart! God is present only in conceal- ment. That is why the possibility of an 'atheistic' self- interpretation will always continue to accompany our faith, as the expression of the ambiguous situation of our nonethe- less unconditional faith. It is precisely because God has re- vealed his proper name in a human and therefore ambivalent form—and we have seen how closely this is connected with God's own being, however mysterious it may be for us—that there will always be a threat, indeed a real human possibility, that man will reject God. But if this possibility is indeed so real, then we may well ask whether we do not use all kinds of concepts uncritically in a *theological* sense, assuming all too easily that they possess the guarantee of faith. And we are therefore bound to ask ourselves whether we are really taking the momentous and widespread fact of atheism sufficiently seriously and whether we are not simply passing it by un- concernedly, to the detriment of the authenticity of our own faith and as a failure to respect our fellow-man who is existentially unable to believe, however incomprehensible this may seem to a believer.

5
CHURCH AND WORLD

However important many of the conciliar decisions about the structures and functions of the church may be, it is living human beings, confronted every day with secular problems which may be of enormous significance for the future of mankind, who ultimately matter. While the Vatican Council was meeting in Rome, all kinds of summit conferences were in progress throughout the world and the well-being of mankind in the immediate and the distant future depended on the decisions made at these conferences. Is the church then simply working for a post-historical future, for the hereafter, while the non-ecclesiastical world conferences are working to build up the world and to improve the welfare of all people, to provide them with a better future here on earth? Should we, and can we, as believers and as members of a church with eschatological expectations, accept this *dualism* between church and world? Are man's great expectations for this earth, which are at present in a state of fermentation, therefore really alien to the essence of man's theologal life in union with the living God? This is the crux of our problem.

It is obvious that it cannot be the church's intention to remove her believing members from the sphere of worldly responsibilities which keep the history of man in suspense. On the other hand, however, the organisation of temporal society lies outside the competence of the church's hierarchy and thus also of a council, in which only the church's teaching office and pastoral authority are directly involved. The hierarchy has, after all, only a moral and religious mission in connection with the kingdom of God. And yet believers have to live their christianity practically in and with this world. Even though the church cannot deny the reality of sin, either in her members (in their activity within the church as well) or in others, in their commitment to a better world on earth,

96

and even though she will—precisely because she proclaims the forgiveness of God—always have to confess and preach the sinfulness of everything that is touched by human freedom, she would be misjudging her real task and leaving the world out in the cold if she were to approach this world simply as an unholy reality which is only in the power of evil and which only belongs to 'this world which will pass away'.

A remarkable change has taken place in recent years. We have become more conscious than we were in the past of salvation as something that is accomplished within the world that we live in here and now. 'Practising christianity' was, until quite recently, a quality alongside everyday life, something that was made true in the quietness of the church or at home in private prayer. The idea at least had gained ground that christianity was simply a flight from the world and a looking towards the hereafter, without any concern at all for life on earth. The world was often seen as nothing more than a springboard to higher spheres where God could be praised and virtue practised. Christians had ceased to be aware of the real significance of the world. Only those who called themselves non-believers seemed to give their attention to the problems of man's existence on earth.

There has been a strong reaction against this. Believing is not adhering, alongside one's relationships with man and the world, to an isolated ideology which regards the development of the nations and the growth of the world with disfavour. Both Catholics and Protestants have forcibly broken out of their ghetto mentality. Religious man has discovered that his religion must also be directed towards achieving unity among the peoples of the world, towards his obligations to the underdeveloped countries and towards dynamic planning for human society of tomorrow. It is in this that modern religious man seeks to realise salvation. From the psychological point of view, he seems to be able to give form to his religion most spontaneously precisely in this.

This new conviction has also made its influence felt in the use of religious language. There is an increasing inclination to call religious concepts by profane words borrowed from genuinely human values. Preference is clearly given to a christianity which, although hidden, is salutarily present in our relationship with man and the world, over and above the explicit confession of a christian church. There is, however, a danger in this rather one-sided emphasis—many believers simply do not know what to do with the 'church'. Sociological research has revealed that people who were previously practising christians, but who now no longer practise, have retained a certain faith in God as the ground of all being and even some faith in the man Jesus, who showed in and through his life on earth the meaning of God's love for men. It has, however, shown that they can no longer accord any place in their faith to the phenomenon 'church'. They would only be able to accept the church, and then perhaps even do so with enthusiasm, if 'church' meant nothing more than the foundation of a community between men, in other words, the true form of fellow-humanity in this world.

I should like to establish this clearly in advance, because I am naturally devoting my attention in this section only to the experience of christianity in the world and I want to prevent any possible misunderstanding. The real significance of the saving necessity of the institutional church is therefore not under discussion here, but positively assumed.

1. 'The world' as the objective expression of the life of grace

The *locus theologicus* or source of all reflection about faith and also of the theology of the relationship between church and world is the historical event of salvation in which God gave himself to us in an absolute and gratuitous manner in Jesus Christ. The man Jesus is the absolute and gratuitous proximity of the divine mystery. Jesus' *humanity* is the objective expression of God's communication of himself in grace and at the same time the objective expression of the free response of this man, the Son of God, to the Father. Christ's human existence, with all its historical conditions and implications, is the personal life of God himself, the Son. The deepest unsuspected possibilities of being man are thus disclosed, possibilities which only become intelligible in the light of Christ. Thanks to Christ, our being men is the possibility of the self-manifestation of the life of grace or of life in union with God. Christ's 'hypostatic union', on whose riches we can draw, teaches us that the whole of the history of mankind is contained in the love of God. The history of this world is therefore not sacralised, because it preserves its specific quality, but sanctified, included in the absolute and gratuitous presence of the mystery.

Although men have various ways of expressing it, it is a universally human datum that our existence as men is steeped in mystery. Christianity only throws light on this datum in its promulgation of the word, which proclaims that the mystery in which our life is grounded has come closer to us in an absolute manner, not only in mystical inwardness, but also in historical tangibility. The whole of the christian kerygma, the whole of dogma, from the Trinity, the incarnation and the life of grace to the church with her sacraments, her ministers and her proclamation of the word and faith in individual and collective 'last things', can be traced back to this fundamental religious affirmation. In her proclamation of the word, the church discloses the implications of this absolute nearness of God in Christ, a nearness in grace which is actively present in the lives of all men as the revelation of reality even before they have been historically confronted with the phenomenon of the church. Acceptance of this nearness is, moreover, the very essence of all saving faith, since believing is placing one's confidence, in and despite everything, in this mystery which has come near to us. This simple reality is of the greatest importance, because it means that the acceptance of actual human existence with all its responsibilities is an act of theologal faith, since it has become clear to us in Christ that human existence can be made the objective expression of the life of grace.

The reader may have the impression that I have strayed from my theme of 'church and world'. I believe, however, that I have come closer to the central core of the question, because two things have been made clear by this brief analysis.

99

In the first place, the absolute nearness of the mystery has reached an explicit, historically recognisable epiphany (as a given reality and at the same time as a task) in the church of Christ. In the second place, it is precisely this epiphany of the church with its concentrated presence of grace that makes explicitly clear and explicitly confesses the wealth (which is perhaps not reflectively conscious) present in the reality of every human experience of existence in the world, namely, security in God's grace. Even in our life on earth, we are with God and, what is more, we are with him not only in prayer and in the worship and the sacraments of the church. Ordinary everyday life with its secular concerns and its work for and with the world is therefore the immediate sphere within which christian life has to be objectivised and its source of strength and inspiration is the direct expression of the life of grace given by the church. Christianity, in other words, acceptance of God as the mystery which comes forward to meet us in Christ, normally has to be accomplished in the context of secular life with its tasks and responsibilities in the world. Paul expressed this idea in a masterly though negative way:

> For I am sure that neither death, nor life, nor angels, nor principalities, nor things present, nor things to come, nor powers, nor height, nor depth, nor anything else in all creation, will be able to separate us from the love of God in Christ Jesus our Lord. [Rom 8: 38–9]

What else does this text mean, other than that true christianity is faith in the absolute and gratuitous nearness of God, in Christ, in all the circumstances of life in this world, and that acceptance of the security of all human history in God's grace is the very substance of christianity? Does it not mean that we are with the living God precisely in and with our world of men? The reality that we call 'world' is given a distinctively theological significance by this insight. 'World' is the reality which, while remaining a profane reality with its own laws and structures and a secular aim of its own, was nonetheless included by God in Christ in the absolute and gratuitous nearness of God. We should not, moreover, regard this world as static—it is something that has been given to man for him to humanise and make a place fit for men to live in, in the service of the whole of mankind. We should not, of course, ignore the fact that the world is marked with the sign of transience and of the creature. Like everything that is touched by the hands of men, the world too is affected by sin. The building up of the world and the development of peoples is therefore a *finite* work of man, participating in the ambiguity of everything that is human and material. The world is non-God, a creature—this is an affirmation of the secular nature of this task. As such, however, creation is a divine placing of realities in their profane, non-divine distinctiveness. It is a divine act which, in contrast to the mythological accounts of creation of Israel's neighbours, was depicted in the account given in Genesis as a demythologised and desacralised act of God, who gave the world to itself, into the hands of men, for the glorifying of God's name. This implies that the history of mankind will always display, in and through God's continuing act of creation, a constant desacralisation of the structures and functions of the world.

Nonetheless, only one aspect of reality is intended in all this, since the bearing, desacralising, silent divine ground of all creatural being has come nearer to us in an absolute and gratuitous manner in Christ. This world, with its profane distinctiveness, is borne into the theologal sphere of the life of grace by man, whose anthropology can ultimately only be fully understood in the light of Christ. This means, in other words, that 'the world' is, in the contemporary saving situation of the incarnation, *implicit christianity*—a distinctive, non-sacral, but sanctified expression of man's living community with the living God—while the church, as the institution of salvation with her communal confession of faith, her worship and her sacraments, is the 'set aside', sacral expression of this implicit christianity. Speaking about the church's relationship with the world is therefore not a dialogue between what is distinctive to christianity and what is alien to christianity, between the religious and the profane, between what is supranatural and what relates strictly to this world. It is, on the contrary, a dialogue—and here we are confronted with the very essence of the whole problem—between the *two complementary forms of experience of the one christianity*, a dialogue between the set aside, sacral expression *by the church* of the theologal life of those who explicitly believe and the secular expression that has not been set aside, *within the world*, of the same life of faith. It is only insofar as this theologal life itself remains implicit and anonymous and is not given its appropriate expression in forms that are specifically those of the church that these two forms of experience of the one christianity can be indicated by the two words implicit and explicit christianity.[1]

Anonymous but real christianity therefore means in this context the secular reality of life within this world which is taken up, in its profane distinctiveness, in the absolute and gratuitous nearness of the mystery, that is, of the theologal life which is in itself the beginning of eternal life and which thus through man involves the secular itself in the definitive eschatological salvation and enables it to participate in this salvation. Within this absolute presence in grace of the mystery and thus within the theologal sphere, which may perhaps be simply anonymous, the building up of the world and work for a better world in the future for all men becomes an activity which *inwardly*, and not only in its intention, has something to do with the dawning of the eschatological kingdom. It goes without saying that the final eschatological consummation of everything on earth will, precisely because of the absolute and gratuitous nature of this consummation, transcend all our expectations and all our building up of this world. Nonetheless, because it is included in the life of grace,

[1] It is clear that the status of implicit christianity can be destroyed by the refusal of man to accept grace. I am therefore not saying that all those outside the church are in themselves implicit christians. Only God can judge the state of a person's conscience. It is worth while placing this on record, however, as the objection that all people who are outside the church cannot justifiably be called implicit christians is certainly valid, just as the opposite is also true —that all explicit, practising christians are not in themselves authentic christians.

everything on earth really shares, in the present plan of salvation, in the mystery of eternity, as the dogma of the resurrection of all flesh and the kerygma of the 'new heaven and the new earth' affirm. There is something irrevocable in commitment to this world, which extends concretely much farther than its purely temporal dimensions might lead us to suppose. God, after all, loves man unconditionally and man is not abstract 'human nature', but a being who, together with his equals in this world, takes the fate of mankind on earth into his hands. It is this man whom God loves eternally and this ultimately gives a divine significance to the building up of the world and the development of all people. After all, if it is true that man is the subject of grace by virtue of his 'receptivity to grace' which is grounded in his spiritual being, then this receptivity to grace means simply this—what is included in theologal intimacy with the living God and thus, transcending himself, participates in 'eternal life' is man himself in his distinctiveness and totality who, as a being who makes history, humanises himself in his humanisation of the world. This total reality receives grace. In the past, an anthropologically false and dualistic view of the conferment of grace and redemption frequently led to our regarding this as a matter of God and man's *soul*. This meant that the whole of man's activity within this world—and quantitatively this was ninety-nine per cent of the factual activity of the majority of men—lay outside christianity. If this view were to persist, it would inevitably encourage the estrangement between church and world, especially at a time when the distinctive meaning of the world is being discovered.

2. Implicit christianity and the church's social teaching

As a consequence of this dogmatic insight, the church's social teaching should not be inspired by a paternalistic condescension as if the church were looking down, from outside, on the low countries of 'the world outside the church', as though she were leaving the holy ground of the *Constitution on the Church* and entering an unholy world which is alien to her. The ground on which the church sets foot in her social teaching is holy ground, already effectively influenced by Christ's redeeming grace even before the official church begins to address the saving word of Christ explicitly to this world. This is why a distinction between the *Ecclesia ad intra* and the *Ecclesia ad extra*, however correct the meaning that can be given to this formula may be, seems to me to be misleading and unfortunate, especially in view of the fact that this distinction unconsciously goes back to the identification of the church with the hierarchy. It was, after all, not said of Christ that he went to a foreign country, but that he came to his own, and this was said of him before there was any question of the foundation of his church. But his own did not receive him and estranged themselves from Christ. What is more, it is clear from the bible that the church and the kingdom of God cannot simply be identified. If all this is disregarded, we find that church statements on social matters tend to become a kind of panegyric in which the church is praised for the social benefits that she has, in the course of history, brought to the 'world outside', while reverent silence is preserved about the recent centuries in which humanisation and commitment to a better future for all men have above all taken place outside and alongside the church. In my opinion, the first task must be official recognition on the part of the church of the holiness of the ground on which the church sets foot when she turns towards 'the world'. Ultimately, this is no more than the confession of her faith in the historical reality of the redemption brought to us in Christ Jesus. In this, the church will also have to take into account the world's affirmation of its own distinctive legitimacy, in view of the fact that the reality of this world does not have to be sacralised, but *sanctified*. The concrete principles of the building up of this world cannot be provided in the light of revelation, but the inspiration and the moral and religious spirit within which this building up must be accomplished certainly can be. That is why the church not only has something to *say* to the world, but also has to *listen* to what secular christianity, be it implicit or explicit, has to say. She has, in other words, to be fully conscious of everything that concrete man in the world—who is,

whether he is implicitly or explicitly christian, nonetheless
with God in this world, because he is included in the absolute
and gratuitous nearness of God who never fails to appear—
demonstrates, in the experience both of the 'secular' world
outside the church and of her own explicit believers among
the laity. This would include, for example, man's illumina-
tion of his own existence, his plans for the future of the world,
his commitment to a better life, more worthy of the whole of
mankind, and his insights into marriage and family life. A
church in monologue with herself is not a partner. If she does
not listen to the world, she will disregard as much human
knowledge, influenced by anonymous grace, as there are
people outside her institutional boundaries or outside her
hierarchy. If, on the other hand, she does listen, attentively
but critically (because she is guided by the revelation of the
word) to the attempts that the 'world' is making to throw
light on the truth, she will not hear strange sounds coming
from outside, but will recognise the voice of her own Lord,
who is not only the head of the church, his body, but is also
Lord of the 'world'. She will hear the Good News which is
always normative for her and which comes to us not only from
scripture, but also and equally from every human existential
experience which is, in one way or another, always confronted
by the grace of the living God. In man's struggle for a better
world, the church has first of all to discover the deepest intention (probably not subject to reflection) which goes beyond
what is strictly confined to this world. Ultimately, there is no
sense in fighting for a better world without implicit faith in
an absolute saving consummation of the individual human
person, even if an ideology has no room for this formal assertion. It is precisely because there is an absolute, transcendent,
eschatological expectation of salvation for man that commitment to the planning of temporal society and to a world that
is more worthy of man is ultimately meaningful.

When the church speaks about the 'world', then, she is
speaking about a truly christian expression of the theologal
life of her own believers and at the same time about the secular expression of the implicit christianity of people outside

the church. In this sense, she is not going beyond the frontiers of the building up of the kingdom of God. In the Vatican II *Constitution on the Church*, she discusses above all the sacral, 'set aside' forms of the experience of grace, the visible forms of grace as expressed by the church. In the *Constitution on the Church in the Modern World*, on the other hand, she is concerned with the worldly and therefore more concealed expressions and objectivisations of the same life of grace— with *secular holiness* and *apostolic secularity*. The unique and absolute nearness of God in Christ and therefore in his church is not dialectically opposed to the nearness of the same God of grace in man's secular activities, but it does illuminate the deepest final meaning and value of these activities. Our profane tasks in this world are therefore not alien to our being christians or a matter of indifference to us as christians. They are rather a distinctively christian duty, the christian nature of which is nourished by the sacral forms of experience of the life of grace which are directly ecclesial. This secular holiness has rightly been emphasised by Dr John Robinson, the former Anglican Bishop of Woolwich, in his book, *Honest to God*. All that he has failed to do is to give sufficient emphasis to the vital importance of the church's expression in her worship and her sacraments of the divine mystery of grace. On the other hand, however, it would be most one-sided and regrettable for the church as a whole (apart from the separate charismatic vocation as expressed, for example, in monastic life) if only the specifically ecclesial expression of the theologal life were stressed and the secular objectivisations of this life were entirely neglected. Some apostles will probably have to get away from the pure proclamation of love and salvation, a proclamation which in practice tends to close its eyes to suffering humanity. What really matters is not loudly proclaiming that love is everything, but effectively caring for people by staying with them. 'As you did it to one of the least of these my brethren, you did it to me' and 'as you did it not to one of the least of these, you did it not to me' (Mt 25:40). This could be expressed in a modern form as follows: your neglect of the underdeveloped countries is a neglect of Christ, an offence against authentic christianity. Surrendering himself to others to the very utmost —this was the messianic act by which Christ founded his church. Wherever men follow this track, perhaps without knowing whose track it is, they are founding a *community* in Christ.

3. The believing members of the church and the future of mankind on earth

So far we have seen that the building up of temporal society has been concretely included in the absolute and gratuitous nearness of the mystery of grace and is, as such, 'implicit christianity'. On the other hand, we have also seen how various activities which were in the past undertaken only by the institutional church for the benefit of mankind—education, social aid, care of the sick, the handicapped and the elderly and so on—have now become secularised and are now the direct responsibility of mankind as a whole. All these activities, in other words, now form part of the secular organisation of temporal society. In connection with the problem with which we are concerned here, the problem of church and world, the distinction within the church between the believing members of the church and their hierarchical leaders is important. This is because the ordinary members of the church may, precisely in their lay state and yet as christians, have duties and obligations with regard to the development of a way of life that is worthy of all men which are not those of the church's hierarchy. After all, Christ did not give the hierarchy any mandate for the building up of temporal society; it was set aside for the gospel. The hierarchy has therefore to keep a vigilant eye on the evangelical and christian inspiration of the task of building up the world. In her teaching office, the church has consequently to safeguard the moral and religious principles of all man's planning for a better life on earth and, in her pastoral office, she has to bar any paths which cannot lead to a way of life that is truly worthy of man. But the hierarchy cannot deduce from revelation and its basic ecclesiastical principles how and by means of what political or socio-economic system this human dignity has to be concretely protected and promoted here and now. Clearly, it is not only the principles of revelation and the fundamental values of human life which the church is bound to safeguard in her teaching office that are involved in this concrete problem. An interpretation of the factual situation by experts and a technical analysis of this situation, which the church's hierarchy, at least as such, has not been commissioned by Christ to make, also plays an equal part here. The planning of temporal society remains the unalienable right of mankind itself, of the believing members of the church together with people who do not belong explicitly to the church. A direct consequence of this is that, in connection with these concrete contemporary socio-political, economic, national and international problems, the church's social teaching is bound to observe very general evangelical and human principles.

But what may be a limitation for the church's hierarchy is not a frontier for the believing members of the church. Here, a wide sphere is open to expert knowledge and to decisions made according to personal conscience on the part of the Catholic laity. It is, for example, not clear, simply and solely on the basis of revealed and human principles, which form of education most fully corresponds at present to the Catholic conviction and at the same time best serves the well-being of mankind as a whole here and now. It is also not clear what degree of political unification in Europe is best for the future. In these questions, more things than simply the general norms which certainly remain in force and must be stressed by the church, but from which a specific policy cannot be directly deduced, play an important part. There may in certain cases be a variety of different solutions which are valid from the christian point of view. On the other hand, it is conceivable that, in other cases, there is only one morally valid and therefore obligatory solution to the problem of educating mankind, in given circumstances, towards greater human dignity, although this one concrete solution still cannot be deduced from the christian and human norms which the church is bound to put before us. Frequently, it is only history that will be able to establish whether a definite decision made by the world was in fact evidence of a prophetic glimpse or whether it was evidence of warped judgement. The Catholic lay community will have to be the active inspirer *par excellence* of this concrete seeking, which can no longer be normalised reflectively, for what will, in the future, be good and salutary for church and world. We are, however, bound to recognise that the Catholic laity still lives very much in the past and that lay christians still tend to cling to earlier structures of the world and either to leave the profane planning of the world to those who are not christians or else to demand too precise orders from the hierarchy. The magisterium has therefore to provide the believing members of the church with a fundamental christian inspiration for their tasks within this world and not with a concrete policy, an economic or social pattern or a concrete position which they are to take up with regard to international planning for a better world.

The whole of man's planning of the world has, however, another dimension as well. Religion, the free acceptance of God's grace and of its specifically ecclesial forms, is also included, as a free human act, in history with its personal, social, psychic and even somatic conditioning. As a result, so-called natural factors are able to exert a positive or a negative influence on man's hearing of the Good News. Terrestrial situations may therefore be seen from a pastoral point of view. Thus, it is possible that the church may really be preaching in the wilderness, because man's freedom is caught up in all kinds of social structures which make it impossible for men to be sufficiently free to listen to the Good News and to receive its grace sincerely. From the pastoral point of view, then, it may be almost as urgently necessary to introduce agrarian reforms and to revise the structures of social relationships in certain countries as to preach the Good News. And I see no reason why even a bishop should not lend his support to such social reforms in a pastoral situation of this kind, without directly entering the field of social politics. To make it possible for men truly to listen as human beings to the

Good News is, after all, part of the mission of all the believing members of the church.

Conclusion: the social teaching of the church

The starting-point for the church's social teaching cannot be a 'dualism' between church and world in which the latter is regarded as a kind of 'outboard' world which can only be meaningful to christianity as providing an opportunity and the matter for the practice of christian charity. The significance of theologal hope, its cosmic significance as well, must be clearly understood, and the close connection between man's great expectations for this earth and the coming of the kingdom of God must be the dynamic idea that sustains and supports everything. In this sense, it is valuable to refer to the theological reflection that was given great prominence years ago at the World Council of Churches when it met at Evanston in 1954, in connection with 'christian hope in the modern world'. Here too, a dialogue with the other christian churches could have a fruitful effect on the precise formulation of the Catholic view in this respect.

Furthermore, the real problem, that of mankind's future on earth in connection with christianity, must be central. A certain Augustinianism, and certainly an Augustinian attitude with regard to precisely those aspects that Albert the Great and Thomas, for example, attacked in the Middle Ages because they were more aware of secularity and the real meaning of 'second causes', must not be allowed to dominate our thinking, even unconsciously. We must be bold enough resolutely to affirm the contemporary meaning of 'apostolic secularity' and, in this context, the whole collective and historical dimension of mankind as well, so as to avoid giving the impression that the special significance of the socialising history of the world is not taken sufficiently seriously.

Finally, we should not take as our point of departure a theological and theoretical conception of the traditional problem (which is, in itself, correct) concerning the relationship between 'nature and supernature'. Our starting-point must be the existential experience of lay christians who, from the vantage-point of their involvement in terrestrial realities and responsibilities, question the place of religion and of the church in their lives. Only in this way will we be able to express in a liberating manner, on the one hand, the church's being non-world, *separata a mundo*, and, on the other, how the 'recapitulation of everything in Christ' within man's life of grace with the living God, the constantly present mystery of grace, inspires a secular holiness and an apostolic secularity which, however, find their source of nourishment within the experience of the church.

To stress the transcendence of grace at the expense of its immanence is always a depreciation of transcendence, or at least a one-sided limitation of this immanence to the sacral, set-aside forms of grace within the church. Nature and history are not, after all, sacralised or deprived of their profane significance by the active presence in grace of the mystery in mankind and man's making of history. They are *sanctified*, included in God's embrace of man. As Thomas said, 'to diminish the excellence of the creature is to diminish the excellence of God'. In this context, we should not lose sight of the fact that, thanks to Christ, the aspect of creation (*creatio*) is, in the present plan of salvation, only an aspect of the *assumptio*. As Augustine said, *ipsa assumptione creatur*, in other words, in being situated creatively in his distinctively earthly quality, man, the creature, is in Christ included in the nearness in grace of the God of the covenant, who definitively loves man in an absolute manner even in his historical attempts here on earth to provide mankind with a better world and a better place to live in.

There is no doubt that this dwelling-place on earth is not outweighed by the personal love of God which comes to us in Christ Jesus. This is why stepping outside ourselves in sacrifice and 'emptying ourselves' will always be a vital reality for all christians. The ambiguity of man's building up of the world indicates that it is man's making. But, on the other hand, it is precisely this finitude that is taken up into the grace and redemption of God. We know therefore that the future of mankind on earth has already been redeemed in advance by Christ. Its transient, earthly aspect has in principle already been superseded by Christ and, as such, it is only a truly human and meaningful future insofar as it is de facto included in the mystery of Christ (though without losing its earthly, profane character by this inclusion).

The church's social teaching must be the proof of the extent to which she understands herself as the eschatological community of salvation. Man in the world has also received, in his distinctively profane quality, the gift of the definitive character of the 'eternal life' which comes, in Christ, to those who step outside themselves in love and who expect salvation, even in its cosmic dimensions, only from God as a gratuitous gift. This gift has, however, already taken possession of us now through the *Pneuma* and therefore, living and active in mankind on earth, also makes this material, terrestrial world, as the space and the sphere of experience of the human spirit, long eagerly for the revealing of the sons of God (see Rom 8: 19–22).

The church must in the first place extend the line that she began so clearly in the Vatican II *Constitution on Revelation* —just as there is a development of dogma in the church's tradition, so too can the church's attitude towards the world evolve recognisably in the course of history. The church does not, after all, perceive all the implications of redemption from the very beginning. She learns from the real development of human world-history with its constantly changing situations. In this way, she herself also makes salvation-history—faith's dialogue with concrete humanity allows this faith, itself governed by the norm of Christ's unique and non-recurrent appearance in the world, to enter history in a process of development that only gradually, tentatively and in seeking discloses the inner riches of faith clearly. Viewed in this light, it is more understandable that there was a time when the world was under the guardianship of the church and there can be no doubt that this situation made a definite contribution to the well-being of mankind on earth. But, although we should never judge the past by modern criteria, the church must humbly admit that mistakes have been made with regard to the legitimate emancipation of this world and that these have partly been the cause of the world's alienation from the institutional church.

It is furthermore strikingly apparent to historians that the church has recourse especially to secular means and positions of power in this world for her mission to the world whenever she becomes alienated from the world at a given period in history. Whenever this alienation is absent or disappearing, however, she abandons these positions of power and chooses to appear as the truly evangelical church, without key positions and points of support and, from the point of view of the world, standing helpless in the world and, precisely because of this, as a powerful and irresistible sign. The power of Jesus Christ, God's servant, now raised by God himself to be Lord of the world, was also present in the impotence of the cross. The church's renewed awareness of herself and the new human and christian appreciation of what 'world' is require the church to take up a new position with regard to the secularised world.

The church sees man's ambitious attempt to transform the world situation into a truly human situation and she also sees the wonderful success of these ambitious undertakings today and their failure tomorrow. Yet, despite this cycle of success and failure, man always continues to set about this task again and again and to begin anew the arduous work of building up the world. A veiled *hope* seems to sustain and strengthen this world in spite of certain signs of despair on all sides and a sense of the absurd in the history of the world. In its teaching the church, 'always prepared to make a defence to anyone who calls you to account for the hope that is in you' (1 Pet 3 : 15), must seize hold of this concealed hope and invite the world to its explicit expectation: 'If you knew the gift of God' (Jn 4 : 10) from which you, world, are unconsciously living! If only you recognised God's gift!

Although it must guard against false human optimism, christian social teaching must also include, in its dynamism, all human expectations. The church loves the world, not only insofar as it is receptive to the life of grace, but also as the world. She loves the world as it is, which means that this love is creative. Therefore, the church equally desires for the world the great human values that it needs so much—freedom of conscience, the personal value of marriage and family life, cultural values, a social, economic and political system in which human and christian life is possible and finally a human world community living in order and peace. The concrete relationship between the structure of the world here on earth and the heavenly social environment transcends all human thought, even when this is inspired by faith: 'What no eye has seen, nor ear heard, nor the heart of man conceived, what God has prepared for those who love him' (1 Cor 2:9). Thus, the ultimate meaning of the building up of this world merges into the mystery which is only accessible to the faith that makes hope live:

> Behold, the dwelling of God is with men. He will dwell with them, and they shall be his people, and God himself will be with them; he will wipe away every tear from their eyes, and death shall be no more, neither shall there be mourning nor crying nor pain any more, for the former things have passed away [Rev 21:3-4].

The church must confess and proclaim this and it is in this perspective of ultimate fulfilment that believing christians, who already possess the earnest-money, the pledge of the Holy Spirit and thus of the eschatological gift, must work for the restoration of this world, despite the reality of sin, which never ceases to undermine the work of redemption that is aiming to make this world into a dwelling-place worthy of man, and even worthy of sons of God. In the meantime, the modest but nonetheless splendidly practical result of this process of humanisation within life in union with God will be that we build up the world in such a way that, in it, men can live a life that is both truly *worthy of man* and at the same time *christian* and in this way more easily accomplish the will of God. In and through this love for the world, included in man's whole personal love for God, God's name is glorified and salvation is brought to men. 'God's glory—living man'.

6

THE CHURCH AND MANKIND

In this chapter my aim is twofold. In the first place, I shall be looking into the tendency in the world *to become church*, the tendency which strives to make the salvation of the church visible in the world and in mankind. In the second place, I shall investigate the tendency in the church of Christ *towards sanctifying secularisation*, that is, the tendency which aims to make the salvation of the church incarnate in the secular reality of the world itself. On the one hand, human solidarity in Christ is certainly the essential core of the phenomenon 'church'. On the other hand, however, we cannot, as believers, avoid giving the church a place as a community *sui iuris*—or better, *iuris Christi*—and this creates a certain distance between the 'church' and 'mankind'. There are frontiers between the 'church' and 'mankind' and yet these frontiers are to some extent fluid. I propose to examine the implications of this problem, both out of love for man who is increasingly moving outside the church and out of faith in the church as founded by Christ.

1. The unity of mankind and the communion of saints

Although mankind also has a biological foundation, the unity of mankind cannot anthropologically be *formally* situated in any possible biological unity of the human race, but must, of its very nature, be the unity of a community of *persons*, a *communio*. Such a specifically human unity can only be built up on the basis of an appeal to values, on the basis of the power of truly human values to found a community of persons. This means that specifically human unity finds its source in the unity of vocation and destiny in life. *Communio* among all men is the immanent expression in mankind of this one vocation. The unity of mankind is therefore essentially not a datum, but a task to be realised.

We know from revelation that this task is in fact a response to God's act of grace. The *koinōnia* or community of all men which has been promised by God is a gift of God—by his absolute communication of himself to men, God has revealed himself as the supreme value in life for man and, in so doing, he has revealed men at the same time to themselves, as the 'people of God'. God's conferment of grace on mankind is at the same time his constitution of mankind as the people of God. The community of all men is the immanent echo in the history of our world of our transcendent community with the living God and the unity of mankind, willed by God, is therefore nothing less than the *communio sanctorum*, the community of sanctified men.

But not only is the fact of this community a gratuitous gift. The way in which it comes about also goes back to a sovereign and free act of God. It is clear from the whole history of salvation in the Old and New Testaments that, however great a part ancient Near Eastern views of life played in this process, God did not intend to realise the unity of mankind around the community-founding value of 'abstract' fundamental values. He wished to gather mankind into a holy community of persons on the basis of values that were prototypically incarnate in living persons. Again and again, 'one of ourselves' was the means of salvation chosen to constitute the 'great gathering' of people from the diaspora, the people of God.[1] The gratuitous way in which God founded a community among men was that of representative mediation—for the sake of one man, freely called by God for this task, salvation (or disaster) was brought to many. The representative function of one man or of a limited group of men (Adam, Noah, Moses, Abraham, the twelve patriarchs, Israel, the King, the Son of Man, the Servant of God, Jesus) with regard to salvation or disaster is essential in the Old and New Testaments.

This manner of founding a community by means of mediation implies that election and universal mission grew towards each other in the bible. Although the process was hesitant and

[1] J. Scharbert, *Heilsmittler im Alten Testament und im alten Orient* (Quaest. Disp. 23–24), Freiburg 1964.

gradual, Israel did begin to experience her election as an example to all peoples—as election in the service of the whole of mankind. In accordance with the Old Testament view, the totality of concrete historical humanity owed its existence to Yahweh's redeeming covenant with Noah after the flood. It is precisely in this connection that a list of all the existing peoples of the world (that is, of the ancient oriental world) was made in Gen 10.[2] What is more, it was in Abraham that all the nations were blessed (Gen 12:3; 18:18; 22:18). The election of Abraham was at the same time God's affirmation of universal salvation.

This idea of one man or a small number of men acting as mediator shows us that people are dependent on each other and that, in bringing his transcendent salvation, God wishes to maintain this structure of common humanity. He wishes to bring salvation to men through men. The idea of 'the first-born among many brethren' (Rom 8:19)—the prototype of human solidarity in religion—and of Israel as 'the first-born son' of God (Ex 4:22), in which both divine election and service to one's fellow-men are combined, was as it were prepared for in the whole of the Old Testament. Moreover, it suggests the fundamental notion that salvation is given by reciprocal service between man and man living in brotherhood in the light of God's election. Israel herself, the people of God, was, in her election, 'the first-born son' of God (op. cit.), first personified in the representative figure of the King, who was therefore eponymously called the 'Son of God' (see, for example, 2 Sam 7:14; Ps 2:7) and finally personified in the figure of the coming Messiah and Son of Man, the 'Son of God' *par excellence*. Jesus was not only man, 'one of ourselves'. He was representatively 'Israel, the Son of God', but in an incomparably deeper manner—the Son of the Father in a uniquely transcendent manner, but at the same time our fellow-man, 'chosen from among men' (Heb 5:1), 'born of woman' (Gal 4:4). Election (the 'Son of God') and fraternal service to men (the 'Servant of God' and of men) found their

[2] See G. von Rad, *Genesis*, London and Philadelphia (Pa) 1961, 140–1.

supreme exponent in Christ. It was therefore in Jesus Christ that the 'great assembly of all men around God' (*hē Ekklēsia tou Theou*, 1 Cor 11:22; 15:9) became a mutual community of men around Christ, a 'church of Christ' (*hai Ekklēsiai tou Christou*, Rom 16:16). In Christ, scattered mankind became gathered mankind (Eph 2:15), based on eschatological man,[3] the 'last Adam' (*ho eschatos Adam*, 1 Cor 15:45). He was a 'life-giving spirit' (ibid)—not only man, but also a man who 'gives life' to his fellow-men.

Mankind thus achieved salvation through the fraternal service of one of ourselves, Jesus Christ, the chosen one of God, the Son of the Father. This reality of Christ, accomplished within our history on this earth and human relationships in the world, has really influenced our history. The new unity or community of mankind, which exists in principle, but is nonetheless real, is based on God's universal will to save men. This, however, is not a purely suprahistorical reality. God's saving will has manifested itself historically and visibly in the so-called 'objective redemption', that is, the personal life of the representative man Jesus, the Son of God, who appeared historically among us. In a man—the *homo principalis* of Irenaeus,[4] in other words, in the man Jesus who is at the origin of the new mankind which he gathered into a community—humanity has already risen through suffering to glory with the Father. The history of Israel, itself part of and embedded in universal human history, was thus given a new significance. For human history itself, wherever this takes place, has in this way found grace with the Father. It has already been definitively appraised by the Father in the *eschaton*, Jesus Christ himself, by the Father's appointment of the humbled Jesus as the glorified Christ, the 'Son of God in power' (Rom 1:4) at the right hand of the Father. Christ is therefore 'the Alpha and the Omega' of human history as a whole (Rev 1:8; 21:6; 22:13). He is not this simply as

[3] See, among others, E. Peterson, 'Die Kirche', *Theologische Traktaten*, Munich 1951, 409–28.
[4] *Adv. Haer.* v, 21, 1 (*PG* 7, 1179); in this work, *principalis* (*archaios*) means 'standing at the head of' and is connected with Irenaeus' theory of recapitulation—Christ is at the new beginning of everything.

the supratemporal, supraterrestrial, exclusively transcendent meaning of our human history. The glorified man Jesus Christ is, after all, a historical man who has entered completion. At one real point of human history, that is, in Jesus, this history itself was definitively completed and perpetuated in the mode of consummation into eternity. In his representative function with regard to Israel and thus with regard to the whole of mankind, Jesus is the prototypical figure of *our* history, the element which has already entered into glory. That is why the Lord is the ultimate meaning which is immanent in our history, even though it is in a dimension which is, for us, trans-empirical. Thus all human history, even where this takes place in so-called profanity, can only be understood in the light of the 'eschatological man', Christ Jesus.

2. The dialectical tension between 'mankind' and the church

Christ has in principle (but really) given mankind a new religious meaning which is immanent, that is, which has been realised within our human history. There is, however, a certain distance between mankind gathered together in principle and the factual, public manifestation of this mankind that has been renewed in Christ. The exponent of this distance and tension is the 'church of Christ'. Within human history, this new meaning acquires a historically visible, public and concrete community-founding character in the church, thanks to free consent to the grace of justification, acceptance in faith of the gospel or the Word of God and reception of the church's baptism in the name of the Trinity. Admission to this church makes Christ's triumphant grace a manifest, historically recognisable fact.[5] The consequence of this is that, in the period between Christ's ascension and his second coming, there will always be a certain difference and a dialectical tension between the *church* and *mankind* (which has in principle (but really) been redeemed).

[5] See, among others, K. Rahner, 'The Church and the Parousia of Christ', *Theological Investigations* 6, London and Baltimore (Md) 1969, 295-312.

The Catholic biblical exegete A. Vögtle has clearly shown, in a series of articles in which he brings out more and more subtle shades of meaning, that Jesus had no intention, in his public preaching at least, of isolating a group of specially chosen Israelites from the whole of the people in order to constitute this group as a separate community.[6] In his public preaching of the kingdom of God and his call to repentance, Jesus obviously did not wish to gather only a remnant of Israel, but the whole of the people and make them the new Israel, the eschatological people of God. It was completely alien to his purpose to form a sect. He radically followed the path of the history of salvation as copied later by Paul— salvation was first offered to Israel and then, in accordance with God's intention, via Israel to the whole world. Jesus' calling of the 'twelve' from the group of disciples who followed him clearly seems to have been an action in the form of a parable which could not be misunderstood by his contemporaries.[7] The twelve patriarchs of Israel were represented in these twelve—further proof of Jesus' desire to obtain the whole of Israel for the kingdom of Heaven. In fact, however, the whole of Israel did not give assent to his preaching. On the contrary, opposition to his appearance increased more and more. As a result of this increasing opposition, Jesus, historically aware of the approach of his death as a violent event, began to interpret and disclose the meaning of this death within the limited circle of his disciples in the light of the

[6] A. Vögtle, 'Das öffentliche Wirken Jesu auf dem Hintergrund der Qumranbewegung', *Freiburger Universitätsreden*, N.F., 27, Freiburg i. Br. (1958), 5–20, esp. 15ff; 'Ekklesiologische Auftragsworte des Auferstandenen', *Actes du Congrès catholique des sciences bibliques à Bruxelles 1959*, 892–906; 'Jesus und die Kirche', *Begegnung der Christen*, ed. Roesle and Cullmann, Frankfurt a. M. (1960), 54–82; 'Die Einzelne und die Gemeinschaft in der Stufenfolge der Christusoffenbarung', *Sentire Ecclesiam*, ed. Daniélou and Vorgrimler, Freiburg i. Br. (1961), 50–9; see also 'Die Adam-Christus-Typologie und der Menschensohn', *Trierer Theologische Zeitschrift* (1951), 209–28; see also p 121 n 8 below.

[7] See A. Vögtle, 'Das öffentliche Wirken Jesu', op. cit., 15; F. Braun, *Neues Licht auf die Kirche*, Einsiedeln 1946, 71; A. N. Fridrichsen, 'Messias und Kirche', *Ein Buch von der Kirche*, Göttingen 1951, 33; see also K. Rengstorf, 'Doodeka', *Theologisches Wörterbuch zum Neuen Testament* II, Stuttgart (1960), 321–8.

prophecy of the second Isaiah, that is, as the death in expiation 'for the many' (for all men) willed by God. Not until he had done this, in other words, similarly in the context of his death and resurrection,[8] did he begin to speak about the church which 'I *will* build' on the rock, Peter (Mt 16: 18–19; see also Jn 21: 15–17), also within the same limited circle of disciples. This implies that the saved people of God became an *Ecclesia Christi* after Jesus' death and resurrection, a historically visible assembly of people gathered around Christ in visible communion with the rock under the twelve apostles. This situation gave the community of Jesus a distinctively ecclesial social structure which did not, as such, coincide with the social structure of temporal society.

On the one hand, then, it is clear that Jesus never referred in his public preaching to a church with forms of organisation and that he stipulated, as the only condition of entry into the kingdom of God, obedient acceptance of his saving message here and now, that is, in the *kairos* of the present moment. On the other hand, it is also clear that he mentioned his church-founding activity in the light of his death as expiation for all men and presented this activity as a post-paschal event ('I *will* build my church'). Scripture thus establishes a clear connection between Jesus' messianic suffering (his going away) and the post-paschal reality of the church. The church is the people of God with a special qualification, namely that she is the people of God who have, by Jesus' death and his resurrection by the Spirit, been made the *sōma Christou*, the 'body of the *Lord*'. On earth, this body was built as church on Peter, the rock. The 'vertical' theme in Jesus' public preaching—the movement towards God, the Father—also became, in the light of the meaning of his death as expiation that Jesus had entrusted to the apostles, a 'horizontal' theme after Easter and Pentecost—that of the building up of a mutual community around the rock. What we have to do with here, then, is

---

[8] See A. Vögtle, 'Messiasbekenntnis und Petrusverheissung', *Bibl. Zeitschrift*, N.F. 1 (1957), 252–72 and 2 (1958), 85–103, in which the author calls the connection between Peter's confession of the Messiah at Caesarea and Christ's promise of the *Ecclesia* secondary, that is, an 'arrangement' by Matthew or the Matthaean tradition.

clearly a mankind redeemed into an ecclesial brotherhood, in other words, the church as a community with its own rites of initiation, its own worship and above all its eucharistic fellowship at table, guided and accompanied by an office of ministry. Thus the death and glorification of Jesus, the Christ, made admission to this brotherhood, to the church in her sacramental, historical and visible form, the condition for entering the kingdom of God.[9] The *communio* of believers, gathered round their bishop (also in *communio* with the rock), *is* salvation—the church of Christ. It is precisely in this *koinōnia* that the Father's absolute communication of himself through the Son in the Holy Spirit must be historically and visibly realised, in a realisation that is the true sign of the vocation of the whole of mankind. In this way, the church is not only a *koinōnia*, a community of grace with Christ and thus a fruit of his redemption, but also a saving institution to which the keys which open the doors to the kingdom of God are entrusted. Unlike the scribes and Pharisees, who excluded men from the kingdom of Heaven (Mt 23 : 13), Christ gave Peter the keys which open the gates to the kingdom.

3. The basis of this dialectical tension

As I have already said clearly in the preceding section, there is certainly a distance between the mankind that has been redeemed by Christ both in principle and in historical reality and the community of Jesus built on the Rock, the institution of the church or 'practising christianity'. If we are to understand this distinction, we must first consider the connection made in scripture between Jesus' messianic death or 'going away' and the church, which is *only* a post-paschal and therefore a *new reality*—new even in comparison with the universal reality which is the people of God. From our point of view, Jesus' death was his rejection by mankind—by the Sanhedrin, Israel's representative, by the pagan world of the Gentiles in the person of Pilate and even by the hierarchy of the future church in the persons of the apostles who ran away and Peter

---

[9] Mk 10:35-40 and Mt 20:20-3; Mk 14:25; see also Lk 22:16 and 18.

who denied him. In his death, Jesus was really alone, crushed by the 'sins of the world', and alone in his surrender to the Father in service to his fellow-men. Death, which brought reconciliation, at the same time caused Christ's empirical absence, in other words, the absence of the source of grace. From our point of view, the rupture in the covenant of grace was made definitive by Jesus' death—mankind banished from this world the 'coming of the kingdom of God' into the world in the person of Christ and thus cast it out of the *communio* of men. Of course, every death implies a physical absence and a breaking off of interhuman relationships with the dead person. But Jesus' death was the death of the only one who could bring salvation. Looked at from our point of view, this removal of the man of grace, Christ, was therefore irrevocable. It was, after all, certainly not thanks to us and not even thanks to Christ's humanity as such that Christ, by virtue of his resurrection, once again entered into living relationships with us. It is only when we have once understood the full implication of Jesus' death that we can completely appreciate the fundamental saving significance of the resurrection which, on the basis of the sacrifice offered, made the sending of the Holy Spirit and the foundation of the church possible. It was in the resurrection of Jesus, the grace of the Father, that redemption triumphed. But this triumph implies that salvation is henceforth situated in the Jesus Christ who is now empirically *absent* from us. We may therefore correctly conclude from this that the ultimate form of our originally sinful condition is 'the situation of a lack of supernatural grace which can only be remedied sacramentally, a situation in which man has found himself since the breaking of the covenant with God and because this act perpetuated itself in the rejection of Christ'.[10] Jesus himself linked this going away with the coming of the Holy Spirit and the building up of the church. He wished to continue to dwell among us as the source of all grace in the church, his body, inhabited by the Holy Spirit. The church, 'this body', thus became for us the condition or, more

---

[10] P. Schoonenberg, 'Natuur en zondeval', *TT* 2 (1962), 199-200; see also E. Schillebeeckx, *Christ the Sacrament*, London and New York 1963, 47-54.

precisely, the incarnate form of our restored association with Christ and our entry into the kingdom of God. Jesus' absence from the *communio*, the community of men, was restored by his resurrection —in the church, his body on earth.

The consequence of this is important, however, and it was suggestively formulated by Thomas as follows: 'From Christ, grace reaches us not via human nature, but only through a *personal act* of Christ himself.'[11] Expressed in more modern terms, this means that the source of the grace of Christ is not human solidarity in itself, but human solidarity with Christ who has, however, disappeared from our empirical horizon since his death, but who wishes to remain present among us post-paschally, by virtue of the Spirit of God, in his body, the church. As the 'body of the Lord', the church forms our living link with Christ—horizontally with the historical Jesus who rose from the dead and appeared to the apostles and vertically with the glorified Lord, thanks to the Spirit dwelling in the whole community of the church, in the office, the word and the sacrament of the church. Thanks to this solidarity of Christ with men, universal human solidarity is given a deeper meaning and the boundaries between mankind and the church begin to blur.

4. The blurring of the boundaries between the church and mankind

A. The world-wide influence of the 'total' Christ

It is clear from what has already been said that the history of salvation is concerned with one covenant in two phases—that of Moses and that of Christ. An absolutely new situation was brought about in the plan of salvation by the death and resurrection of Christ. We have therefore to look for the relationship between the universal people of God, which is co-extensive with mankind, and the church, in which the people of God has been made the body of the Lord.

What the heavenly Christ does, he does in his totality, that is to say, in and with his body, the church. What the church

[11] *ST* III, q. 8, a. 5, ad 1.

therefore does as church, the glorified Christ also does together with the Spirit of God, who is also his Spirit. What is *christian* is therefore also of the church, in an indissoluble, living and organic bond. However much Jesus, the Lord, may transcend his body, the church, his immanence in the church is as extensive as his transcendence above the church, because he is transcendent (above the church) by interiority (in the church). In other words, his transcending of the boundaries of his body, the church, is a gratuitous gift of himself in the church to all men, even those who are (still) outside the church. This at the same time means that the Lord is active in our world even in people who have not yet been historically confronted with the 'church of Christ'. But it also means that this activity of the Lord is at the same time an activity of his body. Every association with Christ, even though it is anonymous, is therefore *ipso facto* also an association with the church. In this way, the church is also the possibility of salvation for the world of men which has not yet perceived and experienced her in the distinctive form in which she appears historically.

In this perspective, the distance which in fact exists between *church* and *mankind* nonetheless acquires a weakened significance—the church is also seen to be actively present even where she is not yet visibly present in her full ecclesial form. Church and mankind cannot therefore simply be opposed to each other as church and non-church. There is, moreover, a great deal that is non-church in the lives of those who belong explicitly to the church and a great deal that is church in the life of mankind as a whole. But because the church is, strictly speaking, mankind insofar as it consents in faith, baptism and eucharistic fellowship at table to being subject to the influence of Christ as such, it is perhaps advisable for us not to use the word 'church' for the anonymous presence of the church in anonymously christian mankind. This situation could be called 'pre-church', but all kinds of objections could also be made to this term. In the real sense of the word, the church is, after all, the saving process by which what the Lord has achieved in the whole of mankind becomes public and is given an explicitly christian presentation—the *koinōnia* of men through confession of God and baptism in Christ which is also an effective sign of the calling of those who are (still) outside the church. On the other hand, anonymous christianity, which we have to accept as a reality, not in the least because of our hopeful trust in the triumphant grace of Christ's redemption ('I have overcome the world') is, of its very nature, an anonymity which inwardly demands its *proper* sacramental visible form. It is precisely because the world-wide activity of Christ's grace is an operation in and through the church, on account of the bond between the Christ who has gone away and the post-paschal reality of the church as the body of the Lord by virtue of the Spirit of God, that this grace is in itself church-founding. This means that, wherever she operates as grace (and this is co-extensive with the whole of mankind and thus with human solidarity) something of the 'mystical body' is visibly realised, although in a veiled manner. Because this grace appears visibly in definite historical forms, that is, in the church, precisely as Christ's grace, this explicit appearance bears testimony to the fact that, wherever this grace is active—and that is everywhere where human history is realised—it also inwardly strives to become historically visible in its distinctive form, that is, it strives to become church. A tendency to become church is clearly taking place in the lives of men. Outside the boundaries of the 'actual' church, because the bond with Christ and his church is only anonymous, this grace will express itself in all kinds of human forms—sometimes in richly varied religious forms and sometimes perhaps in typically 'secular' forms which are unable, in their explicit form, to designate and reflect what is *really intended*.

The fact that the deep meaning that is obscurely present in the dynamic life of mankind is not grasped according to its real significance does not mean that the distinction between 'mankind' and church is only one of 'not knowing explicitly' as opposed to 'knowing explicitly'. It is, after all, true that man only comes completely to himself in expressing himself. What is experienced anonymously always remains a fragile datum if it cannot authentically *express itself*. (This is more than simply a question of 'knowledge'!) Without the church's form and expression of this most profound core of life in Christ, which were given by God in Christ himself, this experience remains a 'light hidden under a bushel', a flickering flame that any draught may extinguish. It is within the sphere of the church proper that God's word of forgiveness is spoken, baptism administered and the eucharist celebrated, and men believe that nothing can separate us from the Lord and that absolute loneliness is impossible for man since God has been with us. And this environment (which is the believers themselves) is vitally necessary if what grace accomplishes anonymously in the lives of men is to be brought to its saving fulfilment. But this special value of the church as a sign and as disclosure requires the church to go back again and again to her authentic evangelical sources and to show herself in forms in which this authenticity will come forward to meet us clearly and impartially.

Thanks to the fact of Christ, there is therefore an inward movement in living mankind towards the church. The church's missionary activity is only the tendency in the opposite direction to this movement, a going forward to meet mankind. This movement 'in the direction of the church', this need of the church on the part of mankind, and, on the other hand, the church's going forward to meet this mankind are *both* the visible forms of the one effective salvation which the Lord is in the *pneuma*, the Spirit of God. In both these forms, Jesus, the Christ, is seeking his messianic community which he gained for himself on the cross in order to prepare it for himself as the spotless eschatological bride for the glory of the Father. The church incognito, as the work both of the Spirit of Christ and of his body, the church, which is indissolubly part of his life, is striving, through the Spirit, really to appear as the 'body of the Lord' which is incorporated through baptism into Christ's death and resurrection. This anonymous church must become a visible sign of the 'eschatological man' Jesus Christ and, in this way, a sign of what human life is in the concrete—a sign, that is, that profound and painful suffering and existence ending in death is not the final word to be spoken about mankind. The destiny of our human life is prefigured in the *kenōsis* and the *hypsōsis* of Christ, his humiliation and his exaltation. The constant struggle for life in mankind, hoping against all hope, is the anonymous echo of this—there is more in it than simply secularity, even though it is perhaps expressed in a purely secular way. Not only are the frontiers between the church and 'mankind' merging in the direction of the church—they are also merging in the direction of 'mankind' and the world. The modern process of desacralisation and secularisation clearly indicates that what was previously regarded as a separate and distinctive activity of the church (dispensing alms to those who were deprived, works of charity and so on) has now become a task undertaken by humanity in general. Many aspects of what in the past appeared as something strictly pertaining to the church have now become a distinctive form of the lives of men in the world. This osmosis from the church to the world can have no termination on earth because the 'old' aeon and the 'new' continue to exist side by side in this world—the coincidence of the 'community of men' with the 'communion of saints' in clear visibility is therefore only a heavenly event, not something that happens on this earth. The merging of the frontiers between the church and mankind can therefore never do away with the dialectical tension between the two on earth, although this does not imply that this tension cancels out the dynamism of the world's tendency to become church on the one hand and the church's tendency towards sanctifying secularisation on the other. It is, moreover, important to stress the fact that this process of secularisation is *sanctifying*, in other words, that it stems from the transcendent community with God in Christ. Anyone forgetting this would, in the long run, let the church merge into an institution like UNO or UNESCO!

Paul has already expressed this idea in his own way, within the framework of his ancient view of the world. According to Paul, Christ fulfilled 'all things' by his death and glorification, that is, 'all things in heaven and on earth', 'visible and invisible' (Eph 1 : 10; see also Col 1 : 16–20), in other words, all created reality. In this context, the biblical exegete H. Schlier was correct in his commentary on Paul's letter to the Ephesians:

> There is no sphere of being that is not at the same time a sphere of the church. The church is fundamentally orientated towards the universe. Her frontiers are only in the universe. There is no realisation of Christ's dominion without the church and outside her and no 'fulfilment' without the church and outside her. The manner in which the universe grows towards Christ is the manner in which the church grows—there are admittedly spheres which are opposed to fulfilment through the church, because they are ultimately filled with themselves.[12]

Paul himself said clearly: 'He (God) has put all things under his feet and has made him (Christ) the head over all things for the church, which is his body, the fullness of him who fills all in all' (Eph 1 : 22–3). The completion of all existence and of all reality takes place through the church.[13] Eschatologically, the church and mankind thus coincide completely.

B. *The unity of creation, redemption and the 'building of the church'*

The fact that the church and mankind are, on the one hand, growing towards each other and that, on the other, there is still an unmistakable boundary, based on Christ's post-paschal 'building of the church on the rock',[14] between them clarify an insight into faith in which creation and the conferment of grace, redemption and the building of the church are seen together in the great unity of God's covenant with mankind.

[12] 'Die Kirche nach dem Briefe an die Epheser', *Die Zeit der Kirche*, Freiburg i. Br. 1956, 169.

[13] Here too, Schlier makes this pertinent commentary on Paul: '(The church) is the *plerōma* of Christ, which means (1) the space filled by him and (2) the space which itself fills by his fullness. She is the filled fullness and the filling fullness of that which has filled and fills the universe. The universe is taken into her fullness as into his fullness and thus itself approaches fullness, that is, church' (170).

[14] I shall be discussing the ideas contained in this statement elsewhere and extending them to the problem of membership of the church in connection with the pluralism of the christian churches.

Grace is God's absolute communication of himself to man and man's personal living community with God—the Father, the Son and the Holy Spirit. It is only in the light of the historical mystery of Christ that we know explicitly that, even in the pre-christian period, grace could only be trinitarian. This mystery discloses for us the secret of all conferment of grace, that is, as community with the Father, the Son and the Holy Spirit. It is only in Christ that the fundamental aspect of every life of grace becomes explicit. This points to the intimate connection between grace and Christ. The fact that the trinitarian character of every conferment of grace remained implicit and anonymous before Christ appeared in our world gives rise to the question as to whether this trinitarian anonymity is not connected with the fact that mankind has, from the very beginning, been orientated towards Christ—an orientation which has, of course, always been implicit. An analysis of the essentially trinitarian character of the conferment of grace or God's communication of himself to man and of the fact that this character was only revealed in Christ shows that the original conferment of grace and therefore the divine constitution of mankind as the people of God were present, for the sake of man's creation, in *orientation towards Christ*. 'Adam' was created in an (implicit) orientation towards Christ and *grace* was conferred upon him precisely because of and in this.[15] This means that man's concrete being itself is a messianic prophecy of the 'Christ who was to come' and the task of forming a true *communio* of men, as the essential task for a community of persons, is a prophecy of the 'mystical body', the church of Christ, which was to come. Thus, although I have followed a different path and perhaps a more radical one, I have come to the same conclusion, at least in the material sense, as Karl Rahner and can affirm, with him, that mankind itself as a whole is the (faithful or unfaithful) people of God and can also, together with him, regard membership of this people of God as forming a consti-

---

[15] I have tried to develop this idea in some detail in 'Die Heiligung des Namen Gottes durch die Menschenliebe Jesu des Christus' in J. B. Metz et al., *Gott in Welt* II, Freiburg im Breisgau 1964, 43–91.

tutive part of our concrete being as men.[16] Concretely, then, every free human act either brings about salvation or is opposed to it. At the same time, however, it seems to me that the manner in which I have arrived at this insight has thrown a clearer light on the objectively new situation in which mankind has been placed since the death and resurrection of Christ. It is, after all, clear from this objectively new situation that salvation is not given in the people of God as such, but in this people of God insofar as it has been made the body of Christ. This implies that the faithful people of God at least have (since the historical appearance of the mystery of Christ) been *made* into a *votum Ecclesiae* by virtue of the sole sanctifying power of Christ in his body, the church. The reasons for this should have emerged from the whole of the foregoing argument, but I will clarify it a little further.

Through man's creation in orientation towards Christ, in which the conferment of grace on man is given, the whole of mankind bears the 'life of the church' anonymously *in itself* as a grace which is either accepted or refused. We may therefore say:

> The relationship with God is always accomplished in and by a people of God, whether it be the still undifferentiated people of God we call mankind, or Israel—in which people the Messianic mould of humanity became increasingly clear—or whether it be, in sharply defined characteristics, the people of God redeemed and constituted as a church by Christ.[17]

The human community of persons is, as created in inward orientation towards Christ, the preliminary plan of the church herself. But it is only a preliminary plan, because the historical appearance of Jesus and his banishment from our human community brought about a completely new situation, especially since the risen Christ built his church and also placed it visibly in the midst of mankind as a community with its own sacramental communal structures, its office and

[16] See Karl Rahner, 'Membership of the Church according to the teaching of Pius XII's Encyclical *Mystici Corporis*, *Theological Investigations* 2, London and Baltimore (Md) 1963, 1–88.

[17] E. Schillebeeckx, *God and Man* (Theological Soundings 2), London and New York 1969, 198–9.

its service of the Word. It is precisely this absolutely new fact of salvation which gives a relative value to the universal reality of the people of God which is co-extensive with the whole of mankind. On the other hand, however, it includes this reality *ipso facto* in a new dimension and makes its implicit acceptance into an objective tending towards the church—a *votum Ecclesiae.* Anonymously christian mankind, already not only in principle, but also really the people of God because of its *creation* in Christ, becomes a true *votum Ecclesiae* only thanks to Christ's death and resurrection and the post-paschal fruit of this redemption, the church. This is so precisely by virtue of the universal activity of Christ's grace *in* the church for the benefit of the *whole* of mankind.[18]

The church of Christ is therefore not so much the final phase of the inner development of the people of God appearing in an increasingly more clearly visible form (although this aspect cannot be denied). Rather, the concretely historical act of Christ's redemption with its post-paschal fruit, the church, *recapitulates* the reality of the people of God created long ago in orientation towards Christ in the death and resurrection of Christ and thus *makes* this reality the *votum Ecclesiae. That* is why we can say *extra Ecclesiam nulla salus*—there is no salvation outside Christ and thus outside his church. At the same time, we must also say that here on earth the church has not yet become perfectly what she has to become. Origen gave clear expression to this idea in the phrase, *ho kosmos tou kosmou he Ekklēsia,* 'the church is the world of men, *de facto* perfectly brought to order (to peace and *communio)'.*[19] The church bears in herself the

[18] Note, however, that I am not claiming that all non-Catholic people are in themselves anonymous christians (just as I also do not maintain that all those who belong to the church are authentically christian). All that I am saying is that anonymous christianity is a real possibility and, in view of the overwhelming power of grace, a *reality* in many cases (although I would not wish to make any statement concerning their number, nor would I be able to). I am well aware of the essential ambiguity of human freedom and its possibility for good and evil. But my trust in God is greater than the ambiguity of human freedom.

[19] See A. Auer, 'Kirche und Welt', *Mysterium Kirche,* pt 2, Salzburg 1962, 492–3.

principles and the incipient reality of this eschatological peace by virtue of the fact that she, the fruit of Christ's redemption, is in the world as the 'body of the Lord' in and through which the glorified Christ accomplishes his world-wide activity in the Spirit. In this way, the church, as the sign for the whole world, is the forerunner of eschatological salvation in our human history. This is the basis of her missionary duty and of the call that she constantly experiences to go back to the evangelical sources of the structures of the church that have developed throughout history, especially at a time like the present, when the image of man and of the world is being radically changed.

C. 'Church' and human solidarity

The blurring of the otherwise enduring boundaries between church and 'mankind' can also be explained in the light of the inner structure of the church. There is no antithesis, but there is a certain distinction in the one church of Christ between the two dialectical aspects of the church as a living community guided by the Spirit of God active in the apostolic office of the world episcopate and the same church guided by the same Spirit active in the conscience of every individual christian. This second aspect of the activity of the Spirit, which shows itself as the activity of christians themselves, also builds up the church and does this to a great extent in the world itself and in the ordinary, everyday things of life, in other words, in precisely the same sphere in which those who have not (yet) explicitly become members of the community of the church are living. Here too, the building up of the church takes on a veiled character.

Because there is, then, a non-hierarchical building up of the church, just as closely connected with the guidance of the Holy Spirit active in the conscience of every individual christian, a real building up and extension of the church is accomplished by christians themselves in the so-called profane world, where the hierarchical church is not present. The growth of the church in the still anonymously christian world is also a factual, although even more veiled manifestation of this same reality, a manifestation which we can, however, only recognise as such in the light of Christ and his visible church.

If, therefore, we wish to look for the significant characteristics which point, in mankind, to a true church incognito (which, because of what she is herself, looks forward to her real epiphany as church), we should look for these not so much in universal human solidarity as such as in the *distinctive qualification* of this brotherhood as revealed by Jesus himself. Jesus characterised this human solidarity as the helping love which goes out to the *mikroi*, the little ones, and the *elachistoi*, the least of men, whom Jesus called his 'brethren' (Mt 25:31–46). It is in accordance with this love that those who belong explicitly to the church and those who do not (yet) belong to the church will be judged at the end of time—'as you did it to one of the least of these my brethren, you did it to me' (Mt 25:40), 'for I was hungry and you gave me food, I was thirsty and you gave me drink, I was a stranger and you welcomed me' (Mt 25:35–6), 'as you did it not to one of the least of these, you did it not to me' (Mt 25:45). Expressed in modern terms, this might mean—your failure to help the underdeveloped countries is a failure with regard to Christ himself, an offence against authentic christianity, and your aid to the underdeveloped countries, not from political motives, but from motives of true human solidarity, is authentic christianity. The messianic act by which Christ founded his church was that of surrendering himself to the very end. Wherever men follow his example, perhaps even unconsciously, they are founding *communio* and church in Christ. The parable of the good Samaritan therefore teaches us, not without a certain sharp thrust at those who belong to the church, that whoever comes forward to help the very first person he meets who is in distress and helps him abundantly with the luxury of excessive love is really founding *koinōnia* —he is, in other words, making this person his neighbour and brother.

This anonymous church-founding activity thus goes beyond the frontiers of the official church, that is, of the church as the sociologically situated, clearly historically visible form of the community of those who confess Christ and take their places in the eucharistic table-fellowship. It goes so far beyond these frontiers that even this abundance of love, however significantly visible it may be in the saints of the church, is not primarily or only realised *historically* by practising christians. And yet it is only where love makes fellow-man into brother that church is genuinely founded. The church-founding activity of love is, in a word, the very essence of the church's being. It was precisely in order to safeguard this essence that Christ founded an office in his church and that he continues to assist this hierarchical office in a special way so as to keep his people in the one community of love and hope, based on the one faith in Christ. Ultimately, however, the church is not so much concerned with this hierarchy as with the church-founding activity of love, and the hierarchy has the function of serving this activity, although this function may be in the manner of christian authority.

Church-founding outside the visible community of Jesus can therefore be found above all in man's unconditional surrender to his fellow-man in disinterested love. In the concrete, one's fellow-man is an offer of God's grace, a sacramental sign of his saving will, but he is this only because of his being created in Christ and therefore because of Christ, the constitutive sign of God's grace. This universal sacramentality of human solidarity is not cancelled out or simply, as it were, syphoned off into the 'formal structures' of the visible church because of the full sacramental form of the humanity Christ shared with us. On the contrary, it is precisely through the historical appearance of *the* man, Jesus Christ, the Son of God, that the sacramental power of grace of human solidarity can be experienced according to its full significance in and because of the Christ who has now appeared. The universal sacramentality of human solidarity is only being made *concrete* in the community which we call the church. The seven sacraments, the church's worship and preaching and the hierarchy's leadership and guidance are only the highest points at which the church's commitment to human solidarity is crystallised. It is clear from this that the church will only appear as the inviting and attractive sign among men when the love of her members for their fellow-men becomes concretely and historically visible (here and now in the present world situation) and is not restricted to those few culminating points in which Christ makes his grace present in a concentrated manner. That is precisely why an increasing desire was felt, during the Second Vatican Council's discussion on the church, to extend these deliberations to a consideration of the active presence of the members of the church in the world. The *Constitution on the Church* inwardly called for *Gaudium et Spes!*

Because of all this, we should not regard the church's representative function in respect of mankind outside the church as a 'representative' function, by which those who do not belong to the church are dispensed from this abundant activity of love and are saved by 'substitution', that is, by the abundance of love that is present at least in the church of Christ. Representation and mediation never mean substitution or replacement in a truly christian perspective—they signify a prototypical reality which communicates because of its abundance, *with the consequence* that others are really enabled to accomplish themselves, by virtue of the grace acquired, what has already taken place before them by the living example of the prototype. In this sense, the church herself lives in the power of the Spirit of Christ for the benefit of the whole of mankind. But it is equally true that this operation of Christ's grace in the whole of mankind through the church also has to gain a visible form, especially in the church's missionary activity. This also means that, in the church's historical confrontation with mankind, those who belong explicitly to the church must *de facto* be the prototypes and the living examples of this superabundance of love and this forfeiting of one's own life for the benefit of others.

5. The secular and sacral realisation of the church's holiness

A certain solution has, I hope, been provided by the argument set out in the preceding sections to the problem posed at the outset of this chapter, namely that a tendency *to become church* is clearly discernible in the whole of mankind and that there is also a similar process taking place in the church, a tendency *towards sanctifying secularisation*. Although certain frontiers remain inviolable—those which are formed by the word, the sacrament and the office, all of which are *serving* functions— the frontiers between church and mankind are becoming blurred. The form of christianity that is completely capable of being integrated in our lives is objectively offered to us in our explicit encounter with Christ in his church. This church ought consequently to be a home that is genuinely fit for human habitation and it is also the church's task to make herself so in different ways at different periods of history. The full religious sense has an explicitly christian form which is experienced within the church. Precisely because of this, christianity—however involved it may be with our everyday cares and tasks and the whole of our activity in the world, in and through which we grow in intimacy with God—also has a sacral sphere that is separate from the history and civilisation of this world, a sphere in which we pray and are simply together with God in Christ. At the purely anthropological level, silence is an aspect of speaking or of social intercourse. At this level, silence has no real meaning in itself, but is merely a function of human solidarity and social intercourse. It is necessary in order to make contact between human beings human and to keep it human. Its purpose is to humanise inter-human contact. Silence personalises speaking —without it, dialogue would be impossible. In a revealed religion, however, silence with God has a *value in itself* and not simply as a function of our intercourse with our fellow-men— precisely because God is *God*. To fail to appreciate the believer's simple, 'inactive' being together with God as the beloved is to ignore the very essense of christianity. It is, of course, true that the whole of our being in this world of people and things permeates this being together with God and does so essentially and not simply as distraction in prayer. We are only able to tell God that we love him or at least that we wish to love him more with words, concepts and images that are taken from our human world. What is more, this being together with God is not individualism, since our prayer is insincere—it is not prayer—if we pray '*Our* Father...' and forget the kingdom of God and our fellow-man. Christianity is not only being together with God in the form that we are capable of experiencing of Christ in his church. It is also *working together* with the living God, 'with the Father who is always at work' (see Jn 5: 17) both in the church and in the world. The religious attitude towards life is primarily a personal association with God, but with the living God who is also the creator of people and things offered to us for us to humanise. That is why man's relationship with his fellow-man and the world is not only cultural, but also essentially *religious*. The *agapē* includes both God and man. The love of God cannot and should not be separated from love of man. Christian love of our neighbour means that *we*, God and I together, love *my* fellow-man. Whereas, in natural human love, God is only the silently present transcendent third, my charity for my fellow-man is just as much *love*, but it is love in the community of love lived and experienced with God. The christian therefore loves his fellow-man with the same love with which he loves God and with the same love with which he and his fellow-man are loved by God. It is only with Christ that one can learn the real meaning of 'being a man for others' (although our experiences with people in the world teach us *how* we have to express our common humanity in particular situations). But, however much membership of the church may be the explicit form in which religion and christianity are lived, the realisation of our christianity takes place in the history of our day-to-day life as human beings in the world with our fellow-men. The authenticity of our personal association with God, of our christianity and our belonging to the church, must therefore be measured against the genuineness of our human solidarity or our real love of men. The source of this christian love of men, however, is to be found in our personal entry into the distinctive forms in which our association with God can be experienced and which are also given by Christ—our listening to the Word of God, our association with scripture and our taking part in the celebration of the sacramental liturgy of the church. In our world, then, there is a *sacral* environment as well as a *worldly* sphere of authentic christianity. In everything that he does, man is either open and accomplishes salvation or he is closed and opposes salvation. We must be with God, not only in church, in prayer, in the sacraments or in reading the bible, in other words, in the sacral forms of religion, but also, and just as much, in our human relationships with our fellow-men in the world and in our daily tasks. Then we may safely say that various types of christianity are possible. Some christians can grow in intimacy with God above all by experiencing the sacral forms of religion and thereby express in a very special way the 'other-worldliness' of the church. Others, on the other hand, can give form to their christianity more especially in the secular sphere—their 'secular holiness' will be a clear expression of the fact that the christian faith is not simply an ideological suprastructure superimposed on human life. These, however, are different emphases of the one christian life which is immanent in this world because of its transcendence. After all, what I have said about the universal relationship between mankind and the church also applies to the individual christian himself—the source of strength for the true christian presence, incognito, in the secular, profane world is always the explicit christian experience of active participation in the life of the word and the sacrament of the 'church of Christ'.

7
THE ECCLESIAL LIFE OF RELIGIOUS MAN

The church is the triumphant grace of Christ the Lord visibly present among us. Wherever this grace becomes visible among us in any way, we are confronted with the presence of the church. My aim in this article is to analyse the apostolic consequences of this reality.

1. The development of the history of salvation towards the people of God of the church

St Augustine described in a masterly fashion how the church, as we know and confess her today, is as old as the world itself. If we disregard certain subtle distinctions in his analysis, we see that he divided this gradual realisation of the church in the history of man into three great phases: firstly, the 'church' of the religious pagan world, secondly, the pre-christian stage of the people of God of Israel and thirdly, the mature appearance of the church as 'the assembly of the first-born' (Heb 12:13). This development should give us a deeper insight into the meaning of the reality of the church.

The 'church' in the religious pagan world

The church was already present, in a vague, but nonetheless visible way, in the life of the whole of religious mankind.[1] The whole of mankind was subject to God's inner invitation which called it to the community of grace with himself. In the pagan world, this vague call, insofar as it was heard and found a sincere response, aroused an obscure awareness of a redeeming God who committed himself personally to the salvation even of these people. This inner religious experience, brought about by grace, did not, however, at this time

---

[1] Augustine, *PL* 44, col. 161, 315 and 974; *PL* 43, col. 609-10.

encounter the visible form of this grace—this remained, as it were, hidden and unknown in the depths of the human heart. Life in this world of creation, however, acquires a deeper significance when man, placed in this world, is inwardly addressed by God. When this occurs, the world of creation becomes an element of this inner, although still anonymous, dialogue with God. If God, who wishes to engage in personal relationships with us, is, however, the creator of heaven and earth, then this implies that the world, our life in the world and our confrontation with being in this world will tell us more about the living God than these are able to do in themselves, more than simply that God is the creator of everything. Life in the world then becomes itself the content of an inner invitation on God's part. It discloses, in a vague way, something of what the living God personally whispers into our hearts by means of his grace which draws us. However vague it may be, it nonetheless becomes a really supernatural outward revelation in which the created world begins to speak the language of salvation to us and becomes the sign of higher realities. The natural event, human life in and with the world, begins to express, through this inward speaking on God's part, more than it is able to do in itself—there is, in all this, a special, even a personal intention which transcends the normal possibilities of created nature and life in the world. The inner grace of God thus reached a certain level of visible manifestation even in the pagan world. The religious pagan world also attempted in this way to give an outward form to its inward expectation. Man could not get away from God because God would not let him go. It was from this search to give form to a deeply hidden, but authentically religious intention that the rich variety of religious life and aspiration arose in the ancient pagan world and, although this search for and this confession of religious intention was expressed in many different ways, it is possible to trace these back to a few main religious themes. It is not, however, easy to disentangle the genuine from the false in these themes. Because they lacked the support of the particular, visible revelation of God, they became a mixture of authentic religion, human, sometimes all too fallibly human experience, dogmatic distortion and moral degeneration. At the same time, however, a germ of genuine holiness broke through here and there and was expressed in mystical prayer. It is only in the fulfilment of God's concern for man in the Old Testament and ultimately in the New Testament that it becomes apparent to us that God was demonstrating his concern for pagan man as well. His revelation has made the themes of the pagan response to this concern clear to us—man's relationship with God is an I-thou relationship of dialogue. He lost this living relationship with God, the relationship of a child with its father, and could not, in himself, find it again. This was evident to him from his life in this world. But it was only in the visible fulfilment of God's concern for mankind, first in the faithful of Israel and then, completely and definitively, in the man Jesus, that the content of truth that was hidden in the distorted myths of the religious pagan world became clear. What had been given a twisted form in pagan man's projections (in which an obscure impulse of grace is nonetheless discernible), and yet was a pale foreshadowing of what was still to come, appeared in its true form in the visible exteriority of the tangibly holy —in Israel and in Christ. The pagan religious community, which was again and again activated by great religious figures, by which pagan religious man was sustained in his life and from which he nourished his life, was the first providential model of the true church of Christ that was to come. The church as the visible presence of grace is therefore a world-wide reality. Indeed, she is even more than this—she is also, as the fathers of the church said, partly unconscious christianity, since, in the order in which we live, all grace goes back to the one mediator, Christ Jesus. Generally speaking, then, we may already say that there is no religion without belonging to the church. Grace never comes simply in interiority. It always comes forward to meet us in a visible form. To try to make a division between religion and the 'church' is ultimately to kill the religious life. Whoever is religious must also be ecclesial.

The 'church' of Israel

The visible form of the grace present in the pagan world (and this applies equally to the religious sense which may be present in the 'modern pagan world') was nonetheless shrouded in complete anonymity. It is as though what God wished to realise in Israel and later in Christ had already revealed itself in advance in the lives of all men, precisely insofar as they were subject to the inner call of the living God. The explicit form of this grace, however, only became clear in God's particular revelation. This first occurred in Israel.

A group of Bedouins of differing ethnological origin, tormented by and weary of forced labour in Egypt, to which their ancestors had been attracted by the fertile Nile Delta, joined together in the great caravan of the exodus. This hotchpotch of different clans, each of which seemed to have its own religion, became one people which united in the desert under the name of God, Yahweh, who had appeared to Moses. This was the hour of Israel's birth as the people of God. The appearance to Moses, as narrated in the bible, was clearly intended to show that this people became one people by a special personal intervention on the part of Yahweh, the living God. After having taken possession of the new country, Canaan, which God had prepared for this new people, Joshua reminded Israel of the strange gods that they had 'served beyond the River (that is, Abraham in Mesopotamia), and in Egypt' (Jos 24:14; see also Judith 5:7; Ex 20:6-9). Yahweh alone had made this people what it was. In stark simplicity, but movingly, the prophet Ezekiel has described this formation of a group of wandering Bedouins into the church or people of God:

> Thus says Yahweh, the Lord, to Jerusalem: Your origin and your birth are of the land of the Canaanites; your father was an Amorite, and your mother a Hittite [that is, a pagan]. And as for your birth, on the day you were born, your navel string was not cut, nor were you washed with water to cleanse you, nor rubbed with salt, nor swathed with bands. No eye pitied you, to do any of these things to you out of compassion for you; but you were cast out on the open field, for you were abhorred,

on the day that you were born. And *when I* [Yahweh] *passed by you*, and saw you weltering in your blood, I said to you in your blood, '*Live*, and grow up like a plant of the field'...
Then I bathed you with water and washed off your blood from you, and anointed you with oil [Ez 16: 3–9].

Israel, the first phase of the church, was the fruit of God's merciful intervention, the prelude to what St Paul was later to say about the church of Christ:

Christ loved the church and gave himself up for her, that he might sanctify her, having cleansed her by the washing of water ...that he might present the Church to himself in splendour, without spot or wrinkle...holy and without blemish [Eph 5:25–7].

The visible religion of Israel, with its believing people, its worship, sacraments, sacrifices and priests was *the first phase of the great church*.[2] This church was already a visible presence of grace, a giving sign of sanctifying grace, not because of a kind of prior activity (which anyway would be very difficult to understand) of the mystery of Christ that was still to come, but because Israel was already a realised part of the mystery of Christ, the fact of Christ in a state of becoming. The church of the Old Testament was the sign and the cause of grace *insofar* as the time of Christ had already been heralded in it. The church of Israel, as the still not fully mature presence of the mystery of Christ, could therefore not give fully mature grace, but only the grace of being completely open to the messiah who was to come—a holy grace of advent.[3]

The essence of the Old Testament revelation is expressed in the following way in various passages in holy scripture: 'I will be your God, and you shall be my people'.[4] To the benefit of Israel, God was to be faithful to this covenant with, and even in spite of Israel. But Israel, in her turn, had to per-

[2] Augustine, *PL* 44, col. 973–4; col. 281, 523 and 845–6; *PL* 42, col. 356.
[3] In this connection, we must realise that, according to the Council of Florence, the Jewish sacraments did not bestow grace; see Denz. 1310 (695).
[4] Ex 6:7; Lev 26:12; Deut 26:17–18; 29:12–13; Jer 7:23; Ez 11:20; 14:11; 37:27; Hos 1:9.

petuate this faithfulness to the covenant by living as the true people of God. This was, and is, the task of the church.

The whole of the Old Testament revelation is precisely this: the history that arose from God's faithfulness and the repeated unfaithfulness of the Jewish people. It was within this dialectical situation that revelation was accomplished. It was God's ultimate aim to call a faithful people into being. Generally speaking, this aim failed again and again—until God himself brought into the world a man in whom the whole of mankind's call to faithfulness was concentrated and who was in himself to fulfil God's faithfulness to the covenant in corresponding faithfulness—Christ Jesus. In the man Jesus, faithfulness to the covenant was thus bilaterally realised in a visible manner. The dialogue between God and mankind which had so often ended in deadlock thus finally found a human sounding-board—both the invitation and the faithful response were accomplished in one and the same person. The man Jesus was the definitively successful covenant, sealed in his blood.

2. The visible church, object of christian faith

Grace became fully visible as ultimate triumphant grace in the man Jesus. Christ is not only the visible fullness of God's grace that is given to us, he is also the full, visible maturity of man's acceptance of grace—the supreme realisation of all religion and consequently also of the presence of the church in every sense. He is simply church—the personal and visible form in which the grace of redemption appears. There is therefore no religion and no church unless in and through Christ. He is this precisely as the messiah—in our name and in the place of us all. It is only in association with this first-born that the church, the 'assembly of the first-born', is a reality in this world. The humanity of Jesus is thus the visible sign in which the mystery of God's redeeming love is given to us in a sensible and vivid way and through which the redeeming God really causes us to enter into his love. It is through this ecclesial reality that we experience the religious reality.

The triumphant grace of Christ is visibly active everywhere

in this world, which has therefore already become 'church' in the broad sense of the word. But the church of Christ in the *full* sense of the word is the *concentration point* of this visible presence of Christ in grace. The fullness of the power of God dwells 'bodily' in this church as it does in Christ. The eucharist is the central point of this fullness.

This church is a visible community of grace, and this community, consisting of members and a hierarchical leadership, is itself the sign on earth of the triumphant grace of Christ. We are bound to stress this point—not only the hierarchical church, but also the lay community of believers belong equally to this striking sign which confers grace, the church. The church, both laity and those bearing office, is the form in which the victory achieved by Christ appears historically. This means that the essence of the church is to be found in the historical and tangible presence in the whole church of the ultimate grace of Christ. Since Christ's ascension, church means the presence of Christ's grace on earth in the whole of this religious community, the redeemed people of God. We should not make the sort of distinction here which was often made in the past between the soul of the church (denoting the inner community of grace with Christ) and the body of the church (denoting the visible society with its hierarchical structure). Church means the visible presence of the grace of redemption and thus this grace itself appearing in a visible form. Any kind of dualism here is pernicious—as though it were possible to play the inner community of grace off against the visible community of grace or vice versa. The church is the grace of Christ placed in the world. Contact in faith with this visible ecclesial presence is therefore a conferment of grace—this is the most profound meaning of 'practising' one's faith. That is why the church is not really only a means of salvation. She is salvation itself, that is, the bodily form of salvation, salvation itself as appearing in this world. In this sense, she is the 'body of the Lord', although she is not simply identical with it. Here too, it is clear that the religious sense, christianity and the reality of the church are indissolubly connected with each other.

As I have already said, this visible appearance of grace qualifies the whole of the church—not only the priestly hierarchy, but also the expressions of the whole people of God. This people of God, as guided by the hierarchy, is the 'sign set up among the people'. That is why the redeeming grace of Christ is visible in his church in a twofold manner. It is *officially* or institutionally visible in the *charisma* of the hierarchical office through the administration of the sacraments, the service of the word or preaching and the governing and pastoral office of the church. But it is also non-officially *charismatic* through the lives of all the people of God living from the impulse of the grace of the Spirit of Christ. Both activities are ecclesial.

In the rest of this chapter I shall concentrate on this second aspect of the ecclesial character of the people of God. This is not because I regard the first aspect as less important, but because I have already dealt explicitly with it elsewhere[5] and also because there is considerable evidence of the prevalence of very wrong views concerning this second meaning of the ecclesial character of the people of God among believers.

Many believers call only what proceeds from the church's hierarchy truly ecclesial. They have a kind of totalitarian view of the church and confuse the absolute claim of the church, in which the hierarchy is really the protector of Christ's visible grace, with a kind of social structure of the church, in which the believers are only executive organs of what the hierarchy plans and wishes to have carried out. This attitude is not only wrong, it is also alien to the essence of the church.

The Spirit of Christ, the active principle of the whole church, guides the church not only in and through the hierarchy, that is, from above, but also in and through the believers themselves, in other words, from below. Office and charisma—both are essential to the whole church and both are subject to the guidance of Christ, the Lord. Both are ecclesial. It is clear to us that the church is a sign set up

[5] 'Evangelie en Kerk', *Tijdschrift voor Geestelijk Leven* x (1954), 93–121.

among the people to refer them to Christ's victory not only in the activity of the church's governing, teaching and hierarchical office, but also, and equally essentially, in the christian lives of her believers. It is clear from their faithfulness to the church, their self-sacrificing goodness and love, the humility and the surrender to faith with which they bear the vicissitudes of life, the christian way of life and sense of responsibility of a father and mother, the purity of heart and spirit which is so evident in their appearance, the voluntary virginity of those who dedicate themselves entirely to Christ and the unmarried state of so many christian women who have not chosen this state, but who do not become bitter and are able to make this fate meaningful as a new vocation. All this is a true expression of the reality of the church, the visible presence of grace among us. The various desires for grace, the manifestation of christian *desiderata*, the emergence among the laity of different initiatives aiming at new forms—in these too, the spirit of Christ is guiding and directing the church. Whatever christian artists, writers and thinkers who live from the eucharistic community of grace release in the mind and spirit of christianity is also a genuine expression of the presence of the church, of the visible activity of grace among us, of the sacrament of God's love of men. Indeed, in certain periods of the church's history, what is done by christian writers and thinkers to stimulate the life of the church even exceeds the visible presence of grace given to us by the hierarchical office of the church. These extremely varied and constantly new and surprising activities of the community of faith of the church ought perhaps to be more emphatically stressed in our own times than the other aspect of the visible presence of grace that is expressed in the church's hierarchy. *Ecclesial* life not only means 'practising' one's faith (in the limited sense of coming again and again into living contact with the sacramental acts of the church). No less essentially, it also means the day-to-day visible presence of our faith, our hope and our love—the visible presence of our holiness itself.

The Spirit of Christ blows where it wills, not only in the ranks of the pope and the bishops, but also in the ranks of the priests and the lay believers of the church. The help of the Holy Spirit which Christ promised to his church is not only a help in the exercise of the hierarchical office in the church—it is also a help in the carrying out of the ecclesial life of the whole of the community of faith. This ecclesial life is, of course, always subject to the control of the authority of the church, above which there is no higher court of appeal other than the word of God. But it is an essential part of the hierarchical authority of the church to give the believing members of the church the opportunity to express their true ecclesial life.

Many different tensions can arise because of this twofold aspect of what I have called ecclesial life. I shall not analyse these tensions here, but simply draw attention to the fact that we believe in a particular church, in the church as she is—not in an ideal, abstract church, but in the living church of Christ, the visible presence of grace among us, in which we nonetheless also encounter sin. *This* church is the object of our faith. In the course of the church's history, people have always emerged who have been so scandalised by the weak form in which the church appears in the world that they have become blind to the visible presence of grace which has always remained unimpaired in the church. Again and again these people have fallen into the heresy which regards the church as a purely spiritual community of those who truly live in community of grace with Christ. They have denied the church the form in which she appears on earth. In this way, the church is deprived not only of her weaknesses and sinfulness, but also of the visible presence of grace itself. We ought to be able to raise the level of our faith so that it is strong enough for us to believe in the church as she is. We should, in other words, be able to believe in the church as the visible appearance of the grace of Christ's redemption and at the same time to accept in surrender to faith that the church, in her head and members, is not yet truly church in everything, but is also an expression of human weakness, lack of understanding, routine, impersonal matter-of-factness and, especially in the past—why should we gloss over the historical truth?—a manifestation of desire for worldly power and even of covetousness. Without doubt, the church as church is holy. She is holy in her essence. In this context, John said, though the church is certainly not something suspended in a vacuum, but a historical reality: 'No one born of God commits sin, . . . because he is born of God' (1 Jn 3 : 9) and 'We know that any one born of God does not sin' (1 Jn 5 : 18). Yet the same evangelist, speaking about christians, also said: 'If we say we have no sin, we deceive ourselves' (1 Jn 1 : 8). What, then, does this paradox mean? It means that everything in the church is not yet fully *church*. The church is salvation in its visible form, the sign that is heavily charged with the reality that she signifies. The members of the church are therefore only able to sin insofar as they positively withdraw themselves from the sanctifying influence of the church. A christian is non-ecclesial, he is going contrary to the church to the extent in which he sins—in himself, and therefore in one place in the church, he is making a division between the sign and the reality that the church signifies.

All this implies that the church of Christ has not yet entered her ultimate phase. It does not mean that, at the end of time, the church will cease to exist and will make way for a purely spiritual communion of grace of the saints. On the basis of Christ's incarnation, the visible, bodily presence of grace is not something provisional, but a definitive reality. It is only in heaven that the church, there too as a visible, exterior presence, will have attained her full growth. It is in the manner of glorification that the resurrection of all flesh will perpetuate and make eternal the history of the church on earth, just as the personal holiness, gained in this life, of the saints will be visible in their risen bodies. All that is wretched, weak and scandalising will disappear from the heavenly church, but it is only then that she will fully and for ever show us her holy face in a visible, bodily form.

The fact that the church, as the terrestrial sign of the triumph of Christ's grace here in this world, is still in a state of impotence and self-emptying simply indicates that the church's glory is still veiled or that there is still a wide margin of weaknesses and shortcomings in the church *alongside* her glories. It also points above all to the fact that the power of God also reveals itself in a process of completion *in and through* the church's faulty wretchedness. The church is great and glorious not because of her power and achievements here on earth, but because the redeeming grace of Christ triumphs in her. Justice is done and, what is more, visible justice is done to the power of God despite human weaknesses and indeed precisely *in* these weaknesses. The church is therefore not only the object of our faith, she is also at the same time a *test of our faith*. She may even be an obstacle and a danger to our faith. After all, believing is not a conviction that is compelled by the evidence of the church's glory. We always believe in the midst of darkness and, viewed in this way, the church's weakness is also a happy fault, causing us to boast only of the glory of God's power. Just as Christ was a stumbling-block for the Jews because, in their view, he set himself up against the one God, Yahweh, so too is the church making a wretched pilgrimage in which the strength of Christ's redeeming grace triumphs. It is here that the strength of our faith in the church lies. This also brings us to the second aspect of the church: the church as a motive for our faith.

3. The church as motive for faith

The church is not only the reality in which we believe. She is also a motive which morally and rationally justifies our faith. The First Vatican Council preferred to emphasise this theme: 'The church is the sign set up among the people, inviting all those who do not yet believe'.[6] It is possible for man to experience from and in the church, that is, not only the hierarchical church, but in a certain sense especially in the manifestations among the charismatic of the ordinary people of God, that God is really among christians (see 1 Cor 14:25). Let us now consider this more closely.

Religious faith embraces two aspects of witness, firstly, the

6 Denz. 3013 (1794).

inner invitation to believe brought about by the grace of God which draws men and, secondly, the historicalisation of this grace, the external 'supply'. The second aspect is a historically tangible reality in the midst of our human experiences, a reality which, in its unity with the inner voice of God, is the embodiment, in the particular circumstances of my life, of God's inwardly inviting grace. God has made his quiet inner call to personal community with himself external. In this connection, we at once think—and it is natural and right that we should do so—of the history of Israel's salvation and of the history of the life of the man Jesus. But, historically speaking, this is already very remote. For people living today, the history of salvation and the church are made concretely present by the christians and the priests whom they meet. Our christian lives must therefore be the specific historical form, the external aspect of God's inner call to grace in the hearts of our fellow-men. Christian life—the fact that we are confronted with saints all around us—is the concrete apologetic argument of our faith. It is by the personal holiness of the christians whom they meet in their lives that people must be made aware of the inner voice of God's grace, in which the sound of the very best of themselves can simultaneously be heard, but is hardly noticed by them. For our fellow-men, then, *encounter with men* becomes concretely the *sacrament of the encounter with God*. Whenever a certain heresy raises its head, not just once in the history of the church, but again and again in a different form, then it is clear that it contains an element of truth. This is the case with the heresy which denies the visible nature of the church because it is scandalised by the lack of holiness of christians. This recurrent heresy draws our attention to the fact that the church is only worthy of belief and only addresses men fully when they are fully aware of holiness embodied in the christians whom they meet. Incarnate christian love, our transference of our love of God to our treatment of our fellow-men as real brothers is for others the great and irresistible motive for adopting the christian faith. It confronts men with the reality of salvation that emerges in the midst of their lives. People then encounter the visible presence of grace on their way through life. They cannot avoid this concrete presence of grace and are obliged to take up a position with regard to it.

But, in that case, it is also necessary for this holiness to be truly visible to our fellow-men. It is here, I feel, that the real difficulty lies in the crisis of the church's apostolate today. So many people have become tired of the church because her outward appearance is so wretched. Augustine complained of this centuries ago: 'Those who were already very close to me in faith', he declared in a sermon, 'have been deterred by the lives of bad and false christians. How many men are there, do you think, my brothers, who would gladly be christians, were they not scandalised by the bad lives of christians themselves?'.[7]

It is certainly significant that the great mass of people in the western world, in which the church has been established for centuries, no longer hear or see the witness of the church. Christianity is simply disregarded by the mass of men. In one way or another, the witness, the striking visible form of Christ's grace, is concealed and kept invisible. We cannot in any sense say that the level of holiness in the church has declined. We can therefore only attribute blame in this situation to one of two facts. Either our encounter with our fellow-men, as the sacrament of our love of God, no longer takes place and we only sanctify each other without any real contact with the world; in other words, christian holiness, though really present, is not sufficiently present among men. Or else, wherever living contact with our fellow-men has really been restored by a new apostolic method, this encounter with other men has not yet become in sufficient measure the manifestation of our inner encounter with God. It has, in other words, only been one or another new form or method of apostolic propaganda and not the sacrament of the love of God.

I believe that both these facts apply to the present situation. If we know that the apostolic power of christianity is con-

<hr>

[7] Augustine, *Enarr. in Psalmos*, Ps 30, Sermo 2, 6 (*PL* 36, 342).

cretely situated in the visible presence of grace, in other words, in our real encounter with men as the manifestation of our encounter with God, we must also know that this is not a question of tactics or of a new apostolic *method*, but of real and unaffected love of our fellow-men. If we, on the other hand, use this structure as a technical method of religious efficiency, we shall debase holiness to the level of a means of propaganda. This will inevitably result in the destruction of genuine holiness and a consequent loss of the apostolic power of the visible presence of grace.

People today are not persuaded to accept higher values by our panegyrics. To put it crudely, they are sick to death of our sermons! They are looking for a power for their lives, a meaning which will give power. They will only be persuaded to accept higher values if these are *made present for them in action*. They must experience from christians that christianity is a power which transforms life. The reproach which the prophet Amos put into the mouth of God is very similar to that which we so often hear today:

> The peace offerings of your fatted beasts I will not look upon. Take away from me the noise of your songs; to the melody of your harps I will not listen. But let justice roll down like waters, and righteousness like an ever-flowing stream [Amos 5:22-4].

Our being and our activity as christians in the world is frequently in such insufficient measure the true visible manifestation of our lives redeemed in Christ. And it is precisely this that is the real presence of the church in the world of the Catholic laity and of all believers. Going to church on Sunday does not set holiness in the middle of the world and until we succeed in doing the latter, we shall continue to obscure the sign which the church must be in the middle of this world.

I for my part am bound to say that the experiment of the worker-priests was typically evangelical, ecclesial in the full sense of the word.[8] And Rome intervened either because of

---

[8] It was typically evangelical at least as a *supplementary* priestly task, because this task is really something that should be carried out by lay

false information or because some or many of these worker-priests had failed to appreciate the deepest meaning of their original apostolate, that of making holiness present in action among people wherever they were to be found and had not continued to translate their intimacy with God into encounters with their fellow-men, but had limited themselves *purely* to encountering and dealing with other men, with all the inevitable consequences of this limitation. However far we may, as believers, go along with our fellow-men who do not believe, so as to share the experiences of human existence in solidarity and together with them, we cannot go along with them as far as the point where the reality of redemption is absent. The presence of a christian in the world, as the great and irresistible motive for adopting the christian faith, is always a presence which comes from redemption, and is thus a presence in and with the living God. It is a redeeming presence.

For this reason, then, we are not able to go along with unbelievers into sinful situations where there is no redemption, like the 'priests of the poor' in Carlo Coccioli's painful novel. What is more, even our inner experience of the wretched situations of lost humanity is different from that of unbelievers. So we must go forward, not with any less pain and tension, but together with God, the joy of our youth. It is in this that the strong appeal and the apostolic power of the visible church is to be found. The miracles which every now and then, and certainly as regular exceptions, occur in the life of the church are the quasi-normal accompanying phenomenon of the presence of saints in the world. They are not in themselves a motive for adopting the faith, but they do point to the visible presence of grace in this world from which the 'miracles' emanate almost as a matter of course like sparks.

If the worker-priests expected salvation from contact with their fellow-men—even though some of them tended to ex-

---

workers and not priests. But the choice made by these priests can be justified as an initiation of lay christians into this task, as the church authorities later admitted.

perience this encounter too little as a sacrament—this was because they were very well aware that christianity possessed the truth, dogma and salvation, but kept them locked in a treasure-chest and had lost the key.

This key is the christian's real encounter with his fellow-men as the expression of his love of God. The christian does not simply throw dogmas to people who are in distress—the commitment of the dogma is the personal commitment of our lives to our fellow-men. Our very lives must be incarnate dogma. Our christian lives are dogma in the form of its carrying out—dogma as a living value which draws men. It is precisely because this visible presence of grace in christians themselves is, at least generally speaking in western christianity, no longer so clearly apparent that western man ignores christianity. If christianity is really to attract the attention of men, there must once again be a collective witness. It is only then that the visible mystery, the church, will once again be central in ordinary day-to-day life and non-christians will no longer be able, and will no longer want to avoid it. So many people today are simply carried along with the current of the world without ever having encountered others in their environment whose lives suddenly made them realise that something more and better can be made of life. Man only discovers his own depths in the eyes of another man—the bad murderer became good when he experienced the deepest possibility of his own heart in the eyes of Christ crucified. For those people who are carried along with the current, we christians must make the church present by the unaffected evidence of our christian attitude to life and thereby arouse in them a longing for salvation, make faith at least possible for them. This is an essential part of the ecclesiality of our being christians. Every person is sensitive to it. When, in a world where it does seem as though people only want to make things difficult for each other, a sudden ray of disinterested and unsparing love breaks through—something from another and higher world becoming visible in the world of men—people are at once disarmed and admit defeat.

This is the essence of the church as the visible presence of grace in this world and of the concrete motive for adopting the christian faith. Our complaint in the twentieth century should not be directed against the 'evil of this world', but against the niggardliness and calculated moderation of the christian witness. And this should, incidentally, be a genuine complaint stemming from the ardour of our christian consciousness, a cry from the heart rather than a sharp reproach or a destructive criticism. If holiness and holy people become invisible, the world becomes shrouded in mist. But, however painful this may be, we should never forget that, despite this lack of the visible presence of grace, grace is still always present in a completely consistent christianity and, as I have already said, is able to fulfil its power even in impotence and misery. The church is also the lowly, humble sacramental sign of the triumphant Christ. This test of faith can direct men's attention to the fact that the church is not the work of men's hands, but God's saving work. It can therefore also be an invitation to enter the church.

It is also possible to add one final consequence to these various considerations. It is precisely because the church is essentially holy, the visible presence of salvation brought in and through Christ, that she has the authority or power to canonise people. Eschatological, triumphant grace is already a reality in the church—this is the 'tangibly holy' element in the midst of our world of experience. In her consciousness of what she *is*, the church is therefore able to recognise holiness in her members and canonise them (K. Rahner). This is the final consequence of God's revelation of himself in and through man.

4. Religion and life in the church

Writers like I. Rosier[9] have sharply posed the problem of 'the practice of religion'. In the usual sense of the word, 'practising' means going regularly to church and regularly receiv-

---

[9] I. Rosier, *Ik zocht Gods afwezigheid*, pt 1, The Hague (1956), pt 2 (1957); see also I. Gadourek, *Cultuuraanvaarding en cultuurontwijking* (Inaugural lecture at Groningen, 16 Dec. 1958), Groningen (1958) and P. Smits, *Op zoek naar nihilisme* (Inaugural lecture at Leiden, 23 Jan. 1959), Assen (1959).

ing the sacraments. Rosier, however, does not equate falling away from the church with dechristianisation. He attributes this falling away mainly, and indeed above all, to the strange form in which the church comes forward to meet us in her liturgy, her sacraments and the whole of her appearance here on earth. He says, then, of the workers who are said to be dechristianised, that they 'really still belong to the church as the community of those redeemed by Christ, but are outside the forms of the church that have developed throughout history'.[10] It is precisely because there is a germ of truth in this view that we should consider it very carefully, so as not to limit the meaning of 'practising christianity' and therefore also of that of life in the church to 'going regularly to mass and confession'.

In connection with what I have just said about the visible presence, in the church, of grace in this world, we should bear in mind that this visible presence is not only found in the sacraments, the ministry of the word and the governing and hierarchical office of the church. It also involves the whole living community of believers in their being and activity in this world. It is a simple fact that the humanity of the people whom he meets makes a far greater appeal to modern man than, for example, the church's liturgical rites (which strike him as rather byzantine) or the byzantine nature of papal and episcopal protocol. This clearly shows that we should, in the modern age particularly, stress the second aspect of church practice, in other words, human solidarity as the extension of the human appearance among us of the redeeming God. This humanity, this divine love of men, must appear visibly in and through christians themselves. As I have already said, this forms just as essential a part of the structure of the church as the sacraments and the liturgy. This visible encounter with God which takes place in encounter with our fellow-men is only given a striking and hierarchical expression, in which God's gift to us is present in a concentrated manner, in the sacraments and in preaching. The reality of the church that

[10] I. Rosier, op. cit., pt 1, p 218.

is present in the lives of christians in the church and in their encounter with other people is, so to speak, present in a highly concentrated form in the sacraments. But the structure is really the same.

There are (seven) great cultic sacraments, but there are many more sacramental expressions in the life of the church. We should not identify the life of the church exclusively with the sacramental or priestly life, as is usually done under the heading of 'Church Life' in certain Catholic newspapers. Under this heading, we are given little bits of news about the pope, bishops and priests celebrating their jubilees and about new churches and chapels, but we never hear a word about the believers themselves! We derive grace not only from the sacraments, but also from being treated as brothers by christians who approach us. These approaches are also 'religious practice' and 'receiving a sacrament' and encounters of this kind can also develop into a true conversion or 'confession'. The cultic sacraments are there precisely so that this more widely spreading church sacramentality is able to become a full reality in daily life. True christian life in this world is, for other people, an 'external supply', and a very striking one, of grace, dogma and preaching. Whenever dechristianised people come into contact with such christians, they really encounter the church as the visible and effective presence of grace in this world. And it is precisely through this encounter that they can be led to the full sacramental practice of christianity, the highest point of concentration of which is the eucharist. In a certain sense, too, this presence of grace in the lives of christians in the midst of people today is a more urgent need than bringing the liturgy nearer to people by giving it a more austere and more modern form. I believe that the modernisation of the liturgy will automatically follow as a direct result of the inner dynamism of the first. Liturgy is not constructed—it is organically the consequence of a new spirit. Once this has taken place, the cultic sacraments will once again begin to make their full and central significance felt among us.

Now that I have deliberately emphasised an element of the life of the church which is not generally stressed, it should not be forgotten too that the sacramental life of christianity, and thus religious practice in the narrower sense of the word, is absolutely central. The sacraments are the essential moments in which everyday christian life is brought into relief, from which the level of christian experience which has already been attained is raised and within which this everyday life must again and again lift itself on to a higher plane if it wishes to avoid becoming a grey and colourless anonymity which will, in the long run, abandon not only the practice of the sacraments, but also christianity itself and, eventually, every form of religion.

There is therefore a deep germ of truth in the rather colourless expression used to describe the christian—'a person who still practises his religion'. The sacrament provides man with the possibility of reaching the highest point in his experience as a christian and in his encounter with God in the form of a priestly encounter with his fellow-man (no one administers a sacrament to himself, but always to someone else, a fellow-man). As such, it is the culminating point of the invitation and conferment of grace by the heavenly Christ who is present in the church. Christian being in the world, encounter with the striking christianity of a fellow-man—in other words, the reality of the church in the broader, but equally essential sense of the word—arouses in people the longing for the fullness of sacramental contact with the church. In other words, the life of lay people and priests, who are also believers in their encounter with their fellow-men, is the door to the hierarchical and liturgical reality of the church's sacramental life.

We have no right, then, to complain about people giving up the liturgical, sacramental practice of their religion if we ourselves are to blame for the absence of the church in their encounter with their fellow-men, so that they do not experience the reality of the church in their everyday lives! This is the consequence of the fact that the church is more than the hierarchy and that christians themselves must make the church present in their being and their activity, and thus also form part of the 'sign set up among the people'.

Viewed in this light, then, it is true that baptised people who have become dechristianised, but who have taken genuine charity and a certain religious sense with them from the church are, in this sense, not only religious and not only christian, but also still sharing in the life of the church. This also applies equally to those who have never been baptised and who have been outside the church from the very beginning. They are never completely outside the influence of the 'church' as a world-wide reality. According to the extent to which they possess a religious sense, they too are, to that extent, practising the life of the church, although they are excluded from (or exclude themselves from) the full, giving self-revelation of the church. This measure of religious practice is, of course, always threatened with extinction in their lives because of the absence of this full contact with the church. But the element of church that is present in their lives can at the same time act as an impetus for them, especially if they are in contact with people who are living authentically christian lives, to come to the church in her true and full form.

Conclusion

It will be clear from the foregoing that the sacramental liturgy of the church is certainly a culminating point in the life of the church, but that we should not identify the life of the church with the liturgical mystery of worship or with the activity of the hierarchical church. The sacraments are only elements in christian life which has far wider dimensions. A flight into liturgy is a failure to appreciate the full ecclesial reality of the church and flight from liturgy is at the same time a failure to recognise the eschatological character of the church and a certain duty to participate with the purely profane world. Christian life is, so to speak, a pendulum movement between these two elements of the reality of the church —between the point where the church shows her hierarchical face (in the sacraments, in preaching, in pastoral activity and so on) and the point where she gives another manifestation of her holiness in her members' task in the world, in their work, their family lives and their encounters with their fellow-men. Precisely because she is only an eschatologically orientated sign of grace, a call to come home, the church points beyond the world to what has 'still to come'. But this at the same time reminds us that we are now in this world and have therefore to live as christians in this world. Her reference to what is still to come is at the same time an admonition that what is still to come is not yet here and that we should not, like the apostles, remain gazing at the cloud into which Christ disappeared and from which he will come again. We must turn towards the world and bear visible witness to holiness there. The fact that we are redeemed must emerge from our encounter with our fellow-men, at whatever level this contact may take place. Is this not the great sign that the church is in this world? She is the visible invitation to love. Thus brotherly love becomes the sacrament of the encounter with God.

8

SUPRANATURALISM, UNCHRISTIAN AND CHRISTIAN EXPECTATIONS OF THE FUTURE

I have quite often been amazed to hear in sermons, or read on the back of holy pictures illustrating an appearance of the Virgin Mary, about the approaching end of the world, or to be informed in pamphlets that the iron curtain would disappear in 1960. I remember being told by a young couple that they were going to postpone their wedding until after 1960 because they both thought that they would not be justified in marrying now, before the great scourge took place! Some time ago, we were overwhelmed with pamphlets, published under the auspices of priests, which proclaimed the day and the hour of the end of the world. On that day, a normal eclipse of the sun took place. Quite often, an appeal is made in these prophecies of the future to authentic or inauthentic appearances of the Virgin Mary. Even when these appearances are genuine, there is a complete lack of critical analysis of the heavenly message and the content of the private revelation is simply identified with the unconscious identifications of the privileged visionary. Quite often too, all this is abused merely to exploit human panic in an unchristian way in order to raise money.

Such practices are unworthy of a christian. That is why I can only be glad that ecclesiastical authority, although always accepting the possibility of attention from above, is becoming stricter in granting an imprimatur to literature of this kind. In times of distress and oppression, the same pattern always repeats itself. The rumour goes round that those who are regarded as oppressors will be converted and that peace will be restored. This happened when the Turks were threatening the christian west—popular preachers foretold the imminent conversion of the Scimitar and a consequent period of peace and reflection. Sometimes, however, this theme of human imaginative projection has been used by the God of revelation to make his saving intention known to his people. The Old Testament contains many examples of this. We too must always remain open and receptive to God, who is so transcendent that he really can enter into the everyday details of our human life. But very often it is man himself who makes his God speak, while God himself remains silent and only points out to us the great Sign of his dialogue, the Word made flesh, in which he has expressed himself 'once for all'. If we examine the current religious sensitivity of believers insofar as they are concerned with the saving character of history and thus with its fulfilment, we can discover three tendencies.

In the first place, there is the nineteenth-century type of piety which is still very much among us, a piety which flees from the world and history and which regards the world not as the true creation of God, but rather as a neutral 'nature', the almost accidental and in any case indifferent framework of the religious life, only meaningful to the 'profane' sciences. Human civilisation is also seen in the same light. In one way or another, and perhaps in a veiled manner, all technical progress is regarded as an impious usurpation of power on the part of unbelieving mankind. This tendency may therefore be characterised as follows: on the one hand, the world is not experienced as God's creation, but as nature, and, on the other hand, piety is experienced as a result of this as a flight from the world, in other words, as a private, bourgeois piety.

The contemporary experience of faith in connection with history also takes a second form, in which time is experienced supranaturally. There is no indifference towards the world, as in the first tendency, but the world is interpreted in a directly religious sense, in the manner of a Nostradamus. These 'supranaturalists' are extremely interested in world history, but not in terms of its inner secular structures. History is directly seen as a sign of supernatural realities and usually in the light of all kinds of private revelations which may be authentic or purely supposed. All attempts made by experts in the fields of sociology, economics or politics to solve human problems of history and all conferences and summit conferences held with the aim of trying to find a solution to international tensions are rejected and condemned by those who maintain this religious attitude to life. All salvation is expected exclusively from prayer.

The expressions of this type of piety are only extreme cases of a radical supranaturalism which neglects the inner structure of the world and of world history. According to this view of the world, history as such is not a part of a fully integrated religious attitude to life. It is, on the contrary, deprived of its historical value and is given a purely religious significance. As in the case of the first type of religious experience, the practical consequence at least of this attitude is that the structures of human life on earth, which are concerned, for example, with attempts to plan and regulate the social, economic and political framework of life, are regarded as atheistic and left to those who do not believe. For all their piety, such believers in fact practise atheism with regard to the world of creation, an atheism that is all the more dangerous because it gives the appearance of piety and an all-embracing religious awareness.

Finally, there is a third type of contemporary religious attitude to the world and its history. This is most characteristically expressed in attempts at a new spirituality such as are found in the works of Leppich and Quoist. In other words, the world and world history are really experienced as God's creation and, what is more, as the creation of the God of salvation and, although the phrase, 'the world of creation', may, for reasons of existentialist sensitivity, be avoided in this context, the world is not experienced as neutral nature or autonomous civilisation, but is included, in accordance with its inner structure, in a living dialogue with the God who addresses man and who is addressed by him. But, despite this positive aspect, this third form of contemporary piety is nonetheless one-sided. It is far too restricted to the individual level of experience. Great scope is given to human history in man's personal community of grace with the living God, but this history is not seen as the *collective* history of salvation of humanity that has been called to be the people of God. It is not seen as a history in which the God of salvation really weaves a meaningful thread in a dialectical relationship with man (in a covenant situation, to use the biblical term), in and through the secular structures of legitimate social, economic, political and scientific forms in the world on the one hand and the absolute principle of human freedom on the other, thus leading history towards its ultimate fulfilment. Certainly, theologians are investigating the basic historical lines of the Old Testament and their work is gradually making it possible for us to follow God's line in the history of the Old Testament, but it gives the impression that this line came to a dead end with Christ's resurrection. Apart from a number of examples of apocalyptic charlatanism, where are we to find any theology of God's plan in the history of the church and the world since the resurrection of Christ? Just as there was a divine aspect present in the history of the Old Testament, so too has this aspect always been present in the history of the church—in this sense, there is no difference between the Old and the New Testaments, as though the history of salvation ceased with the death of Christ!

It is clear, then, that we already possess the first basic lines of a biblical theology, but, so far at least, there is still no sign of any *theology* of the history of the church. This is not meant as a criticism of theology, which can only gradually become fully conscious of all its tasks in its reverent and groping advance into the mystery of the reality of salvation. What is more, any theology of history since Christ's death and resurrection will inevitably be precarious and essentially incomplete. A theology of the history of the world and the church will only be possible when we are able to look back from the *parousia* at all that has happened throughout time, just as a theology of the history of the Old Testament and of the prechristian period was only possible when men were able to view it from the standpoint of the incarnation of the Son. This does not mean that the history of Israel ought to be regarded only as 'our custodian until Christ came' (Gal 3 : 24), as an extrinsic addition, viewed in the light of the fact of Christ who was still to come. On the contrary, the history of Israel was an intrinsic preparation, even though the real depth of the christological aspect of Old Testament history only became clearly visible, or at least explicit, in the light of the historical fact of Christ. Although it was not explicit for the Jews of Old Testament times, this history was nonetheless *inwardly* christological. It was indeed the growth of the mystery of Christ. It was this mystery in a process of becoming, with the result that it already bestowed grace, even though this was not complete grace—this full grace had still not come into being and only commenced to exist in the historical appearance of the God-man himself. Old Testament history, then, was inwardly the grace of the 'God who was to come'. Protology and eschatology imply each other. The beginning of creation and the end of time include each other and the biblical view of the eschatological kingdom is therefore able to express both with the same images of cosmic peace experienced while walking with God in the garden. They imply each other, not only in the living idea of God's providence that transcends history, but also in the very historical fact of the mystery of Christer and, as a consequence and in the light of this, both in the history of the Old Testament and in the contemporary fact of our created, human existence as men who make history and who are subject to God's call to salvation.

It is precisely because of this mutual implication of the beginning of creation and the end of time (Genesis and Revelation) that even history since the death and resurrection of Christ is 'our custodian until Christ comes', a movement towards the *parousia*, inwardly and not simply as an extrinsic later addition. It is precisely because of this that the eschatological significance of the history of the church can and must be to a certain extent—certainly not fully, but in meaningful fragmentation—already clear in this world to those who, confronted with history, listen to God's word, think about what they have heard and consider it in holy reflection. We should, after all, not forget that the analogy between the history of the world's salvation since Christ's resurrection and the history of the Old Testament does not hold good in every instance. Every history is certainly *open* to human possibilities, because it is the work of human freedom. The life-project of man and humanity will never be closed and man will never be finished with himself and with the history of mankind until his last word has been definitively spoken—at death in the case of the individual person and at the end of time for humanity as a whole. But here we should bear in mind that this total openness of the whole of human history has, in a very central aspect, been 'established' by the death and resurrection of Jesus Christ. God has spoken his last, definitive word about humanity in the man Jesus, whose resurrection, ascension and sitting at the right hand of the Father is the culmination of his becoming man. This is the fundamental meaning of the christian assertion that revelation is closed. The saving significance of the history of the church is therefore, in a certain respect, really different from that of Old Testament and pre-christian history, which was not simply an open history of the kind that all human freedom, even post-christian freedom which is making history, sees before it. It was also open precisely as a history of salvation and a history opposed to salvation. God's ultimate intention for humanity had at that time still not been made public. History was still faced with the possibility of a totally new historical event which could radically change its whole meaning, an event, in other words, which God himself was to bring about in Jesus, the man who lived among us. In this sense, then, the ultimate meaning of human life was still completely open. It was only in Christ that God fully expressed the meaning of human life and history, and this statement remains among us as an indestructible fact that can no longer be changed. 'I have overcome the world' (Jn 16: 33)—*nenikēka*—and this conquest is an accomplished fact which cannot be repeated, changed or reversed.

This basic pattern of the meaning of human history has been fully portrayed in Christ. No new constitutive facts of salvation can occur in our history as they could in pre-christian history. Although our history, as a revelation of human freedom, remains open and therefore continues to be directed towards a future that is unknown to us, the pattern of this history and of all future history has been established in the living form of him who called himself the Son of man. In this sense, our history (which really continues to be history) is already at an end in Christ, the prototype of mankind. The *kenōsis* and the *hypsōsis*, the humiliation and the exaltation, the power which comes into force in weakness, will continue to show, in constantly varying forms, the same face that resembles Christ. But human freedom, which is always making history, will at the same time continue, under God's guidance, to give this face a secular stamp of its own, about which the last human word has still not been spoken and cannot be spoken until all time and growth has ceased at the *parousia*, the general resurrection of the dead and the last judgement on all living beings by the God-man.

It will therefore be clear from what I have said that the end of time is, on the one hand, an accomplished fact and that, on the other hand, it still has a history. There are phases in the 'last things'—the phase of the history of the church, the post-terrestrial phase from the death of every individual to the general resurrection and finally the completed *eschata* in the eschatological kingdom of the Father at the *parousia* of Christ. Christ's resurrection from the dead is at the very centre of these last things—he is the *eschaton*, the fulfilment of time. God, of course, and God alone, is the *prōton* and the *eschaton*, the first and the last, the *alpha* and the *ōmega*. He is this in himself, but we call him this with regard to man, insofar as he is God for us, a God who turns his face towards us. This face which God turns towards us is, concretely, the man Jesus. The man Jesus is therefore the First and the Last. By his Spirit, the Father creates a new heavenly humanity in Jesus' resurrection, a humanity of the Son made flesh. In this way, the Lord of the 'new creation' and the *eschaton* is already an accomplished reality in his humanity.

This also defines the method of eschatological theology. The theological treatise on the last things has to be written in the light of the present situation of the history of the world and the church, that is, not from the vantage-point of the last things and looking back at ourselves, but from our own situation and looking forwards to the last things. What is more, it is only in this way that eschatology can be 'demythologised' in the genuinely Catholic sense of the word. From the vantage-point of our own religious situation, which derives its meaning from the eschatological event accomplished in Christ, we arrive at a 'protology', a theology of the beginning, and an eschatology, a theology of the end of time. God's utterance is not like a purely human utterance, an utterance about something—it is an utterance that somehow brings about what it utters. In our believing existence in grace in this world, we already carry the germ of the *eschata* in ourselves. The source of eschatology is God's utterance insofar as this has achieved anything in us, namely human redemption, in other words, the redemption of that spiritual reality which lives in a world of men and things by reason of its own corporeality. This reality was touched by God's act of redemption and so carries the *eschata* in itself and these last things are only the implication of man's real community of grace with the living God or of his refusal of grace.

What has revelation to tell us about the end of the world? The Old Testament expression, 'the last days', or, more correctly, 'the last of the days' means the future and it is from the context in which this expression appears that we must decide whether or not it refers to the eschatological future. In the New Testament, however, the *eschaton* or 'the last of the days' means the eschatological time that commenced with Christ's appearance on earth and above all with his death and resurrection. These 'last days' are different from the 'last day', which coincides with the 'day of the Lord' or the *parousia*. The eschatological time therefore has a twofold meaning—the whole period on earth of the history of the church in this world is known in the New Testament as 'the last days', but the end of this period culminates in the concluding events of world history at the end of time, which will be followed by the day of the Lord and the general judgement of all mankind. Present history is therefore at the same time a prophecy in action of what the 'eschatologically historical' time, which will close the history of the world, will be. God's revelation never takes place in a vacuum—it always has a social context, so that it is necessary for the biblical theologian to look for the historical circumstances which gave rise to this revelation and partly determined its explicit form, its expression and its formulation.

What is very striking in this connection is that everything that the apostolic church has to tell us in scripture about the concluding events at the end of the history of the world was seen in the light of the church's experience at that time of incipient falling away from faith, of heresies and of the oppression of the first generation of christians. These two perspectives seem to merge into one another and overlap. Although I cannot go into this in detail here, it is clear that the great eschatological 'signs of the times' which are to announce the approach of Christ's *parousia*—a massive falling away from faith, the presence of the Antichrist and the violent oppression of believers because of God's kingdom—form the pattern of the whole history of the church. In other words, what will take place at the end of the history of the world is no different from what the first christians experienced and no different from what we are experiencing now in the twentieth century and will be no different from what has been experienced throughout past history and will be experienced in the future. In the concluding phase of the history of the world, however, these experiences will be more strongly accentuated and assume greater proportions.

A great ultimate and eschatological phase of world history still lies ahead of us in expectation, but this phase will be a continuation of what constitutes the basic pattern of the whole history of the church as a movement towards the *parousia* of Christ. The Book of Revelation especially enables us to some extent to share in and experience what will happen in that time. It is, however, an event with which we are already familiar. The Book of Revelation depicts a situation which has always been the constantly recurring fate of the church militant on earth, although it takes new forms and changes with the varying circumstances of history, civilisation and government. The eschatological time is seen from the point of view of our own time, because our own time is already an eschatological time—we too are living in the time of eschatological pains. Wherever Christ approaches us, Satan is also at hand and makes himself felt in the oppression of believers. The most important thing for christians, however, is that, wherever distress is greatest, Christ is also near. At all times, believers are aware of the nearness of Christ in their suffering for the sake of the kingdom of God. But this nearness is still not the great *parousia* of the Lord.

Thus we see that there is a double thread running through history which is leading the world on towards the end of time—the thread of good and the thread of evil. The approaching kingdom of God is revealed in the first and the second is the thread of Satan, who, as Christ said in his eschatological discourse, scents carrion like a vulture— wherever the kingdom of God is approaching, Satan appears to combat it. World history grows slowly from within towards the end of time and thus becomes ripe for the Antichrist, just as it at the same time becomes ripe for the *parousia* of the Lord, but no one—neither angel nor man nor even the Son of man on earth—can tell us *when* this will take place. This is God's secret. It is a truth which has not been revealed be- cause it has no saving value for us and because it is not yet a reality which intimately concerns us. It is also a secret for the devil who consequently lies in wait for every sign of holiness in the world and is at work wherever christians confess the Lord.

Scripture predicts all this, not in order to make us pessi- mistic and gloomy, not so that we shall make excuses for our- selves because of oppressions that afflict us, not for the sake of the kingdom of God, but on account of our own unchristian behaviour, and certainly not in order to proclaim apocalypti- cally and ridiculously the ripeness of our own time for the *parousia*. Scripture tells us this to give us consolation, a con- solation which is applicable not only to christians of the

eschatological time at the end of history, but also to christians
living in all periods of history, because, since Christ's ascension, time itself belongs to 'the last days', even though these
days may, if they are measured according to time, have lasted
for a long time already and may even last for a long time yet
and even though the first christians expected that these days
would not be long delayed and we tend to think that it will
probably be a long time before they come. This additional
appreciation is of no importance, not even in scripture—it
does not in any way affect the heart of the matter. All that
scripture says is 'he who endures (in affliction) to the end will
be saved' (Mt 24:13). That is all. Again and again throughout
history, after a first crisis in connection with this during the
earliest christian period, the church has continued to warn us
against all prophecy concerning the approaching end of the
world or Christ's *parousia*.

And yet, at every period of history, people go beyond this
scriptural admonition and, especially in times of oppression
and alarm, these charlatans are able, in the light of their own
so-called private revelations and of their own quite unbiblical
attitude, to prophesy the day and the hour of the *parousia*.
And pious people always fall for it! It seems to form part of
the psychology of people in distress. There is an enormous
documentation, including such 'data' as mixed swimming
pools and wars in which 'women wear trousers like men',
which are claimed to be proclamations of the end of the world
and 'one of the most unmistakable signs of the end of time is
the emergence of the new state of Israel'. Why do books of
this kind receive an imprimatur? They undermine faith and,
even if they are accompanied by an orthodox faith, they still
make men behave without their normal moral sense of
responsibility, cause them to panic and above all violate the
moral gift of freedom.

Even when these books make use of genuine private revelations, they tear what is revealed from its context and approach
the revelations with a less critical attitude than that with
which exegetes approach the sacred text of holy scripture.
If I may be forgiven for saying so, this can only be called

ridiculous charlatanism and, as such, an immediate danger to the soundness of the christian faith. What is more, these charlatans also discredit the deep meaning of the charisma of private revelations by displaying this charisma in a shop-window full of fetishes, idols and little fancies of the Nostra-damus kind. It is not those theologians who may perhaps make mistakes or are ahead of others in their studies who are the real freebooters on whom a careful watch should be kept— it is these hawkers of suspect religious goods who speculate (in good faith, I believe) on people in distress against whom we should be on our guard. They abuse God and distort the true religious meaning of profane history insofar as this is borne up and guided by God, not only as the creator of the world, but also as the creator who is also our redeemer, the God of salvation. The messages of Fatima have, for example, been put to a great deal of wrong use—quite apart from the fact that these have first to be sifted critically from the latent identifications which Lucia herself gave to them years later. These all too zealous attempts are a travesty of the true event of Fatima, the ultimate significance of which is only that Christ is the Lord of history, including contemporary history, and that we must have confidence in this, however badly things turn out in this world. No private revelation can re-lieve us of the duty to assume full responsibility in the history of this world in a christian spirit and at the same time in accordance with the legitimate structures of earthly activity. Surely it is quite mad that some of the so-called appearances of the Virgin Mary, the authenticity of which has not even been confirmed by the church, should be put forward as among the greatest events that have taken place for twenty centuries.

Much more could be said about this subject, but I will conclude with a warning given by Rome to Catholic adventists of this kind:

Like all mothers, the church has the heaviest and most difficult of tasks and, like all mothers, she has sometimes to act and sometimes to be silent and to wait patiently. Who would have imagined fifty years ago that the church would today have to warn her children and even some of her priests against appearances which are reputed to have occurred and against so-called miracles, in a word, that she would now have to warn against all those facts which are regarded as supernatural, the fame of which has spread from one continent to the other and from one country to the other and which almost everywhere attract the attention of men and excite them? ... Now the church must warn her children by the voice of her bishops and by repeating the words of her divine Master (see Mt 24:24) so that they should not be easily led astray by such occurrences and so that they should come to believe in them only after mature reflection and after the results of the most authoritative investigation. In recent years, we have witnessed a great increase in people's passion for miracles, even in the religious sphere. Great crowds flock to places where so-called appearances and miracles have taken place, while, on the other hand, staying away from church and neglecting the sacraments and sermons. People who do not even know the first words of the Apostles' Creed behave with ardent religiosity as self-appointed apostles. Some of them do not hesitate to speak about the pope, the bishops and the church's priests in very disapproving terms and even express great indignation that these do not go along with the people and join in the excited enthusiasm and the exaggerations of certain popular movements. However regrettable it may be, it should not cause us any surprise ... We should not believe that one can be religious just as one would like to be— one must be truly religious. Just as deviations may and in fact do occur in the case of other feelings, so too are there deviations in religious feeling. Religious feeling must be guided by reason, nourished by grace and directed by the Church, like the whole of our life, but even more strictly. There is religious instruction and religious training. Those who have so frivolously disputed the Church's authority and religious feeling are now faced with impressive explosions of instinctive religious feeling without any rational clarity, without any awareness of grace and without any restraint or sense of direction. As a consequence, they resort, in the most lamentable way, to disobeying the authority of the church, which is forced to intervene in order to check this movement.... The period through which we are now passing lies between the two extremes of overt and irreconcilable irreligiosity and of unlimited and blind religiosity. Persecuted by the one and compromised by the other,

the church can only repeat her maternal warning, but her voice
is not heard in the environment of denial of the one extreme
and in the environment of exaggeration of the other ... We
have holy scripture, tradition, the supreme shepherd and a
hundred pastors all around us. Why, then, should we show
those who attack and despise us that we hand ourselves over to
imagination and senseless exaggeration? 'Christians, behave
more seriously', Dante wrote long ago, and gave believers the
same advice that we give them now: 'You have the Old and the
New Testaments and the Shepherd of the Church who guides
you' and he concluded, as we now conclude: 'May this be
sufficient for your salvation.'[1]

[1] Mgr A. Ottaviani, *Osservatore Romano*, 4 Feb. 1951.

9
CHRISTIANS AND NON-CHRISTIANS:
1. THE THEORY OF TOLERATION

1. The dialogue

It was the French phenomenologist, G. Gusdorf, who made the striking statement, 'To come into the world is to begin to speak'.[1] Speaking—dialogue—is essential to a person's incarnation in this world. Later on in his book Gusdorf says, 'In speaking man must express the best of his being'.[2] Our deepest conviction must be offered in dialogue. It will therefore be obvious that I, reflecting about the significance of the dialogue between various ideologies, will do this from my own Catholic manner of believing, remembering also that this faith is a gift to man, that is, to this particular, personal, historical man, living in community with others and constantly confronted, by his existential experience, with new problems. Faith presupposes being man. This consequently means that this being man is the communal basis for every dialogue. I will now try, systematically, to reveal the fundamental implications of this previously given fact.

1. Every man is concerned with the fact that he must give a meaning in this world to his human existence and that he must do this within the sphere of his encounter with his fellow-men. This being man, this co-existence with our fellow-men, implies that our fellow-man is a condition of existence for us, just as we are a condition of existence for him. In planning a personal way of life or a definite course in life, we are, while preserving our own personality and ensuring its growth, dependent on each other in mutual communication. The relationship of dialogue, in all its forms, is one of the

[1] *La parole*, Paris (1952 and 1956), 8.
[2] ibid, p 83.

most characteristic and striking aspects of this co-existence. We speak with each other about the meaning of human life.

What is presupposed in this situation of dialogue? First and foremost, our acceptance of the existence of a universally valid truth which is recognised by everyone. In a situation of complete relativism, there can be no meaningful speaking. But, although the truth itself is universally valid and absolute, man's view of the truth, or his possession of it, participates in everything that is human—in man's imperfection, his relativity and his historicity.[3] Thus, although every affirmation of the truth is, on the one hand, inviolable in its absolute character, it is, on the other hand, also open to growth and amplification, precisely because a human insight never exhausts the truth and always leaves a remnant of strangeness and obscurity. What is more, man's insight into truth is always both historically and personally situated. This does not in any way lead to a complete relativism, but it does mean that differing, mutually complementary and correct insights into the reality in which we live are possible, quite apart from the insights which are false because of human fallibility.

It is clear from this human structure of the witness we bear to truth that, although the truth is absolutely valid, man's insight into it and his communication of it can never lead to absolute unanimity, even though a difference of opinion will only be possible within the sphere of mutual understanding. The condition which will enable us to reach the greatest possible unanimity of which man is capable is therefore an attitude, in the presence of every affirmation and evidence of truth, of openness and receptivity to the views of others. It is only in an atmosphere of courageous defence of our own witness to the truth and of sincere openness and readiness towards the possibility of its amplification by other insights that a genuinely human dialogue is possible. Moreover, since man is a being whose humanity is guaranteed only when he

[3] P. Guillaume provides typical examples of the psychological implications of the 'perspectivism' of man's consciousness of truth in his *Introduction à la psychologie*, Paris 1946.

bases his life on an inner conviction about what is good and true, the situation of dialogue implies that each partner must have reverence for the inviolable dignity of the human person, including his view of life, which may, according to our own conviction (which claims to be absolute), be wrong.[4] For us, reality as truth is only a value as we discover it more and more as truth. No man may give his assent to something and let his life be guided by it if it is contradicted by his own personal and sincere sense of truth, for the simple reason that no truth exists in concrete which has value for me if the spirit does not recognise this as such. It is only within mutual personal love in reciprocal and positive tolerance that the defence and the propagation of one's own conviction, which one regards as of value for all men, are justified. It is only then, too, that a genuinely human dialogue is possible—a dialogue that does not lapse into pure relativism on the one hand or dishonest 'irenism' on the other, an irenism which, for the sake of peace, levels out all differences of opinion and blurs all distinctions and only stresses the points of agreement, which are in any case frequently only verbal. Dialogue of this kind is no more than a flirtation, not a serious undertaking.

The fundamental theme of every dialogue is this—we all participate in the basic fact that we *are there*, although we did not previously will or choose our existence. Without being asked, we are in a world that we similarly did not ask for. We are personally looking, in community and above all in dialogue in all its forms, for the meaning of this human existence. If this human existential experience is accepted by all partners in the dialogue as a communal basis, its further content is not equally accepted by all the partners, with the result that a fruitful dialogue may come about on this basis— at least to a certain point. We should, after all, not try to conceal from ourselves the fact that the limitation and the impotence of human dialogue is also a reality. Not everything

[4] A great deal has been written recently about tolerance. Here, I will mention only two of the best studies: Karl Rahner, 'The Dignity and Freedom of Man', *Theological Investigations* 2, London 1963, 235–63; Humanus, 'Persoonlijke en burgerlijke verdraagzaamheid', *Kultuurleven* 25 (1958), 245–57.

is solved simply and solely by talking about it. The partners in dialogue meet, after all, in order to defend their own convictions—each is determined not to let anything of his conviction be violated, because he sincerely believes that his own view of life presents itself with indisputable evidence and a firm guarantee. This clearly shows that man's view of life is not a purely intellectual matter, but a problem which directly affects the whole of human existence.

To summarise, then, it is possible to say that man's common search for the value and meaning of human life, and, in this sense, for true humanism, forms the basis of every dialogue. But in this context, two directions are immediately apparent.

We can either call the reality in which we live a *mystery* which we go forward to meet, not with an absolute will to power, but in humble and open love, which may or may not be based on a consciously religious attitude. Or we may regard this reality as a purely secular matter, in which the mystery has no place. In the first case, we do not hold this reality in our grasp—it embraces us. From the very moment that we encounter the reality precisely as a mystery which claims our surrender—from the moment, then, that we go forward to meet the reality in love and openness towards the mystery— we are already implicitly on theistic ground. Even before there is any explicitly religious attitude, when faith, hope and love exist with regard to reality, this attitude can only be consistently explained by an implicit relationship with a person who addresses us through this reality. According to the Catholic faith, this honest and sincere going forward to meet the reality in a provisional and veiled manner is a confrontation with God, whose mystery flows out into the terrestrial reality, so that acceptance of this reality as mystery is synonymous with acceptance of its creatural character—in its source, this reality is spiritual, an expression of a personal love. And it is only on this basis that our surrender becomes possible and meaningful. I therefore believe that anyone who gives his life a consistent direction in all sincerity and openness to the mystery of reality and in accordance with the unveiling of meaning which he gave in conscience to this mystery will implicitly—thanks to his impartial love—reach God, who addresses him in and through this reality. God is already with us at the pre-reflective level of our being in this world in the sphere of human encounter. According to our Catholic faith, then, God himself is the one who is communally present in every dialogue, including dialogue between theist and atheist. God himself is the ever-present but unseen partner in all dialogue.

This, however, is denied by secular humanism and this brings us to the second direction. It is pointless, in discussion with an atheist, to inform him reassuringly and understandingly that he is in fact an implicit theist. This kind of attitude ultimately implies that we are not taking him seriously. If he says that he is not an implicit theist, then we are bound not only to accept his testimony as such, but also all the consequences of this, namely that it is impossible to regard the worldly reality as a mystery to which one can give oneself in faith. From the very moment that the reality is regarded as purely secular there is no more place for the mystery that calls for our surrender. On the contrary, from the purely secular point of view, man is lord of the world. In itself, nature is meaningless and alien to man, something that offends him because of its lack of declared meaning. Nature is the reality which does not care about man. It is a reality which has no meaning without man, who humanises, spiritualises and makes this world meaningful and no longer uncanny, but familiar to man by his seeing, hearing and feeling, his civilisation and technology. The only mystery that is to be found in nature outside a theistic perspective is that which in this nature still escapes man's grasp—its non-humanity. It is a temporary mystery of sub-humanity which needs to be given meaning by man. It is secular man's task to humanise, spiritualise and give meaning to this dull nature without problems.[5] In this perspective, belief is pointless. No one can give himself in faith to something which has no

---

[5] The philosophical backgrounds to this view have been analysed in a masterly fashion by D. de Petter in 'De oorsprong van de zijnskennis volgens de H. Thomas van Aquino', *Tijdschrift voor Philosophie* 17 (1955), 199–254.

declared meaning in itself, but which has to be given a meaning by him.

But this situation within the world is also accepted by christians, so that it too forms a communal basis for dialogue. The entire question is, after all, whether or not everything has been said about man in this exclusively secular view of life. Does it or does it not provide an answer to the problem of man as a *totality*? Or is not man thereby renouncing himself and his own humanity or state of being a person in favour of a merging into nature and history? We are therefore faced with the question as to whether true humanism is not violated if we do not look for the meaning of human existence in the direction of self-transcendence, by which man is raised in his humanity to the superhuman level—to the life of an infinite person, God. The fact that this is so according to our Catholic faith means that our dialogue with atheism contains an element of hope—we know that there is an absolute person, God, who is personally interested in our human problem and in our ideological dialogue, someone who unveils the very meaning of life for us in his grace in such a way that we, either accepting or rejecting, are bound to take up a position with regard to this. This reality, moreover, brings us to a new implication.

2. Our explicit acceptance of the mystery of reality and therefore of its theistic background opens the way to our acceptance of God's *personal* dialogue with us in the revelation of Christ Jesus. We are thus convinced that the medium in which every dialogue in fact takes place is the Lord, Christ himself, and can say, together with our Protestant brother in faith, Professor R. Mehl of Strasbourg, that Christ is the one who is 'communally present' in every dialogue.[6] Of course, the non-christian does not know this, nor does he accept it, but we, in faith, are sure of it. It makes our dialogue especially hopeful and indeed redeeming. The human existence of our partner in dialogue has already been touched by Christ even before he

---

[6] *La rencontre d'autrui* (Cahiers théologiques 36), Neuchâtel and Paris 1955, 57.

is addressed by his fellow-man. If what Gusdorf says—'every word, spoken or heard, provides the opportunity for an awakening, the discovery perhaps of a value of which I had not yet been aware'[7]—is true from the phenomenological point of view, then christians are *a fortiori* convinced that every word and everything that the believing christian says in dialogue expresses a truth which is also, in one way or another, unconsciously and anonymously, actively present in the life of his partner in dialogue, even though it may be in the manner of total or partial refusal. Our dialogue is never a first break-through in the person of the other—it only has the function of making explicit and conscious the great conversation that takes place personally in Christ between the living God and every man. It is therefore possible to add to the foregoing that Christ himself is the one who is 'communally present' in a very special way above all in ecumenical dialogue between christians and that he is striving personally to lead our conversation towards the full truth that he is himself.

Dialogue 'in Christ' moreover stands the best chance because Christ has made human co-existence into a bond of love. This love allows the other, in serving freedom, to speak. In this way, the dialogue becomes a real encounter.

3. Finally, I should like to discuss the last basis of every dialogue between men, a basis which I propose to call by the possibly risky phrase, our communal unbelief. Let me explain what I mean by this. At first sight, dialogue between non-Catholics and a Catholic believer gives rise to a difficult problem. Listening to the other is an inward aspect of every sincere dialogue. This sincere listening and readiness to allow one's own view to be possibly corrected by that of another would seem to be impossible, especially for a Catholic, for whom the word of God, heard in scripture and in the scripture-permeated tradition of the church, has already determined the meaning of human life and established it dogmatically. We Catholics give ourselves unconditionally in faith to this reality of salvation. But does this unconditional

[7] *La parole*, 62.

surrender to the authoritative word of God not make dialogue
with a Catholic inauthentic, unless the Catholic simply plays
the part of the teacher and his partner in the dialogue settles
down at his feet like an ignorant pupil in an attitude of
humble listening? I am not referring here to speaking which
bears witness, the 'ministry of the word' (Acts 6:2-4), in
which the minister of the word in faith really appears in the
name of God, but to dialogue between those holding different
views of life. Is dialogue of this kind with a Catholic not impossible? Or should the Catholic try to set aside his faith, as
a personal conviction, for the time being during the dialogue?
This would, however, be completely inauthentic.

In the first place, I freely admit, as a believer, that a
dialogue between a Catholic and a non-Catholic does sometimes, often or very frequently—I leave it to everyone to
decide from his own experience of such dialogues—take on
this kind of appearance. But, leaving caricature aside, the
question really is—is the impossibility of dialogue with a
Catholic attributable to the very nature of the Catholic faith
or not? I cannot here discuss in detail all the aspects of this
problem and will therefore confine myself to one aspect only.

What has already been said about the imperfection of man's
possession of truth also applies to faith, which transcends all
verbal and conceptual expression. In the midst of this darkness of faith and all kinds of uncertainties in a constantly
changing historical situation, the christian himself is still in
search of a fuller faith and of a more perfect and deeper
meaning of faith for human existence. Faith provides no cut
and dried solutions. With faith we have no magic spell which
can explain the whole problem of man in the twinkling of an
eye. Faith is a perspective for life. 'Faith is not something by
means of which man is changed at one stroke as if by magic
into believing, so that, lying *buried* in faith, he almost disappears as a man and becomes a stranger to all that is human.'[8]
Man believes. Even more than other men, the believing chris-

---

[8] D. de Petter, 'Het filosoferen van de gelovige', *Tijdschrift voor Philosophie* 21 (1959), 8.

tian is a man full of problems.[9] There is a constant tension between his faith and his human experience. There are in fact, in the assumptions on which the christian believer bases his thoughts and actions, all kinds of *human* insights, views and opinions, which have developed as a result of his human experience, in addition to his faith. In the concrete, all these assumptions form a single psychological whole, within which faith is not always maintained in a pure and sound state. Believing man has again and again to place faith and experience opposite each other so as to purify his faith. Because of this, there is always a seeking restlessness in living faith, making faith a constantly renewed personal choice. It is therefore possible to say that a 'communal disbelief' is the basis for every human dialogue between the believer who believes in the transcendental and what I may call the 'believer' who believes only in the intramundane. In this way, the seeking of all men for the full truth is the communal basis of every dialogue. Believing, not believing and believing differently are all situations within which our common humanity is placed, but in no sense factors which make dialogue about the real meaning of this common humanity impossible. In human dialogue, in which our humanity is always at stake, what is ultimately at issue, then, is this basic question—has this humanity, together with man's ability to give, in freedom, a meaning to life, itself the last word, or is this human word, even though it may be an absolute 'no', in the long run only a penultimate word, so that only God has the last word, a word that we know is not a *verbum irae*, a word of anger, for all men who are sincere, but a *verbum misericordiae*, a word of infinite mercy. It can therefore be regarded as characteristic that the reality of God's revelation, Christ Jesus, is known as the 'word of God'. By definition, Christ, the God-man, is *the* dialogue—man's dialogue with God and the dialogue between men themselves within the dialogue with the living God.

---

[9] See G. MacGregor, *Christian Doubt*, London 1951, in which the author warns believers against dogmatism in the shape of a narrow-mindedness and self-satisfaction and shows how faith does not preclude problems, but, on the contrary, opens the way to them.

2. Toleration

Man's capacity to know is orientated towards the absolute
and towards truth, but is never able to grasp this truth
exhaustively. The same truth can therefore be approached
from different, mutually complementary points of view.
Moreover, since man's. activity in knowing is a personal
activity, closely linked to various situational aspects, his insights can never lead to absolute unanimity. Although in
itself truth is one, absolute and unchangeable, man's view of
this truth participates in the characteristics of his humanity—
it is imperfect and relative. This means that, insofar as it is
our possession, the truth is always open to growth and
amplification. Association with those who think differently
from ourselves may therefore mean a widening of our own
horizon. This is a first and as it were philosophical basis for a
tolerant attitude towards the statements of others.

The problem of toleration, however, goes further than this.
It also arises in connection with affirmations and views of life
which strike us believers as untrue. A solution to this problem is at the moment being sought by Catholics in two
different directions.

A. *The problem in history*

(i) *Medieval views and the* ancien régime

According to the medieval view, untruth—although it had
no right to exist in society—had to be tolerated in certain
circumstances so as to prevent worse evils and above all to
open the way to possible conversions to the truth. This was,
in principle, an attitude of intolerance. In practice, however,
it was usually softened by a certain toleration in the sense of
patient endurance. It could, in fact, be called a tempered
intolerance.

This view of toleration is still quite widespread in the
church today, although perhaps in not so crude a form, and
is not confined simply to the Catholic church of southern
Europe. The view of intolerance is still insisted on *in thesi,*
whereas *in hypothesi,* that is, because society is in fact mixed,

a certain measure of toleration is, in practice, advocated, as a 'lesser evil' that has to be accepted so as to avoid a worse evil or simply because there is no alternative. The real danger is that, when they constitute the majority in the state, Catholics who hold this view are often inclined to be intolerant towards those who think differently. On the other hand, when they are in the minority, these same Catholics frequently demand that the state should be tolerant towards them. This ambivalent attitude is motivated by the assertion that only the truth has a right to exist and that untruth has no right to exist and can therefore only be patiently endured.

Broadly speaking, this was the current view—of Catholics and non-Catholics—up to the French Revolution.

(ii) *The birth of the modern democracies and 'Human Rights'*

At the time of the break between Catholics and Protestants in the west, these views were in fact still held on both sides, but there was—at least after the first bloody conflicts—a powerful inclination to be tolerant in practice. This tendency was expressed, on the one hand, by the Edict of Nantes (1598), which clings to the basic principle of intolerance on the part of Catholics, who, for practical reasons, took measures of toleration in favour of the Huguenots. On the other hand, it was also expressed, for example, in the later Act of Toleration (1689), in which the same basic principle of intolerance on the part of the Anglicans was in practice weakened by measures of toleration in favour of the Catholics. In the gradual growth of national consciousness, however, a new value began to emerge and erupted with great violence at a definite point of time—during the French revolution. The 'rights of man' were championed, and this phrase contained an affirmation of the functional laicity of the state and thus the separation of church and state. This new conviction was expressed especially vividly in article 10 of the *Déclaration des droits de l'homme et du citoyen*: 'no one may be disturbed because of his personal, even his religious views.' In article 11, moreover, freedom to express one's opinion, for example, in the case of propagating one's own view of life, was safe-guarded. This was in fact the birth of our modern view of toleration—an idea that soon found general acceptance and was opposed almost exclusively by the Catholic church (see below). This same idea has, since the time of the French revolution, become so widespread that 'freedom of opinion, conscience and religion' was included in the 1948 *Declaration of Human Rights* of the United Nations Organisation. This was not simply a practical demonstration of favour, but a fundamental declaration in principle of respect for the human person as such and for his inviolable possession of personal conscience and freedom. Toleration is therefore no longer simply a favour granted for practical reasons, some-thing which is based on a principle of intolerance, but a moral value which is promoted for its own sake.

(iii) *The reactions of the church and the theory of 'Thesis and Hypothesis'*

From 1789 onwards, and throughout almost the whole of the nineteenth century, the church opposed 'liberalism'. This struggle reached its climax during the pontificate of Pius IX, that is, between the years 1850 and 1880. If the church's resistance to liberalism is to be interpreted correctly, it is important to bear in mind that the declaration of the prin-ciple of the rights of man was initially accompanied by a strong anti-Catholic tendency. In addition, the principle of freedom of conscience was also put forward in the form of indifferentism and this was something that the church could not, of course, accept. As this anti-Catholic tendency dis-appeared and the principle of freedom of conscience gradually became dissociated from indifferentism, the church became more and more open to the positive value of liberalism.

The first sign of resistance on the part of the church was Pius VI's encyclical *Quod aliquantum* of 10 March 1791. The religious freedom that had been granted, the pope main-tained, had as its sole aim the eradication of the Catholic religion and was therefore a 'monstrous right'. The French bishops, on the other hand, made a distinction between the special legality of the structures pertaining to this world and the supernatural order and were therefore able to accept the new French constitution. The pope, however, stressed the fact that the state might not affirm itself as the ultimate reality. There were practical agreements between church and state under Pius VII, but, from the doctrinal point of view, no agreement was reached in the argument. The struggle became violent during the pontificate of Pius IX, who published the encyclical *Quanta cura* together with a *Syllabus* of current errors. What the pope was attacking in these new tendencies was the moral attitude of man (individually or in community) who believed that he could be self-sufficient and had no further need of God and his commandments. But the other side gained the impression, from Pius IX's protest, that the church was opposed to all progress. It is clear from the impassioned literature of this period that even many Catholics feared that the division between the church and the world would be sealed by the attitude of Pius IX. Between 1864 and 1914, church and society were in a state of war. In America, which stood apart from the struggle, the bishops wrote that, in their opinion, both sides in the European struggle were wrong (Mgr Ireland).

Previously, the 'liberal' Catholics had tried to save what they could. These Catholics—and especially de Lamennais—were able to accept the basic principles of the declaration of the rights of man and even believed that it contained greater pastoral possibilities for christianity. The idea that acceptance of religious freedom and freedom of conscience did not in itself necessarily imply indifferentism gained ground and two different movements arose, often known as the French school and the Belgian school. The Belgian school—more than ten priests collaborated in the drafting of the new constitution—had a more pragmatic than doctrinal orientation and accepted freedom of worship only in fact. The French school, on the other hand, aimed to provide a doctrinal basis for this practical attitude. It was from this movement that the idea of 'laicity', the tendency for the recognition of lay status, as distinct from 'laicism', the lay attitude of hostility towards the church, was born.

When Pius IX's *Syllabus* appeared, Mgr Dupanloup especially tried to find a solution to the problem by making a distinction between *in thesi* and *in hypothesi*, interpreting 'freely' the strict attitude of the pope.

During the pontificate of Leo XIII, there was a certain, though not very important change in the church's attitude. Leo's encyclicals, *Immortale Dei* (1885) and *Libertas prae-stantissimum* (1888), opened up the possibility of accepting what was later to be called 'laicity'. Leo maintained that liberalism, in the sense of freeing man from his subjection to the absolute, could never be accepted by the church, but that the church did not deny the 'civil and political freedom of nations'. In this way, Leo XIII gave the condemnations of Pius IX the more subtle shades of meaning they needed. He stressed that the church condemned freedom of conscience, of worship and of the press under certain conditions. She condemned freedom of conscience 'if this meant that everyone might worship God or not quite indifferently, according to his own choice'. She condemned freedom of worship if this was based 'on the principle that everyone was free to confess the religion that pleased him or even to profess no religion at all'. Finally, she condemned the freedom of the press which was not limited by any ethical norm, with the consequence that nothing of the fundamental natural principles on which society was based 'remained sacred and intact'. These three freedoms, however, Leo insisted, 'could be tolerated' in the light of a higher good—public peace—and out of respect for the human person. Leo XIII affirmed far more clearly than the Roman theologians had done in the past the competence of the state within its own sphere. Nonetheless, he continued to condemn the division between church and state, although he expressed his approval of the situation in America in his encyclical *Longinqua Oceani*, adding, however, that this situation should not be regarded as ideal.

Under the pontificates of Benedict XV (1914–22) and Pius XI (1922–39), the church gradually became more open to the idea of toleration and this process has continued up to the present. Good relationships between church and state were restored under the pontificate of Pius XI (the concordats), although this pope still repeated in his encyclical *Maximum gravissimumque* of January 1924 that his mild attitude did not mean that the condemnations of his predecessors ceased to apply—'We continue to condemn laicity'.

All the same, Pius XI made an important contribution to the modern Catholic idea of toleration in his letter, *Non abbiamo bisogno*, by making a distinction between freedom of 'conscience' and freedom of 'consciences'. By freedom of conscience, he meant that man is, in conscience, naturally free to satisfy his religious need by following any religion at all. This, in other words, was indifferentism, an attitude which the pope of course rejected. By freedom of consciences, on the other hand—a concept often known, confusingly, in non-Catholic circles, as 'freedom of conscience'—he meant that man's personal conscience cannot be forced by any external power so that he has to live in accordance with any view of life which is different from the one which he, in conscience, inwardly regards as true. This was, then, the first statement on the part of the church officially of her acceptance of the principle of toleration as a basic attitude.

Pius XII went even further. In keeping with the idea of world peace and the internationalisation of nations, which could not possibly be built up on the unity of belief, this pope recognised that a 'Catholic nation' had the right to give its approval to, for example, an international charter in which freedom of religion and of worship was included. He considered the affirmation of the 'sound and legitimate laicity of the state' to be one of the basic principles of Catholic teaching.[10]

In our own time, partly as a consequence of the new French constitution with its fundamental principle of 'the State is lay',[11] a sharp distinction has been made between laicity, as a juridical statute of the state, and laicism, as an affirmation of

[10] See the *Osservatore Romano* of 25 March 1958.
[11] 'L'Etat est laïque'.

a view of life. The assembly of the French cardinals and archbishops declared in 1945 that laicity was acceptable even to Catholics.[12] In 1958, five French cardinals made a firm stand in favour of a carefully distinguished laicity against an integralist minority which could not reconcile itself to the affirmation that 'France is a lay . . . republic'.[13] Long before this, in 1946, an article with a similar trend of thought about 'laicity' and 'laicism' had even appeared in the *Osservatore Romano*. The writer of this article even said that there was a biblical foundation for the view that the state should not impose any religion on its subjects. Cardinal Lercaro also went a step further than Pius XI in his affirmation of the principle of the freedom of 'consciences' in expressing the official view of the church by basing civil and practical toleration directly on reverence for the free self-determination of the human conscience and on the demand that truth must be accepted as truth and indeed must be accepted on the basis of a personal conviction of truth and on no other basis. This was in principle a declaration that the older distinction between *in thesi* and *in hypothesi* was no longer valid. In addition, Cardinal Lercaro also said that we are only on the threshold of an authentically Catholic view of toleration.[14]

B. *The foundation of the modern view of toleration*

Although the movement which insists on the validity of the theory of thesis and hypothesis still has firm adherents in Catholic circles,[15] most Catholic theologians are looking for a different basis for toleration. They have only very gradually come to realise that civil toleration is more than simply the

[12] See *Kath. Arch.* 1 (1946–7), 4–5.
[13] 'La France est une République . . . laïque.'
[14] See *Kath. Arch.* 14 (1959), 393–404.
[15] See Cardinal Ottaviani, *Il balluardo*, Rome (1961). This book, like the Cardinal's earlier lecture given at the Lateran University (see the *Osservatore Romano* of 4 March 1953), is characteristic of the whole movement. It is well known that Pope Pius XII felt, at the time of the Cardinal's lecture, impelled to dissociate himself from the Cardinal's opinions in a speech which he made to Italian Catholic jurists on 6 December 1953; see *Herder-Korrespondenz* 8 (1953–4), 173. Cardinal Ottaviani does not seem to have changed his opinion in his subsequently published work, *Institutiones iuris publici ecclesiastici*, pt 1, Rome (1958–60⁴).

consequence of the fact that society is mixed, although this concrete situation has of its own accord raised the problem of peaceful co-existence, firstly on the practical level and then on the doctrinal level. There is therefore a tendency to base toleration on principle and, with this aim in view, even to link it with the age-old conviction in the church that the acceptance of faith must be a free act. I should like now to examine this view more closely under four headings.

1. Many Catholics no longer regard toleration as an attitude based on opportunist motives, however noble these may be, but as a pattern of behaviour based on an ethical principle, that of justice and love. This view of toleration on the one hand honours the objectivity of truth and therefore has nothing to do with indifferentism, but on the other hand also takes the knowing subject, the human person, into consideration. Truth alone is the distinctive value of a knowing consciousness. Therefore truth is for everyone the norm towards which the whole of human life must direct itself. But this truth is a subjective and concrete norm only if man is conscious of it as such. Thus, the truth as known by man is the directly subjective norm of human action. On the basis of human personalism, then, no one has the right to accept something as true—and to direct his life in accordance with it—if this is contradicted by his conviction of truth. A man may not accept anything as true and live in accordance with it unless he is somehow or other—naturally or supernaturally—convinced in his conscience of the truth of it. We ourselves do not *determine* what truth is (this closes the way to indifferentism) —our spirit *discloses* the truth and it is only as disclosed that the truth acts as the norm in respect of our thought. Toleration is therefore the positive respect that we have for the personal witness to truth borne by others, even if this may be objectively wrong, precisely because the person can only live fully and worthily as a man on the basis of an inner conviction about what is good and true. As a person, a man can only live in moral responsibility in the light of his own inwardly guided freedom, that is, in the light of his own conscience and his

personal view of truth. Toleration is therefore a direct consequence of the objectivity of the truth as it is revealed to man's understanding of the truth. It is at the same time a reverence for the human person. There is no room here for a distinction between the value of the human person, who must be respected, and his personal convictions, which may in concrete be wrong and which consequently would not merit this respect and can only be 'patiently endured' for higher motives. Man is a person precisely in his personal convictions about life. As a direct result of this, then, the tolerant man not only respects the personal convictions of others, but also acknowledges their right to regulate their conduct, even in public, in accordance with those convictions. Surely it would be a pharisaical attitude to respect different views of life, yet at the same time to deny to those who held those convictions the right to express them in society? The human person is, after all, a unity of interiority and exteriority and respect for the other's person therefore also applies to his expressions of his personal convictions. To recognise the freedom of conscience of others, but to deny them the objective conditions of existence which are necessary if this freedom is *de facto* to be exercised is in fact duplicity and intolerance. Toleration presupposes, then, respect for the person in his convictions and in his outward expression of these convictions.

One objection that has been raised here, namely that evil and error have no right to exist, is based on a misunderstanding. Truth and error are, according to this view, regarded as legal subjects, the one possessing all rights, the other possessing none at all. But only a person is a legal subject and a person has the right to accept something as truth if it appears to him, in all sincerity, as the truth (even though it may, objectively speaking, be an error). Thus, an erring person also has rights. Toleration is therefore an ethical and social task for every man. This toleration applies both at the individual level of mutual encounter between persons and at the social level of 'civil' toleration. This means that the state may not impose any view of life on its subjects, but must take care that they are all free (and thus that they also have the objective conditions of existence in which this freedom will prevail) to be able to lead their lives according to their personal convictions.

In this sense, freedom of religion and conscience is a value in itself which must be respected even when Catholics are in the majority and must be protected by positive legislation. According to this modern Catholic view of toleration, then, the state, as an auxiliary organ, also has the duty to serve the growth of life and educational possibilities of the various groups among its subjects with differing views of life, at least according to proportional equality and distributive justice.

2. This justification of a principle of toleration does not refer to what has been called 'irenism'. The christian whose attitude is irenic is simply intent on not contradicting those who think and believe differently from himself and on camouflaging and concealing his own conviction. Toleration as an ethical task is not indifferentism or irenism, but something that is always accompanied by zeal for one's own conviction, so that it does not in any way exclude a militantly defensive attitude. Anyone who is convinced of the value which truth has for human life will after all strive, from love of his fellow-men, to enable others to share in his conviction of truth. All that toleration does exclude in this connection is the use of methods which are contrary to due reverence for the free act of recognition of this truth on the part of others and by which the truth is forced on them. Invitation, testimony in word and in life, dialogue and argumentation—these are suitable methods for persuading someone to change his conviction. Toleration is therefore always accompanied by a healthy zeal for one's own conviction, but 'in the noble gesture by which I, with all my heart, grant my fellow-man the freedom of his own conscience, there is something painful which I accept' (J. H. Walgrave), because, although toleration is in itself a positive ethical good, division in views of life and convictions cannot, as such, be called a value. It is only in this sense that the positive virtue of respect for the convictions of others acquires the distinctive character of 'toleration' and 'patient

endurance'. It is only in this sense, too, that there is an element of (abstract) truth in the theory of 'thesis and hypothesis', that is, that a world in which all men are christians because of their inner convictions remains the ideal for the christian believer.

3. In concrete, toleration is not unlimited. If it is founded on respect for the freedom of man's conscience and derives its ethical significance from this respect, this means that it will also protect this freedom of conscience against unjust and violent infringement. Toleration can therefore legitimately change into resistance. Toleration in principle becomes meaningless when confronted with intolerance in principle or in fact, because it would, in that case, destroy its own inward foundation. The state is therefore also bound to resist every form of propaganda or every organisation which violates man's freedom of conscience. Toleration can, therefore, in an extreme situation, resort to armed resistance. Only a very small number of modern Catholics do not accept this inner consequence of toleration and have a pacifist view of toleration, thus rejecting all use of force in an extreme situation.

4. Finally, I should like to say a few words about toleration within those communities which man joins of his own free will, communities such as the church. In view of the fact that membership of such a community is based on an identical, personally accepted view of life which should be the unifying factor of the whole group, this membership is meaningless if one of the members personally holds a different view of life. If, therefore, he openly disputes the conviction which is the reason for the existence of the community, it is obvious that it is the right and frequently also the duty of this community to condemn him and, if he persists in his different view, to expel him from the community. (In the case of the church at least, this will be done with the aid of her own spiritual resources.) Whenever it is a question of differences of opinion within the one Catholic conviction and confession of faith,

however, the problem is, of course, different—in that case, the principle of toleration still holds good.

Conclusion

The above interpretation of toleration has not yet been accepted in all circles of the Catholic church, but it does have a firm foundation in the dogma of the act of faith as a free act and it does at the same time respect the objectivity of the truth. On the other hand, the earlier Catholic view of toleration is still a serious stumbling-block for non-Catholics and it would therefore be of great benefit to the whole world if the church were solemnly to accept the 1948 *Declaration of Human Rights* and place this in a specifically christian perspective. The objections of those Catholics who refuse to accept this idea of toleration can be partly explained in the light of the sophism that 'untruth has no rights'. Their objections can also be explained partly by a rather naive mentality —they are too ready to doubt whether the views of those who think differently from themselves are really sincere and whether they are acting in good faith. History bears witness to the fact that such a view of truth can easily lead to intolerance. A further reason for their objections is an inclination to see the truth in too static and abstract a light, separate from knowing man. Finally, these Catholics may also be prompted by the fear of having to abandon established positions of power if they adopt a more tolerant attitude.

Ever since the time of the French revolution, a clear development in the direction of the modern idea of toleration is discernible in the guidance given by the church's hierarchy. In this connection, however, it is important to remember that the church, and especially her hierarchy, not only proceeds from unassailable data of revelation, but is also in fact a child of her time (and often of a time long since past) and that she consequently also judges in the light of assumptions and opinions which do not form part of revelation, but are the legacy of man's consciousness at a definite stage of his development. This means that it is possible for this human consciousness to be already well developed in certain Catholics, but, in others, even including members of the church's hierarchy, it may be 'retarded'. What is more, it is also possible for the church to adopt a more liberal attitude towards the more developed communities, for example, but for her attitude towards the less developed nations to continue to be determined by the earlier ideas. This position can undoubtedly be justified. But, in the light of the present internationalisation of life (which means that what happens in Spain, for example, can have repercussions on the whole of the world), this certainly raises problems in connection with world opinion.[16]

---

[16] The following books and articles can be mentioned in connection with the whole problem of toleration: J. Leclerc, *Histoire de la tolérance religieuse au siècle de la Réforme*, 2 vols, Paris 1955; A. Latreille, *L'Eglise catholique de la Révolution française*, 2 vols, Paris 1946–50, *Tolérance chrétienne et communauté humaine*, Tournai 1952; R. Aubert, *Le pontificat de Pie IX* (=Fliche and Martin, *Histoire de l'Eglise*, pt 21); K. Rahner, 'The Dignity and Freedom of Man', *Theological Investigations* 2, London 1963, 235–63; J. H. Walgrave, 'Persoonlijke en burgerlijke verdraagzaamheid', *Kultuurleven* 25 (1958), 245–57; *Person and Society* (Duquesne Studies, Theological Series, 5), Pittsburgh Pa. 1965, 163–74; A. Dondeyne, *Geloof en wereld*, Antwerp and Bilthoven 1962, 213–30: English translation: *Faith and the World*, Pittsburgh (Pa) 1963.

10

CHRISTIANS AND NON-CHRISTIANS: 2. PRACTICAL COOPERATION

1. Social structures, social work and charity

In connection with the humanist, christian and Catholic literature dealing with the relationship between social work (in the specific sense of the word) and man's view of life, I should like to clarify a few theological concepts which are in constant use in the discussion that has arisen. Several fundamental questions have been brought forward in this context. To what extent does the charitable element still play a part in the present-day activity of social work? What are the relationships between the personal and the functional aspects of social work? Has social work carried out by believing Catholics a special mark of its own and does it require its own institutional forms? And finally, how can this Catholic intention in social work be reconciled with the social worker's task of accepting his client completely in his own individuality without exerting social pressure on his convictions? If I envisage them correctly, these are the problems with which christian social workers are at the moment faced.

A. Christian 'Charitas'

(I) THE CONCEPTS CARITAS AND CHARITAS[1]

(a) In the universally christian sense, *caritas*, charity, means the divine virtue of love both of God and of men. It is a love which is given to us in Christ by the Holy Spirit. Ordinary human love differs from christian *caritas* not because God is

---

[1] Professor Schillebeeckx here uses two words, *caritas* and *charitas*, current in Dutch, but not in English, to make a distinction between the specifically christian, divine virtue of love of God and man (*caritas*) and 'charity' in the looser, more restricted sense of 'good works' or 'charitable' works (*charitas*). Although they sound unfamiliar to English ears, I have, for the sake of clarity, retained these two terms in the English text. The adjective 'charitable' is also used here in the second sense. *Transl.*

absent from authentically human love, but because his presence in human love is merely indirect, silent (at least in itself). There is, in other words, no lived personal community of love with God in this human love (even though true *caritas* is anonymously present in this human love to the extent to which it is an authentic giving of self). *Caritas*, on the other hand, is first and foremost and explicitly a lived personal community of love with God, in which this *caritas* comes forward, together with God, with God's love itself, to meet our fellow-man. It is possible to say that *caritas* towards God is, as it were, implicit in our love of our fellow-men and that it develops in an explicit dedication to God and our fellow-men. The christian's encounter in love with his fellow-man is therefore a silent invitation to this fellow-man to community with the God of love.

For the christian every activity, even the most profane, must be borne up by this divine virtue of love. It is only when social justice, for example, is included in and integrated with this christian love that this justice is a christian virtue in the full sense of the word. This means that every activity carried out by a christian, however much it may be, in its essence, determined by its own object, and however profane and secular it may be in itself, must nonetheless be the expression of *caritas* towards God and men. The social work performed by a christian cannot be an exception to this—it is the incarnation of christian *caritas*.

(b) In the christian tradition, *caritas*, charity, has also acquired a more particular, limited meaning, for which the word *charitas* is often used in the Netherlands. Whenever universally christian *caritas* is directed in external activity towards our fellow-man *in a situation of distress or need*, it acquires a special mark. This is traditionally expressed by the adjective 'charitable' and has been technically formulated in the phrase 'spiritual and corporal works of mercy'. General christian *caritas* has thus acquired the significant meaning of *misericordia*, mercy, because it deals with a need. In this sense, not all external acts performed out of love are 'charitable' acts, but only those which are concerned with a lack, a deficiency, a need or a misfortune.

Although in our own times we have come to realise more fully that those who are suffering distress have a certain *right* to help and assistance, the christian significance of merciful love has in no way been changed. Out of justice, I give my fellow-man what is due to him—out of love, I give with an open hand, gratuitously. The good Samaritan was, as a man, bound to help the man who was lying half dead by the way-side. But what Jesus was seeking to point out in this parable was a generosity in the care of our fellow-men, in which what is not obligatory is given—a personal relationship of love which is not measured out, but which is unsparing and lavish in pouring out oil and wine. Thomas was therefore right in saying: 'merciful love does not destroy justice. On the contrary, it can be said to be *plenitudo iustitiae*, a fullness of justice'.[2] The person is the source of many different rights with regard to his fellow-man, but being a person is also an appeal and an invitation to love which gives more than the strict obligations of justice. Loving *as* Christ loved the world is here the measure of love which is immeasurable. It is only in gratuitous love that justice reaches its ultimate fulfilment.

(II) CHARITAS AND PROFESSIONAL SOCIAL WORK

In the past, a sharp, but false distinction was always made between the inner spirit of *caritas* and outward actions. It is, of course, true that two aspects can be distinguished in *charitas*, in the second and more limited sense of the word— the *motive that inspires it* and the *outward activity in rendering assistance*. The motive that inspires *charitas* is, however, not purely inward—it is made present precisely *in* outward rendering of assistance and it only becomes an authentic reality in this outward activity. The spirit of love is situated precisely in the outward act, not behind it in a kind of enclosed inwardness. The spirit of love is therefore not simply an inner intention. This inner intention is, after all, quite often a pure ideological suprastructure and may have nothing

[2] *ST* I, q. 21, a. 3, ad 2.

to do with the true inner orientation of our outward acts in which we can still hardly see the true authenticity of our intentions. We often delude ourselves into thinking that we are doing something out of love!

In *caritas*, man is turned towards his fellow-man—each makes the other, as a person, the object of care and disinterested service. In this *caritas*, man lives for the other in a community of personal dedication—a personal *communio*. He experiences his being a man as a being a man for the other and he lets this giving of himself be the offer of God's love for man. In this, the outward activity of rendering assistance is the 'instrument' of our effect on the other, the *sacrament* of our effective love—that whole of meaningful and effective gestures in and through which we give ourselves to other men and thus experience and bring about the unity of love in an incarnate manner. It is by expressing itself in the outward activity of rendering assistance that this unity of love is constituted, not alongside it or above it. The motive of love which inspires us to render assistance is identical with the rendering of that assistance.

The fact that this motive of love or spirit of love is not to be found in a purely enclosed inwardness, but precisely in 'the world', in the very activity of rendering assistance, has all kinds of consequences, but especially in two directions, suggested by the distinctive nature of incarnate love.

In the first place, it has consequences in the direction of the motive of love or the charitable disposition. The community-forming factor in the association of the welfare worker who provides assistance and the client who is in need of assistance is not only the outwardly performed work, but also, and above all, the disposition which is personally directed towards the other *in and through* the outwardly performed work. What we have here is a totally human social activity directed towards the other. The social bond does not come about simply and solely by means of the outward achievement —it is the personal disposition which forms the community, realises the *communio*, in and through this achievement. This human and social activity is a community of persons, which offers the serving person to the other in and through the quasi-sacrament of outward service. Without this inspiration, which makes the 'outward body' itself alive, the outward achievement is dead and lacking in any real result. A technically perfect service in which assistance is rendered without this inspiration is, seen from the personalistic point of view, asocial—it does not form a community.

What is more, the opposite is also asocial. A so-called inner disposition to *caritas* without the outwardly performed technical work soon deteriorates into a morality of good intentions. Outwardly perfect structures, on the other hand, can in practice propagate an inhuman, unchristian spirit.

The external work of the social services is, in our own times, becoming more and more highly organised and institutionalised. It is becoming a rationalised system. So-called charitable work is being carried out less and less by isolated individuals acting on their own initiative and directly inspired by motives of mercy. The social services are increasingly becoming an activity undertaken by permanent, well organised and even subsidised institutions which perform the work with much greater technical competence. In many countries, there is, in addition to the Ministry of Social Affairs, a separate ministry for 'social work'. Social work has become a profession. These objective structures can only further the disposition of love of the giving persons who are concerned. After all, the real meaning of love is attained *in* the welfare of the other—it is not the subjective experience or the satisfaction of the one who gives. Love therefore requires as high a degree of technical competence and of professional skill as possible, precisely because it has the real good and welfare of the other in view. Otherwise, a disincarnation of love is bound to take place, with fatal results in two directions. On the one hand, social and charitable work becomes completely preoccupied with technically perfect social work, in which importance is attached only to technical administration and the client is neglected as a person and reinforced in his loneliness. On the other hand, the genuine disposition of love, wherever this is maintained, continues to make use of primitive means and consolation is derived from the thought that this is done out of love.

It is therefore possible to say that the development of the more personal form of charitable work towards a rationalised system does in fact imply a real advantage for those who receive assistance and it is, after all, towards this—the realisation of the real welfare of our fellow-men—that the disposition of *caritas* is directed. On the other hand, however, it is also important not to forget that this is, partly at least, a pious wish, because there is certainly an ever-present danger that a rationalised system—which must, in the very nature of things, contain a strong element of economics and calculated matter-of-factness—may well deaden the spirit of true gratuitous love and blunt the delicate sense of loving intuition. Social work, in that case, derives its perfection from the practical efficiency with which distress is relieved—it still continues to be social work, even though it is done without love. But this is a failure to appreciate our fellow-man, who is, after all, an appeal to our loving care. In this case, social workers become officials who are certainly more effective than those who did charitable work in the past in the relief of tangible distress, but who leave the human person himself far more than in the past a victim of the deepest human distress—a victim of loneliness and of the cold absence of true love with its often 'useless' but meaningful attention. Authentic social work must therefore include both elements—the disposition of love and the outward achievement—and it must do this in such a way that the personal inspiration of love creates, through the quasi-sacramental medium of the outwardly performed service, a real community. It is only then that the rationalised modern system can be truly incorporated into social work and at the same time transcended.

B. *Social work and the Catholic view of life*

(1) MAN'S SOCIAL NEED AS AN EXISTENTIAL NEED

The fact that social and charitable work, in accordance with its own object, the relief of social need, has been transferred to the sector of 'social justice' does not imply any change in the problem of its christian significance. Social justice is a christian attitude if it is included in the dominant motive of christian love which recognises and presupposes the distinctive value of justice but sees it as part of a greater totality. In formal terms, *caritas* is not the exercise of our human mode of existence (that is love in general); it presupposes this love in general as a basis but is itself the exercise of our community of grace with God, the act of a new mode of existence which originates in Christ. The fact that non-christians—or those who call themselves non-christians—and the state have become aware of their duty in this sphere does not free the christian from the distinctively christian character of his obligations in this world towards his fellow-men which he must see placed in the perspective of redemption.

Social work is directed towards man in specific or general situations of social need or distress. The reality to which we refer when we use the term 'situation of social need' is very varied, but it can be seen above all in a twofold perspective. In this light it will also appear that the social provisions made by the state cannot be regarded as real 'social work'. It is possible to distinguish two aspects in this social reality.

In the first place, there is the aspect of personal community or intersubjectivity, in other words, of personal encounter. This is truly human and not purely spiritual, and it comes about through all kinds of outward activities and through outward institutions and arrangements. Viewed in this light, the institution itself also forms part of this aspect of personal encounter and is the expressive form, the *signum efficax*, of the personal community—it is, in other words, the incarnation of this personal community.

In the second place, however, these institutions and structures are not *purely* the expression of the human community of persons. The incarnation of this personal community is at the same time an alienation. The structure thus objectivises and at the same time alienates from the personal community. As such, the structure acquires a certain independence with its own laws in human society. Seen in this light, the social reality is a massive fact, something that precedes the activity of the person in making it incarnate and, in its incarnation, this personal activity thus becomes, consciously or unconsciously, partly dependent on and influenced by the element of alienation contained in these structures. In the concrete, then, the structures can be both a help and a hindrance to real personal encounters or to the human social reality in the full sense of the word. These social structures can therefore be felt as asocial by our present-day experience of the community, even though they were created by an earlier experience of the community precisely as the effective sign of the social experience of that period.

There are, then, in my opinion, two directly necessary directions which the social services must take as a result of these two aspects of the reality of man's situation of social need.

a. On the one hand, there must be social provisions which come to grips with the objective structures. This seems to me to be the special task of the authorities, encouraged and helped in this way by the trade unions and by social policy generally.

b. On the other hand, the sphere of 'social work' does not seem to me to be so much part of the sector of structures, institutions and functional relationships, as of the field of personal encounter, of personal social relationships. Despite perfect structures, individuals and groups of people can still find themselves in a situation of real social distress. What is more, social need is ultimately *personal* need. Distress is not simply physical or psychological—it affects the whole person. In one way or another, it is an 'existential' need which can only be approached in a personal (and professionally expert) encounter. A case of this kind, or rather, a personal problem of this kind is what concerns the professional social worker. What is involved here in a very special way is a witness of love, of *caritas*, in the form of expert technical skill, varying in accordance with whether the situations of social need are particular or general, and this 'expert' witness of love is furthermore involved in such a way that expert professional skill forms an element of the truly personal encounter. It is this that characterises social work, because even social action which really affects the structures (and does not, as such, come within the sphere of 'social work') is, if it is carried out in the light of christianity, truly a witness of *caritas* in the form of expert technical skill. In social work, however, what is in the very first place involved is the personal encounter itself, which, because of man's particular or general social needs, requires a special expert professional skill. The point of departure is therefore different.

(II) THE SECULAR AND THE RELIGIOUS DIMENSION OF SOCIAL WORK

Since social work is, because of its very nature, situated in a characteristic manner within the sphere of personal encounter, it is obvious that it starts from a definite *image of man*. The meaning of man's physical need, for example, changes according to whether man is regarded as a purely physical and mental being, as an incarnate person or as a man redeemed by Christ and called to a living community with God. Localised needs, of course, have a certain measure of independence and these can be approached equally with definite techniques, whether the client and the social worker are or are not believers and whether they are buddhists, christians or nihilists. But the total, existential approach to man in a situation of social need will be different in the case of a humanist, a christian or a Catholic. And it is the person as a totality who is approached by the social worker. There is, of course, a basic level common to both believers and un-believers—our common humanity. On the other hand, how-ever, belief in God is not simply a suprastructure built on to this humanity—it points rather to the *personal* meaning of humanity. Religion is—often negatively, as a refusal—at the very heart of reality and above all at the heart of our en-counter with our fellow-men.

Social work is not an activity aiming at conversion. The structure of every activity must be formed on the basis of the inner direction of its meaning (on the so-called *finis operis*, as distinct from the *finis operantis*, which is possibly different). In the case of man in a situation of social need, the inner meaning on which the structure must be based is the relief of distress. This has led some people to conclude that social work has therefore to be given its structure without regard to the many different views that man has of life. I am bound to reject this conception emphatically. Ultimately, this view implies a belief that faith—christianity—is simply a suprastructure added to the human, social reality. I am convinced, however, that christian faith and *caritas* on the one hand become objectively visible in social and charitable work, which inwardly becomes a reference to the christian redemption of man in his totality and consequently also in his social distress, a reference which makes this redemption present, and that man's social need on the other hand is a *personal* need and therefore has moral and religious implications. Because of the existential unity between human life and christian life, the religious or the so-called 'supernatural' element is not, for all the relative independence of the secular element, simply a subjective aim (*finis operantis*), but truly an inner direction of meaning, even though this transcends social work itself within this world. It is therefore a *finis operis*, not a *finis operantis*. The Catholic view of life is not outside the structure of Catholic social work, but quite certainly within it. Social work carried out by Catholics is social work which appears publicly and visibly as a *referential* and *realising* *sign* of man's redemption by Christ. Christian love is not a 'value-free' love. Social work in a disrupted family, for example, acquires a different orientation through its intention of *caritas* if it is done in connection with believers who accept the indissolubility of marriage as a *task*. There are therefore certain situations in which so-called social and charitable action is bound, because of the christian and ethical implication of *caritas*, to take an entirely different form when it is carried out by a believer from the form which it will take when carried out by a social worker who does not believe, even though we need not doubt the latter's loving care in such cases. The 'non-directive' method can hardly be accepted as a universally valid principle. All the same, the principle of free acceptance by the person receiving assistance also applies to the Catholic social worker—his rendering of assistance must never be allowed to become a spiritual guardianship or a constant or ill-judged pointing to moral and religious values. There is certainly a kind of paternalism that is alien to the world and a doctrinaire insistence on principles which can be a special threat to the Catholic and make his social work ineffective. This attitude can be as harmful to social work as the 'principle of neutrality', not only in the technical aspect of the work, but also in the personal approach to the client. The first attitude makes man inaccessible to the very varied reality of the life that a person in a situation of social distress can be leading. The second attitude reduces man to a totality of structures and functions which are only open to a purely technical influence.

If this delicate and non-moralistic attitude applies to clients who share the social worker's faith, it also applies even more to those who believe differently or to those who do not believe at all. And yet, even in the case of the second, the social worker's approach in the total and existential sense is not 'neutral'. An appeal to the client's religious conviction, in the case of a client whose faith is different from that of the social worker, may form a necessary element of social assistance. The social worker may perhaps have to appeal, even in the case of someone who calls himself an unbeliever, to his client's deepest and perhaps unexpressed longing for a 'surplus' in life which he cannot in fact find and yet seems to lack. Of course, the only suitable answer to a question that relates strictly to this world is an answer that relates to this world, but a question relating to this world may perhaps conceal a question that transcends this world. An unconscious but real need for salvation may be latently present, partly determining the client's social distress. Many different contemporary theologians have pointed to the presence of real but anonymous christianity among people who have given up active membership of the church and even among those who have never belonged to the church. God's grace opens men's hearts to his redeeming word, which they must, however, receive from their fellow-men. The religious word must therefore always be an answer, but it may perhaps be an answer to a question which is not recognised by the subject who is asking. The social worker's word and his existential and 'non-neutral' attitude may therefore ignite what was smouldering in the life of the client and waiting for a spark.

The social worker, however, needs subtle intuition if he is to do this—he must not use sentimental phrases or argument addressed exclusively to the intellect, but unobtrusive words and sensitive reactions which can be heard and understood in the heart. The social worker's whole attitude, his whole approach, must make the good news of the christian message present as an existential experience and he must do this less by what he says than simply by his actions. The christian message is, after all, a message of love and the proclamation of this message must therefore above all be part of the personal approach of the social worker, who will, if necessary (in accordance with the demands made by the specific situation), make his Catholic identity known to the client. Christianity is—as we see in the man Jesus, the Son of God—the descent or appearance of merciful grace *in* the human word and in the human approach which, although simple, goes straight to the heart of one's fellow-man. Since the word of God became man, every human word has had within itself the power to open every human heart to this divine word. The deeply human thus becomes itself the vehicle of grace. As soon as social work ceases to be a purely rational system, a pure technique, and becomes an incarnate act of love, then it is no longer neutral or non-directive, because love itself, as the supreme *human* and *christian* value, includes, in the mode of existential experience, a view of life and the world and is at the same time essentially a carrying out into the world of the christian message. But this 'directive' character of love is, of its very nature, not a guardianship or a failure to appreciate human freedom. On the contrary, it is an appeal which respects the other's freedom and at the same time opens the way to a liberating perspective to which the other has perhaps not yet given his consent, but of which he has certainly had an obscure presentiment. In this sense, social work as a social and charitable activity of its very nature contains within itself the possibility of the client's conversion. This is the supreme possibility of social work, which is one of the many incarnations in this world of Christ's redeeming love which affects the *total* man. The 'spiritual perspectives' of social work are therefore—with the help of technical methods—ultimately a question of the resourcefulness and intuition of *caritas*, going out to man in need as a particular person in his historical context.

There is no doubt that there has been progress in science and technology—progress by means of rationalisation. But this progress only manifests one limited dimension of our humanity. For authentically human progress, this technical rationalisation is only a means and a condition and, in the long run, we would only be helping to dehumanise mankind if we were to identify activity to promote the spiritual health of the people and social work with the spread of more efficient techniques. It is not the process of rationalisation which determines the basic event in man, but the releasing of human freedom as a giving assent to authentic values in life. Science and technology cannot do everything, but this little bit merits our full attention. It is only in this way that we can synchronise professional technical skill with the specifically spiritual perspectives of totally human life.

We ought therefore not to treat the problem of confessional groupings in all secular activities in exactly the same way. If there is no longer any question of situations of social need and marginal situations, this separation will tend to be a handicap. In the field of social work, however, in which our fellow-man is affected in his very being as a person, the relationships are different. A specifically Catholic *institution* for social work ought, in my opinion, to be above all a service institution, a high-level organisation, giving advice both in the technical sphere and in the sphere of the ethical and religious dimension of social work. The setting up of a Catholic institution of this kind is a question of christian efficiency and of prudent guidance and the objection to confessional groupings does not apply here. Generally speaking, we may say that, when it is a question of structures and functions, we are on profane ground and, even though the christian can and must be resourceful and act as an inspiration here, confessional organisations would seem to be an obstacle. As soon as it is man in his personal quality who is directly involved, however, then what is at stake is the totality of man and ultimately the very meaning of our being as man and this meaning cannot be divorced from the ethical and religious dimension. In this case, the problem appears in quite a different light.

On the other hand, however, we should not forget that various views of life, however much they may differ from each other, may in fact be united in a common basic intention of *caritas*, even though this may possibly not be conscious. Sincere, loving and understanding association with one's fellow-man is not a monopoly of the christian. Despite his christian view of life, the christian may in fact be a less good social worker than the unbelieving humanist, for example. There are, after all, christians who are, because of their character, unsuitable for this kind of work. On the other hand, there are also non-christians who are specially gifted for the task of associating with their fellow-men and helping them in the most precarious and complicated situations.

It is certainly true to say that social work is not simply a skill, but an art, in which the imponderable elements of personal encounter are of great importance and pure technique never has the last word. It is even possible to say that purely scientific assistance only provides solutions to problems on the fringe of human life. Assuming that all man's material, psychical and social needs were met, the question 'and what now?' would still remain—a question that arises from the mystery that man is, and will continue to arise, a question about the very *meaning* of man's existence. And this question is in fact implied in every material, psychological and social need experienced by man. The greatest danger to our western civilisation is that we believe that science will enable us to solve the mystery that man is. Accepting this would mean promoting our humanity in a metaphysical void and thus by-passing the deepest questions about life. Now that we can, thanks to rationalisation and the scientific system, increasingly realise the conditions under which man is able to appear in true *freedom*, it is becoming more and more necessary for *values* in life to be shown to men by living example, values in the light of which they can build up a life that is really worthy of man. When human freedom has itself been freed from all kinds of impediments which deprive it of its freedom, then this freedom is faced with the task of making itself into what man, in the light of *values* or objectively valid norms, himself judges that he ought to be. But in that case, it is important that we should not put forward as a norm what is really no more than a hallowed social pattern of the past. The metaphysics of man and ultimately man's understanding of himself in the light of God's revelation will, in the long run, have to be our guarantee that, when all man's special needs—his physical, psychical, psychological and social needs —have been solved by all kinds of rational techniques (and we have by no means reached this point yet), man will not appear to have been left behind with the most profound human experience of loneliness—uncertainty about the real meaning of his human existence.

2. The Catholic hospital and health service

Recognition of secular reality may well be regarded as a central event in the modern world. Man is looking for a social system that is economically, politically and socially more humane, and he is doing so because he is determined to make the world a better place to live in and its system more in accordance with the material and spiritual aspirations of the whole of mankind. In the course of this striving towards the secular reality, all the Catholic institutions that are either remotely or intimately concerned are being subjected to discussion and reassessment. The Catholic hospital service is no exception. Its value too is being seriously questioned. I propose to subject this whole problem to a loyal analysis.

First of all, then, I shall deal briefly with the contemporary phenomenon of laicisation. Then I shall examine the meaning of the adjective 'Catholic' as applied to the modern human reality which we call 'hospital'. Finally, I shall consider, separately and theologically, the question of the hospital in the specifically Catholic context.

A. *The hospital in the secular planning of life*

I have already pointed out elsewhere[3] how various elements of humanity which were in the first place called into existence by religion have again and again in the course of history been transferred to the world and, having become laicised in this way, have been included in the secular structures of life. In the past, it was almost exclusively christians, prompted by *caritas*, their love of God and their fellow-men, who showed mercy to the poor, the sick and the needy and cared for them in what were, in those times, known as houses of God, hospices and almshouses. The care of the sick was, as I have said, almost exclusively the work of christian charity, an extension of the early christian *diakonia* or care of the poor.

Together with the rationalisation of society in the light of technical and scientific advances, this classical structure has been completely changed by the modern view of man into what is now called the modern hospital service. In the present struggle for man's true recognition by his fellow-man, we are devising a grandiose plan for a society which will provide all men with the guarantee of greater equality of opportunity in life and at the same time offer them effective freedom. In this search for a more humane economic and social system, man has also become aware of his social rights in the sphere of medical and allied treatment. Care of the sick has thus legitimately become one of the branches of the social services which society provides for its members, irrespective of their metaphysical, religious or philosophical background. It has

[3] 'The Search for the Living God', *God and Man* (Theological Soundings 2), London and New York 1969, 18–40.

become a part of the specialised organisation of temporal
society which is mankind's task within this world. In view of
the enormous progress that has been made by science and
technology, this development of the hospital service is such
that this aim can no longer be achieved effectively by leaving
it merely to private initiative. The state is inevitably more
deeply involved in the health service as a part of the social
services as a whole. A highly organised society under scientifically justified state control is a prerequisite for modern care
of the sick.

The necessary consequence of all this is the secularisation
of the health service. Care of the sick has become a part of
social justice. Some christians regret the passing of the old
idea of *caritas*, but in so doing they are forgetting the real
meaning of this secularisation. If we, *as believers*, wish to define our attitude towards the problem of care of the sick, we
must of necessity take as our point of departure recognition of
and full consent to this so-called secularisation. There are two
reasons in particular for this.

In the first place, this transference of value only means
that care of the sick was, in the past, the exclusive fruit of a
religious experience of God, whereas now it is also found
outside the sphere of the church and has become a general
human achievement in the secular sphere. The development
of man's consciousness, in part historically influenced by religion, has led to a greater sensitivity to general human values
in life. It was precisely because this sense of human value was,
in the past, not given a *human* expression in the world—it
was not even expressed in human terms by Catholics themselves—that Catholics, and indeed all truly religious men, in
the meantime, from motives of religious mercy, gave effective
assistance wherever social justice was still not recognised in
this sphere. Religion provided for this need in the absence of
a real sense of purely human value.

Catholics and indeed all truly religious people can only
welcome unconditionally that fact that this sense of human
value has developed to such an extent that it is now clearly
and concretely expressed. To give someone in the form of

alms something to which he has a right as a human being may well be charitably intended, but it betrays a fundamental lack of clear-sighted *caritas*. However well it may be intended, this paternalism which condescends in mercy may well contain a fundamental failure to appreciate the primary condition for true love—justice. Love has, after all, to give existence to justice. The minimum demand for love is justice, which is the presupposition of love and indeed to some extent enters into the very essence of love itself. Before a human person can be received into a loving I-thou relationship so as to give form to the truly human community of persons, this love demands the recognition of the other person in his inalienable personality and independence. If this demand is not fulfilled, the other person may no longer be regarded as the ultimate value and may, in the worst case, even be regarded purely as a means of personal self-sanctification. Finding no point of rest in itself, justice attains its fulfilment only in that which it makes possible and on which it is based—disinterested love in the *communio*, the human community of persons. Even without any background of a religious view of life, this structure of community-forming love based on justice is demanded by any personalistic and soundly humanist philosophy.

The fact that what was previously mercy has now become justice is a clear indication that man's awareness is becoming increasingly interior, profound and spiritual. At the same time, it also means that *caritas* itself continues to call forth an increasingly deep sense of justice, to regard charitable elements as pertaining to justice and thus, as disinterested, overabundant and brotherly love, to grow towards the full human form of the love of Christ which is, from the human point of view, senseless: 'God *so* loved the world.'

In the second place, this transference of value has an even deeper and more universal significance. Secularisation, which has made care of the sick a secular task incumbent on the state, is really a rather unfortunate description of what is in fact a much deeper christian reality. In itself, secularisation is not laicity. We christians all too easily tend to leave the secular ordering of temporal society to unbelieving mankind. We tend to forget that the so-called profane aspect is a part of the total religious attitude to life.[4] In other words, the phenomenon of laicisation or secularisation is itself an event which takes place within christianity and within the church, within the people of God itself. Laicisation and secularisation are ambiguous words. They mean that, within his dialogue with the living God, the christian comes loyally to recognise the reality of the world. This recognition, however, forms a part of the christian's total religious attitude to life. Christian 'laicisation' is therefore quite different from the 'laicity' of the atheist, who experiences the reality of this world as the ultimate sphere of life.

The ordering of temporal society, which includes the health service, is therefore quite definitely a task to be undertaken by the Catholic lay community. In his being in this world, the christian believer is with God. In his believing existential relationship with God, the christian has the positive task of actively giving meaning to what pertains to this world. In his consciously experienced relationship with the living God, his serious task within this world remains inviolate. As the institution of salvation, the church—and therefore the church's hierarchy as well—has an exclusively supraterrestrial mission. She does not have this task within the world. But the church is also the lay community of believers. These lay believers also belong to the world and have at the same time a terrestrial task to perform in it, a task with a directly terrestrial aim—that of humanising the world and mankind. Viewed objectively, purely profane or atheistic laicisation is a *hairēsis*, a removal of the profane reality of this world from the totality to which it belongs, in other words, from man's existential believing relationship with the living God. Because this secular sphere of life has its own laws within man's total religious relationship with the living God, this removal is, however, both practically and technically possible. The consequence of this is that the fully human

---

[4] See E. Schillebeeckx, 'Dialogue with God and Christian Secularity', *God and Man*, 210–33.

ordering of temporal society, which includes the social services and care of the sick, must in fact be carried out both by believers and by those who do not believe.

This organisation of temporal society is, in accordance with its directly inward structure, a structure having its own laws, a specifically human task in life which is, as such, distinct, related therefore to this world and, in this sense, non-christian. It belongs to the secular structure of our being man in this world. At this level, then, the christian believer cannot make anything exclusively his own, nor can purely profane man enjoy an exclusive monopoly. Everyone who is at all sensitive to the value and dignity of man can collaborate in this task. Both the christian and the atheist are on their own ground here. Neither the christian nor the atheist is, in this field, an outsider. As believers, however, we also affirm that this communal sphere of work, which is the real sphere in which man as such lives, is only a part of a reality which, because of its creatural condition and because of man's personal and religious sense of life, has deeper dimensions than those accepted by unbelievers. This brings me to the second part of my examination of the problem.

B. *The catholicity of the health service*

(1) CATHOLICITY IN THE INFERRED AND APPLIED SENSE

The care of the sick is, as I have said, a part of the social services and as such an element of man's organisation of life within this world. This organisation is not a fixed datum, but a human task. It is a social task accomplished by man's free will in confrontation with the historically changing world of man. This freedom is not, however, value-free. It is, because of its created condition, a freedom that is subject to norms and sustained by a human judgement of values. Man's task of setting life within this world in order (in this case, his provision of a health service and his care of the sick) must be inspired and governed by the fundamental values in the life of an incarnate person, faced by changing historical situations, which is what man is. Illness is not simply a defect in the human biological organism. It is, in the purely human sense, an existential need experienced by the whole human person and therefore a living problem which cannot be solved by medical care and nursing alone, but which also requires a personalistic attitude which takes account of the great values of life. Even at the purely secular human level, the care of the sick has also to be governed by these inviolable values which constitute the person. These values can, in principle, be distinguished by every man in the light of his condition as a spirit incarnate in this world.

Man, however, finds himself in a situation which is, in the religious sense, opposed to salvation. For this reason, his sensitivity to these general human values which are of primary importance in the care of the sick becomes blunted, with the consequence that it is difficult for him to form a correct judgement about these fundamental human values, apart from the influence of the religious sense of these values in particular historical forms. It is only within his existential religious relationship with God that full justice can be done to the human element as such. In this sense, then, it is possible to speak of the christianity and catholicity of the health service. Religion makes man sensitive to those values in life that he ought, as man, to appreciate. Thus religion is, in this sense, a source of inspiration for the truly human care of the sick, an activity which is always in danger of being deprived of true humanity if it is not done within the context of religious feeling. Whenever, then, religion helps to bring about truly human care of the sick, it is possible to speak, in the improper sense, of the catholicity of the health service. Nonetheless, in itself, the care of the sick remains a human task within this world and, in this sense, non-christian.[5] But,

---

[5] The secular autonomy of the social services is therefore not nullified by this. The result of this human structure of the health service is, however, that the church's teaching authority possesses competence in connection with these fundamental values. Revelation is, after all, unthinkable without man's acceptance of these natural human values. The church, as the guardian of revelation, has, by virtue of the fact itself, control of these *praeambula fidei* among which the basic values of the human person must above all be included, that is, recognition of the inalienable rights resulting from the value of our being man. These rights are unchangeable in their basic outlines,

in the concrete, this is all simply an aspect of the real catholicity of the health service, a problem which I will now examine.

(II) THE REAL CATHOLICITY OF THE HEALTH SERVICE

We know through faith that the humanisation of life in this world is not the ultimate meaning of man's life. The *personal* meaning of his life is more than human, suprahuman, divine. This meaning cannot be won on the basis of human and worldly powers. It is only in an act that transcends itself that man can receive the personal meaning of his life as grace from God. This means that all man's organisation of life in this world, including his provision of social services and care of the sick, finds its ultimate significance only in a religious view of life. His setting in order of temporal society is included in a total religious attitude to life. This is all the more true of the care of the sick, since the problems of illness and death only acquire ultimate significance within man's immediate religious relationship with the living God. The christian's 'presence in the world' in helping and caring for the sick becomes, in the concrete, a presence in the light of redemption, a redeeming presence *in and with* the living God, with whom the christian is personally in communion. The christian's being in the world is a *believing* existence in all of its aspects. The christian's participation in the social services and the care of the sick thus becomes a believing activity. He is in the same genuinely human world as the unbeliever, and both he and the non-christian devote themselves to the care of the sick. But the christian knows, in faith, that his social work in this world is (apart from the fact that it is something for which he receives a salary) also an aspect of the personal relationship between a God who loves man, gives to him and calls to him and man who is called and responds in love. Care

---

although they only gradually penetrate in their full scope to man's consciousness. The christian lay community itself has, on its own responsibility, to carry out the technical organisation of society as a whole, which includes that of the health service, in the perspective of this human source of inspiration sanctioned by the church.

of the sick thus becomes an act of a totally new mode of existence, that of our 'being in Christ' together with many brothers. Divine *caritas*, as the centre and the heart of our christian existence, is not an expression of our being man, but of our intimacy with God, the very act of life of reborn man. Brotherly love is therefore a concrete form of this love of God. And this was made possible by God's love appearing among us in Christ in the sacramental form of a truly human brotherly love. This love is thus at the same time apostolic— its inner dynamism is the salvation of men.

The catholicity of everything the christian does acquires a pregnant fulfilment of meaning in the care of the sick. In the first place, the catholicity presupposes everything that has been said about the secular social services. It recognises the special sphere and the directly human aim of the secular hospital service with its scientific and technical structure and equipment. For this reason, a Catholic hospital must above all be a good hospital and in no way inferior to other hospitals in its provision of medical care and nursing. Catholic *caritas* is directed towards effectively helping those who are ill. The development of the more personal form of charitable work into a more professional system has been practically advantageous to those receiving help and care. *Caritas*, moreover, does not derive its distinctive significance from any form of subjective experience or self-satisfaction, but from the well-being of the other person. In present circumstances, it is only effective when it fully accepts the inner structure of the modern hospital service. The modern hospital service, with its rationalised and specialised structure, provides christian *caritas* with far greater opportunities of expressing itself in effective forms. *Caritas* itself therefore demands a recognition of the total reality in this world of the social services. The catholicity of the health service will therefore only be truly seen when the whole of this system is involved in christian *caritas*. This brings us to the heart of the matter.

First and foremost, although the health service forms part of the social services in general and is expressed in terms of social justice, Catholic care of the sick places this distinctive structure within the framework of christian love. Love, the fundamental inspiration of christian life, acquires a special significance in the context of this external human activity which is directed towards the distress of one's fellow-man. This is the reason for the frequent references in the tradition of the church to corporal and spiritual works of mercy. Not all the external acts which are performed out of love, but only those acts in which the christian helps his fellow-man in a situation of corporal or spiritual distress are known as acts of *caritas* in the narrower sense of the word. Thus the name *caritas catholica* retains its full significance even though social justice is also included within this meaning. *Caritas* here calls justice into being. In the case of a patient presenting himself as someone entitled to treatment, *caritas* will mean that the christian will treat the patient as his neighbour in the christian sense of the word. In the Catholic care of the sick, the sick are regarded and treated as persons subject to God's prevailing personal love in which we all share. The christian bestows the same care as the non-christian, but in his case this care is experienced in an entirely different light, which is also expressed in the care of the sick itself. It is experienced as a *gift from God* himself to mankind *via* the human service of *caritas* in the care of the sick. This christian care of the sick is no longer simply a particular function in the general process of the humanisation of mankind. But within this humanising process the christian's care of the sick becomes a 'sacrament of grace', an instrument of christian *caritas*. In the historically tangible forms of medical attention and nursing it becomes an expression of God's redeeming love of man. The health service is therefore not only an instrument by means of which we cooperate with others in this world in order to raise the life of mankind to a truly human level. It is also a holy sacrament through which we experience in a properly incarnate manner the unity in *caritas* between God and men and between men themselves.

Even when seen in the perspective of a sound philosophy, expert and externally perfect care of the sick is, from the personalistic point of view, asocial if it is carried out without inner inspiration. It is not simply the external social activity that forms community. The human element in social life is to be found in the community of persons which is brought about via the bodily care of the sick. This structure of the human community of persons, in which the bodily care of the sick plays a part, is given a deeper dimension in christianity. The Catholic care of the sick does not derive its perfection only from the practical efficiency with which distress is relieved and enduring health is restored—such external service is not the same whether it is performed with inner *caritas* or without it. *Caritas* does not simply give this service an individual supernatural merit. Although it occurs frequently, such individualism of intention or disposition is unchristian. Both the inner disposition and the external activity are contained in an indissoluble unity in the attitude that is truly social and above all social in the christian sense, and they are both present in such a way that the personal experience of *caritas* brings about the real community of persons through the quasi-sacramental medium of the external expert service. The external service must be the visible form of the inner disposition of *caritas* and thus an offer of and an invitation to personal love. It is only in this way that the rationalisation and specialisation of the hospital service can be united with the interpersonal character of love and Catholic *caritas*. Further, it is only within this unity that there can be any real question of an *apostolate* and especially of an apostolate by expert members of the health service. The primary apostolic value of the Catholic care of the sick is, after all, to be found in the rendering of medical and nursing assistance as the incarnate witness of Christ's love which addresses men personally through this outward act. This unity of inspiration and incarnation is so strong that (except in cases of emergency or in circumstances over which the person has no control) the inner disposition of the christian worker cannot make up for what may be lacking in technical efficiency in the work itself. Modern scientific and technical equipment and service are here at the service of *caritas*. As a consequence of this, *caritas* no longer has, in the present highly organised structure of medical care and nursing, the sensational attributes that it had in the past, nor is it so directly linked with the person himself as it was before. This does not mean that it is any less true *caritas*. This modern structure contains a positive invitation to the person to give himself even more in disinterested service, in which witness to the hidden, almost anonymous life can reach truly mystical heights.

The motive of Catholic *caritas*, which includes the social services and at the same time also transcends them, is not immediately man in distress, but the love of God himself for man, a love which is unconditional and which gives everything, a love which is disinterested in its service of man, a love which is not directed towards man because he is loveable, but does not draw back because he is unloveable, a love which goes beyond ingratitude, sin and hostility and for preference goes out to those most in need of help. The practical consequences of this love cannot be enumerated here, but they are far-reaching.

The fact that the immediate motive of the Catholic care of the sick is not human distress and not even the human person in his situation of need, but the love of God does not mean that we should not love man, but only God, or that man is not an ultimate value in himself. Christian *caritas* goes out to man himself in his concrete existence, but it does this as the love that God has given to us in the Spirit of his Son. This is why *caritas* is even more intimately related to the person of our fellow-man than purely secular care of the sick and why the truly human dimension of the social services only gains a perspective of unexpected depth in christian *caritas* (which is, however, also possible in anonymous christians).

C. *The Catholic hospital*

What I have said so far has been concerned with the essence of the Catholic care of the sick and not with the question as to whether this service should or should not be carried out in a specifically Catholic hospital. This is, after all, not the direct consequence of a Catholic health service—a clear distinction must be made between these two questions. A Catholic doctor or nurse can care for the sick in an essentially Catholic manner in a non-Catholic hospital.

The question of a specifically Catholic hospital is therefore not one of principle. It is rather a practical pastoral question. There can therefore be many different solutions to this problem throughout the course of history. Indeed, we may go further and say that we Catholics may differ in our opinions about this problem even in the present situation. Catholics in different countries and even within the same country may legitimately hold different views, without one group being entitled to accuse the other of lacking a Catholic understanding of the problem. In any case, the following principles must be borne in mind in this context. In principle, christians have as much right as non-christians to organise themselves freely. On the basis of a natural and sound personalism, it is hardly possible to accept action on the part of the state which would make all private initiative impossible. In a mixed society such as our own, if the full witness to Catholic *caritas* becomes practically impossible or at least difficult outside the context of specifically Catholic organisations, Catholics can then avail themselves of this right to organise themselves freely. The Catholic hospital is then not only the exponent of social service in a society that is inspired by truly human motives, but also a visible sign of that divine *caritas* which aims to bring salvation to mankind via the technical and medical care and the nursing provided by those who believe. Such a Catholic hospital serves both a competent health service and a true christianity which expresses itself in the care of the sick. The Catholic spirit can penetrate the whole of this working community from top to bottom and Catholicity can become visible in the entire structure of the hospital. No-one would deny that a Catholic hospital of this kind is in itself the optimum condition for a truly religious care of the sick. It should, however, also be borne in mind that such a hospital is an institution with an immediate secular aim, that of providing a genuine health service in the technical and personalistic sense of the word. Two important consequences are implied in this. In the first place, a Catholic organisation of this kind, with a directly secular aim, does not come directly under the guidance of the church's hierarchy, but under that of the Catholic lay community,[6] which has to perform this task on its own responsibility and in the light of a human and christian inspiration. As in the case of every expression of Catholic life, the bishops ought to be able to exercise control over the Catholic hospital service.[7] The priests concerned, however, are either purely theological advisers or else, like industrial chaplains, priests who find a sociological basis for their distinctively priestly, pastoral task in this particular group of people, that is, the medical, nursing, administrative and domestic staff of the hospital and, of course, the patients themselves.

As soon as a truly christian life of *caritas* becomes manifest in a hospital that has been set up by Catholics (this is something that is at least implicitly recognised as such by the church), then we may speak of an authentically Catholic hospital.

The second consequence of the Catholic hospital's having an immediate secular aim is that the Catholic hospital cannot possibly be regarded as a second-class state hospital. What has come from the people themselves, including the Catholic section of the population, is no less a part of the state structure than what has been directly set up by the state itself. Anyone who denies this is clearly placing the interests of the state above those of the people. Further, it is also important to note in this context that a Catholic hospital that is recognised by the state and receives a subsidy from the state does not in any way lose its Catholic character.

[6] By lay people in this context, I mean those who are not priests. Religious brothers and sisters are therefore also included within the category 'lay' in this connection. It is difficult to see why preference should be given to members of religious orders, for reasons of principle, in the Catholic care of the sick, but it cannot be denied that they have a very special function in this service. The religious state is, after all, the visible form in this world of that aspect of christian *caritas* which provides a sign of the *eschaton* that transcends this world. The character of *caritas* must therefore be powerfully expressed in a visible manner in the care of the sick when this is done by members of religious communities. This, however, does not occur automatically simply because they are religious.

[7] See *Codex iuris canon.* III can. 1515–16, §3; II can. 336.

A Catholic hospital certainly realises the optimum conditions for the Catholic care of the sick. For extrinsic reasons, however, the Catholic hospital service has many disadvantages. In a mixed society such as our own, such a situation inevitably leads to divisions along confessional lines. It is becoming increasingly clear that only our fellow Catholics are reached via the Catholic hospital. The apostolic function is not hereby lost, but the missionary aspect of the witness of *caritas* is not given any opportunity to express itself. It should, of course, not be forgotten that the real apostolic significance of the Catholic hospital is to be found in the apostolate of the care of the sick—the Catholic hospital is not an institution set up for missionary purposes. The Catholic hospital should not be expected to have any other purpose than the one for which it was created. The real purpose and consequently the real limits of such Catholic organisations should be loyally accepted. The Catholic hospital continues to realise fully, as a Catholic hospital, the essence of the *caritas catholica*, even in these circumstances. But—and this is not unimportant— full and visible justice is not done, in these circumstances, to the christian theme of *caritas*, which is, after all, universal and is, for the sake of God, directed towards all men and especially to those most in need of help. In fact, in these circumstances, care of the sick is limited to Catholics. The universality of *caritas* is undoubtedly restricted—not inwardly, certainly, because it is not Catholic *caritas* itself which makes this selection, but in any case externally. What is more, there is also an element of competition between the Catholic and the non-Catholic institutions and quite often a struggle for positions of power. The church, which should be the universal invitation to love, thus becomes, at the secular level, an organisation in competition with other similar organisations. The disadvantages of this can, of course, be eliminated to some extent by *humanising* this competition and this struggle for power. But this situation as well as our understanding of the very essence of Catholic *caritas* certainly draw our attention to the *purely relative* value of a Catholic hospital. *Caritas catholica* should consequently not be entirely and exclusively bound to and restricted to the specifically Catholic hospital. The catholicity of the care of the sick also demands that not all the available Catholic doctors and nurses working in the hospital service should be employed exclusively in Catholic hospitals. The witness of *caritas* must be able to be heard elsewhere as well. The catholicity of the care of the sick must act as a leaven in non-Catholic hospitals as well. Dialogue and loyal cooperation with non-Catholic hospitals are also required by the purely relative value of the Catholic hospital.

Finally, the Catholic hospital is not in any respect an unchangeable demand of Catholic *caritas*. It is certainly a fundamental demand of catholicism that it should be able and allowed to testify to itself in this world and in its activities. But this essential demand is not identical with specifically Catholic organisations.

Perhaps, in our own age, we have more need of a 'period of transition' in which the presence of catholicism in the world is increasingly obliged to assume new forms. No true appraisal of changing historical situations will be made by theological principles alone. A sensitive examination and interpretation of the spirit of the age and the spiritual situation in which man lives and wise christian guidance must also play a part in this. We have a duty, as christians, to try to discover the direction in which man's development is moving so that we are not taken off our guard by what might otherwise be abrupt changes in the social system. Instead we should actively prepare the way for and accept a new existence that will be intense and splendid for our faith, but also possibly more difficult to follow. If everything that is taking place in the world is taken carefully into account, it must be clear to every thinking man that it is not enough to oppose the unmistakable development of mankind by clinging inflexibly to established positions. More than ever before, we need in the present age what Professor Albert Dondeyne has called a 'morality of the period of transition'. Institutions in this world that are concerned with the spread of the kingdom of God go back, in one way or another, to the supernatural mystery. These institutions must, however, be overhauled again and again in the light of this mystery. Although we may still accept these Catholic organisations today, their very catholicity requires a certain flexibility and independence with regard to the institutions, which may perhaps, as a result of the development of mankind, be taken from us. What was, in the past, a help to the effective and missionary confession of religion and perhaps still is a help today, may, in the future, be a hindrance. The same christian spirit that, in the past, set up these specifically Catholic organisations may perhaps have to take the initiative and, in the light of the same apostolic inspiration, change to a different system, if Christ is to be preached and the sick are to be effectively helped with expert skill in the light of a Catholic inspiration.

It is, however, in no sense my intention to put forward a case for the abolition of the Catholic hospital service. I am only pleading for the necessity of a Catholic morality of the period of transition. But in this connection it should always be remembered that the ordering of life in this world should never be taken out of the hands of the Catholic lay community, as though lay Catholics had no say in the organisation of society and were inferior citizens of the state and the world. On the contrary, this work of organisation is the real lay christian task of the people of God, their own distinctive sphere of activity. And if they at the same time play a part in ensuring that the hospital service is not simply conducted with scientific and technical professional skill, but is also carried out with due consideration for fundamental human and christian values, then the catholicity of the care of the sick will be revealed in its true form.

MAN AND HIS BODILY WORLD

1. The christian approach to human bodiliness

After treatment of the human body from the anatomical, physiological, biochemical, psycho-pharmacological, psychological and philosophical points of view, we may well ask whether any aspect that lends itself to a theological approach to the human body still remains to be discussed. To this I must reply that, so far, only the philosopher and the psychologist have considered the human body. Because of their own special method, biologists—I use this word here and shall continue to use it in the rest of this chapter as a collective name for all those engaged in all branches of the natural sciences that are concerned with the study of the living body —consider only the body of man, not the *human* body, which, in its very humanity, lies outside the scope of their method. But it is certainly possible to say that there is indeed nothing left for the theologian to consider—just as the philosopher does not dwell on that aspect of the human body which is left after that body has been considered in all its aspects from the scientific point of view, but studies the *totality* of the human body, so too does the theologian reflect, not about a partial aspect of human bodiliness, but about its totality, insofar as the experience of faith sheds any light on it. And, since theology is a reflection in the light of faith about the content of human experience which has already been made explicit in the natural sphere by philosophy, the theologian has constantly to return to the anthropological insights of the philosopher and include these in the totality of faith. The theological approach is only possible through living contact between faith in reflection and human experience and the insights of the positive sciences and philosophy.

A. *Biblical and renewed anthropology*

It is, in the first place, particularly significant that what revelation has to tell us about man is very different from what most biologists, philosophers and theologians have to tell us. Even when the latter consciously try to avoid platonic, and above all cartesian, anthropological dualism, what they say still betrays an implicit dualistic assumption. This emerges clearly in the so-called psychophysical problem. What is the explanation for the fact that any interference with the body has an influence on psychical and spiritual activities? The one has an influence on the other—there are somatical activities and psychical consequences or psychical activities and somatical consequences. A certain dualism is therefore taken as the point of departure—one talks about body and soul—and the whole problem consists in *reconciling* these two data. Not experience, then, but a definite theory is taken as the point of departure, and, what is more, a theory which already provides a solution to the problem and indeed a solution in a wrong sense, that is, in a purely dualistic sense.

But is it perhaps not because the question has been wrongly posed that the so-called psychophysical problem is insoluble? There is, after all, a tacit assumption of dualism in the formulation of the question. If, however, we contrast this implicit dualism of our acquired image of man with man's spontaneous, even primitive mode of experience as seen in all those peoples who were not influenced by the dualistic ideas of the Greeks, we at once encounter a completely different image of man. Such a view prevailed in the world in which God's revelation took place directly—the world of Semitic thought. And, even though we must continue to make a distinction between the Semitic image of man and the specifically biblical anthropology (the two are not necessarily identical), we are nonetheless bound to say that the view of man that prevailed in the Semitic world was undoubtedly able to express more purely the distinctive nature of man's supernatural and christian salvation. In contrast, the dogma of the redemption of the whole of man by Christ was con-

stantly threatened by Greek dualism—it was precisely this
way of thinking about man that gave rise to the heresies
concerned with man's redemption in the early church.

It is a striking fact that *our* terms 'body' and 'soul' were
completely unknown to the writers of the Old Testament,
who saw man as a self-evident unity. For them, the whole man
was body and the whole man was spirit. Man was not a body
and in addition also a soul. Not the body, but the *human*
body was, according to biblical anthropology, the whole man.
'Flesh'—in Latin *caro*, in Greek *sarx* and in Hebrew *bāśār*—
meant simply man as a reality, the source of bodily and non-
bodily phenomena. Soul and human body—these were, for
the Old Testament authors, synonymous. This moreover
applied not only to the body as a whole, but also to all the
parts of the body. The liver, the kidneys, the hand, the blood,
the face and so on—these were all both bodily and spiritual.
These parts of the human body were not used metaphorically
by the Semite who thought within the framework of divine
revelation—as we, for example, use the heart as the symbol
of love—they formed part of his total anthropological vision.
The face *was*, for him, the person who was turned towards
him, and seeing someone 'face to face' meant encountering
him directly as a person. All the parts of the human body
thus had, in the biblical view of man, both a bodily and a
spiritual meaning, not in any dualistic sense, but in the sense
that a spiritual activity took place within a bodily activity.
For the Semite, increased beating of the heart was love itself,
as human love—only when thus bodily manifested, was
love a human reality. A bodily expression was always an expression of the *whole* of man, just as a non-bodily or spiritual
expression also concerned the whole of man. In its primitive
expression of God's creation of man, the bible does not say
that Yahweh first formed man's body from the earth and then
blew the soul into it—such dualism was alien to the bible.
What it says is that God fashioned the whole man and made
a *nepheš* of him, that is, a living man.

What is the underlying intention of this primitive idea of
man? It is that the whole man, man as a unity, is the work of

God the creator. Man is, in his totality, a living soul. The Old Testament writers were so deeply convinced of the anthropological unity that they situated the whole man, after death, in the underworld, where he led—body and soul—a shadowy existence. Here, however, Semitic thinking did not faithfully reflect the data of revelation—*something* was correct in Platonism, namely that man was primarily spiritual and only secondarily, although equally essentially, bodily. Towards the end of the Old Testament, therefore, we are aware, with increasing clarity, of a new emphasis within this monistic view of man—an emphasis on the transcendence of a spiritual principle over man's bodiliness. This spiritual principle does not, however, in the later books of the Old Testament, transcend the *humanity* of man's bodiliness, since this to some extent coincides with man's transcendence over material nature.

It is clear, then, from this brief outline of the biblical view of man that being man was, for the authors of the Old Testament, a special mode of bodily existence. For the Semite, the whole of man was body and the whole of man was soul. Man's soul was both something of the body and something of itself. The *soul* was the distinctively *human* mode of bodily existence and the body had this thanks to the *spirit*.

This view may well be regarded as primitive, but it is undoubtedly the spontaneous expression of pre-reflective experience. It is, moreover, characteristic that twentieth-century existential thought, which has constantly aimed to throw light on precisely this pre-reflective experience, has come to almost identical conclusions and, what is more, with the same one-sidedness that characterises the original Semitic thought.

Thus, Merleau-Ponty, who may be regarded as the exponent of this tendency, has said seeing as man sees and being spirit are synonymous. Under the influence of an implicit dualism, we, on the other hand, would put the matter spontaneously in the following way—as a result of an external stimulus or of an internal biological stimulus within the body, the central nervous system, the reticular formation and a number of other biological structures in our body come into operation. In this way, the stimulus becomes ultimately a sensory perception—I see, I hear, I feel. We forget, however, that we have already introduced a spiritual factor here, since we say *I* see. But where does this consciousness of self, this *I*, come from? So we go on to put it in this way—*behind* this sensory perception lurks a soul with a spiritual capacity to know, a soul that derives something from what is seen or heard that the eye has not seen or the ear has not heard. The reality of experience, however, is different. My seeing itself is not a seeing if it is not a *human* seeing—*I see* and I see *knowingly*. Human seeing is always a knowing seeing. The transcendental is always expressed in the biological and psychical—I know *in* perception, not after it. One of the principal elements in *Gestalt*-forming seeing is, as our colleague Calon has explained, identification—the identification of what is perceived as a definite something by an *I* that knows. There is no *human* perception without identification and there is no identification without human perception. This is furthermore confirmed by the pathology of perception—the authentically human element in the perception of mentally disturbed people is either not at all or else only partially present, so that the vague seeing of such people more resembles the 'nocturnal', purely subjective and biologically determined seeing of the animal.

It is clear, then, from the foregoing that we are spirit in our body and that our body too is spirit, although in the bodily mode. Biologists can therefore never make any statement about this human body as such. They can make statements about man's body, but not about the human body. That is why the problem of freedom does not arise for the biologist in his capacity as biologist. This reality does not come within his scientific vocabulary. The only thing that the philosopher and the theologian can ask of the biologist as such is that he should, regardless of what they may say about man, remain conscious of the fact that this one aspect of the reality of man which he studies cannot be regarded as a total image of what man is. The human 'soul' has no place in the biologist's vocabulary. As soon as he does begin to talk about the 'soul', he at once abandons his scientific point of view and takes up a different point of view, concerned with man as a whole. From the human and christian point of view, this more integral viewpoint is, however, necessary, so long as we do not forget that this is a much wider field than that of biology and that, in this wider field, laws and structures which are different from those of the biological reality are brought into play. The specialist in the sphere of biological science as such can therefore say nothing about the relationship between the soul and the body, although the results of his investigation, together with the data of general human experience, provide us—that is, man as man and as a believer and, at the reflective level, the philosopher and the theologian —with the facts with which we are able to determine this relationship.

What, then, is the *datum* that we are studying in these papers in its full scope? The immediate datum of human experience is man who is a corporeal being. This is the first basic datum. But something special has also to be taken into account in connection with this corporeal being, man—there are discernible phenomena that, with all the good will in the world, cannot be reduced to pure corporeality, because they display qualities that are diametrically opposed to the being of this corporeality. As our colleague Van Melsen has pointed out in the previous lecture, the animal being merges into its environment and only does what has been previously determined in its biological nature. Even acts of so-called intelligent behaviour in the animal are unintelligible without the activation of biological factors—this is clear from our observation of the training of animals, which is ultimately based on Pavlov's reflexes of a biological and psychical nature. The so-called psychical element in an animal is a purely biological mode of being. It cannot be distinguished from the natural impulse of the animal—it is the distinctive manner in which the natural impulse of a biological being appears. What is perceived simply has the value of a stimulus which sets the coercively predetermined nature in motion towards biological stimuli.[1]

The same also applies to man. In his case too, sensory knowledge—which our colleague Prick has called the biological and psychical element—is in itself biological corporeality. It is not an objective knowledge, but a psychism in which the 'knowing' aspect cannot be distinguished from the striving aspect—the biological and psychical element is *inwardly* at the same time a dynamic striving towards or turning away from what is positively or negatively valuable in the biological sense. This explains why so-called intelligent behaviour in animals displays so much that is comparable with certain acts of human behaviour.[2]

But this is only one aspect of what the reality of man reveals to us in experience. We are well aware of aspects which are associated with man's activities and which are distinguished by characteristics that are quite opposed to those previously mentioned. There is, for example, man's technical activity. He is educated, not trained like an animal. It is always possible for man to sacrifice his life for higher values. He is active in the spheres of science and art, he experiences beauty and fashions language. Finally and above all, he has a moral and religious attitude towards life. It should therefore be quite clear that, although there are remote, but nonetheless striking resemblances with the animal world, a different active principle is obviously involved in the case of the corporeal being we call man, a principle which, despite the fact that it is manifested only in and through the body, is not inwardly bodily or biological. What is peculiar to man, in other words, what is specifically human and makes man distinct from all animals is, then, that he can freely choose to *distance* himself from his environment and his biological structure. He can not only approach reality insofar as this reality is biologically interesting to him—he can also approach it in itself, as an absolute value. This shows that his know-

1 See E. Straus, *Vom Sinn der Sinne*, Berlin 1956[2].
2 See F. J. J. Buytendijk, *Mensch und Tier*, Hamburg 1958.

ledge transcends the purely biological—that he also has objectively oriented consciousness.

There are, in other words, activities in the corporeal being that we call man which indicate a completely unbiological reality—freedom. As in the case of animals, there is also in man a determined biological and psychical consciousness which is activated by an external stimulus or an internal biological stimulus and this consciousness is of its very nature also a striving towards the biological as a pleasant experience. But man also possesses, unlike animals, the astonishing faculty—a faculty which is based on his inner conviction, his sense of the ideal and ultimately on his objective consciousness—of being able to say no to this tendency which is in itself biologically determined and psychical.

On the basis of this, we are bound to conclude that there is also a spiritual principle active in man. This spiritual principle is not a postulate or a fruit of religious awareness—it is a pure fact of experience, the explicitation of a datum of experience. It is not even a conclusion, in the sense of an inference drawn from experience. It is experience itself that has been made lucid from within by phenomenological analysis. This means that man, whom we experience as biological nature, cannot, however, be identified with this nature —he *is not* this nature, he only *has* it. Or rather, he *is* this nature, but he is also more than this nature. And, what is more, he is more than this biological nature *primarily and in the first place*, since it is precisely in this that the corporeal being that we call man is distinguished from the animal being—and here I am consciously dissociating myself from the view held by Merleau-Ponty, who ultimately denies man's value as a person. Man is therefore, in his distinctive quality as man, a being in whom an absolute beginning is present, a freedom, with the result that, as man, he does not go back to ancestors and is also not an aspect of a cosmic evolution or a natural series. Appearing in nature, he *confronts* this nature —he is an *I*, a person.

But he is a person of a very distinctive type. He is not a

creative I, but an I who can only make his freedom felt with regard to a natural biological impulse in confrontation with which he has to appear as man giving meaning. He is an I, a freedom which is at every moment called to appear as man giving meaning in the situation in which this freedom is always involved by its bodiliness. Thus we conclude that man is a person, but a person who only comes to himself by constantly going outwards in and through his body. The human person, then, comes to himself in going outwards.

Instead of approaching man from below, it is also possible to view him from above. Man is a spiritual freedom which is essentially conditioned by a body. His bodiliness enters his free act. In everything that he is, man is, in his distinctively human quality, at the same time bodily. Thus we can say that the human spirit is *spirit (subsistens) in the mode of self-participation with the body (forma corporis)*.[3]

The body is thus only human insofar as it shares in the spiritual mode of being of the soul and the soul is only human insofar as it communicates itself to the body. It is in this that the essence both of human spirituality and of human bodiliness is to be found. Insofar as man is authentically man, there is, then, a quasi-identity between what we call soul and what we call body. Within this unity, however, there is complexity and distinction—the spirit is incarnate in an *alien* bodiliness which it humanises, but with which it can never fully identify itself, since this would eliminate bodiliness. All dualism is pernicious, but it is impossible to deny the existence of a certain 'duality' within the unity of soul and body. This can help to explain the fact that man is not yet, here on earth, fully man and that his bodiliness in the same way is not, in all its aspects, human bodiliness. My body is not, in all its parts, equally *my* body. This moreover applies to such an extent that man, in his least humanised aspects, merges, so to

---

[3] D. de Petter, *Het persoon-zijn onder thomistisch-metafysische belichting*, the text of a paper given in 1948 to the Nederlandse Vereniging voor Thomistische Wijsbegeerte, the Dutch association for Thomist philosophy, and later included in De Petter's collected studies, *Begrip en werkelijkheid*, Hilversum and Antwerp 1964, 186–216.

speak, into the material universe.[4] It is not possible to draw a clear dividing line between man's body and the bodiliness of his environment, as Alexis Carrel explained in a masterly, poetic manner in his *L'homme, cet inconnu* and, as an atomic scientist has said, quite correctly, whenever a child cries in its cradle, the heavenly bodies vibrate. Man's body is really a piece of the material universe. It is only human insofar as it shares in the spirit. Man is therefore that piece of the cosmic world in which it, at that one point, becomes the expression and presence of a spiritual and transcendent reality. Being essentially in the world, man transcends it. But he is a transcendence which can only make himself felt in this material world, the appropriate environment of his human life. Since, then, the essence of man does not consist of a combination of soul and body, but of the spirit's communication of itself to the body, it is also clear that if this participation is disturbed or impeded, for example, by sickness, drunkenness, an injection or pathological disturbances, man himself is disturbed or impeded in his state of *being man*.

As transcending the body, the spirit cannot really be influenced by the biological. But man is only man insofar as he has a body which really *lends itself to* this communication of the spirit. In this very special sense, we may say that the spiritual aspect of man is dependent on the bodily aspect. If man's body is affected, for example, by an injection, *man* himself is affected and therefore his spirit as well, since man is spirit in his body. Because of the—admittedly complex— unity, the one 'is' the other. Because of man's distinctive quality as spirit in the mode of self-communication to the body, a somatic event has a psychical aspect and a psychical event has a somatic aspect. We can therefore extend what the atomic scientist said and say that the heavenly bodies vibrate whenever man thinks and wills. Man's thinking and willing may be spiritual and therefore of quite a different order, but they are *also* a mineral and biochemical event. It is also true in the case of man that every interaction of two molecules

---

[4] S. Strasser, *Het zielsbegrip in de metafysische en in de empirische psychologie*, Louvain and Nijmegen 1950, 100–39.

takes place according to mineral laws and not because of a push given by the psyche. What causes different cells to combine with each other is not psychism or a 'life principle', but the chemical affinities of, shall I say, protein complexes. But all this forms a substantial unity with the human activity of the spirit, so that an act of human will is really a biochemical process, as the biologists tell us. This means that the biologist only sees the biological aspect of this act of the will, the biological aspect that is essentially connected with the act of the will, but the act of the will completely transcends this aspect. The clenched fist, the surge of blood and the whole of this biological tension 'is', in quasi-identity, human anger precisely as human, that is, as inwardness which constitutes itself as inwardness by incarnation in the bodily (sincere or simulated, since the free will can, in this case, direct the incarnation). This makes it possible to understand how a disturbance in this biological structure is also a *human* disturbance—a disturbance in the life of the spirit.

What is so unsatisfactory in the way in which the so-called mind-body problem is presented is that the soul is regarded as a pure spirit which is—God knows how—connected with the body. In this way, the problem is insoluble. The situation is quite different if the body—as *human* body—is regarded as an *aspect* of human subjectivity, an aspect of the *I* itself. Cartesianism, which reduced the unity of the soul and the body to an external relationship of two more or less independent parts, gave rise to the mind-body problem and at the same time made it impossible to solve this problem by presenting it incorrectly. This dualism dehumanised both the human spirit and the human body—the spirit became pure interiority and the body pure exteriority. This is precisely the definition of dualism.

All this points ultimately to the fact that being man is not something that is ready-made or given, but a task to be performed. The point of departure is a fundamental freedom which is given by God and which is initially, so to speak, at zero, but which has to make itself gradually felt as a result of varying contacts with the world through the body. In this sense, the spirit opens up in and through bodily events. If we spontaneously think of our being spirit by taking, as our model, biological nature which is in itself fully equipped from the very beginning, we view it incorrectly. This spontaneous view of our being spirit is, in other words, a view of the spirit as a 'nature'.

We should, however, put the problem in the following way. Man, in his fundamental freedom, possesses the ability to *make* himself free and thus, as man, freely to give himself a definite character as he himself wishes. Man's being is therefore a being-of-possibility which has to make itself—this is the distinctive attribute of the spirit as compared with the bodily nature with which the spirit is connected. The foetus is man in a very distinctive mode, just as the child is man in the mode of a child, a mode in which the human element hardly comes into play. Because of the complex unity that man is, all kinds of bodily, biological and psychical and social conditions are required for this fundamental freedom to be released. It is therefore even possible for the internal and external conditions of life to be, in certain cases, such that this fundamental human freedom is never able to come into play. If, for example, a biologist demonstrates that a certain injection into the human body makes man perform an action which is predictable or that a certain stimulation of the cortex of the brain always evokes the same fantasy, the only answer that we can give to this is, very good, I accept this fact, but I must add that this man is simply not acting as man—he is still within the purely biological sphere, that is all, and the element that is specifically human—and this is a task—has not been able to come into play. This should not surprise us as soon as we are aware that being man is a *becoming* man and freedom is a *making* free, a task and not a reality which is already given and finished, as it were, behind our body, even before we make our appearance actively in the world.

At the same time, all this also points to the profoundly human significance of the biological sciences. They are called so to influence the body by their scientific control of matter that the body can really make itself available to the spirit's communication of itself to the body and thus to the world. They form an important element in the general process of the humanisation of man and the world as mankind's task within this world. They can also make it possible for man to live freely and thus morally and religiously, although it is up to human freedom alone to determine precisely how man is to give value to his life—for good or for evil.

B. *Creation and evolution*

We must, however, return to the sphere of pure theology. The reality which I have just tried to clarify can only be understood in its full significance in the light of our consciousness as believers.

We know, from the dogma of creation, that the soul was created in a special manner by God, that is, as an absolute beginning without horizontal precedents or bonds. In figurative language, we may say that man, as a spiritual being, comes directly—vertically—from the hands of God. Let us, however, try to understand this properly. Everything, including the material world, comes directly from the hands of God. God did not first create a primordial atom or a primordial mist, from which the whole of the world later came into being from within by means of gradual development, without any further activity on the part of God the creator. It is up to the natural sciences to demonstrate to us whether there is evolution—philosophy and theology cannot make any judgement here. But if there is evolution, we are bound to say that there is, horizontally, certainly a vast process of development, but that precisely this development, vertically, is the object of God's creation. God's creative activity cannot be added to the inward forces of evolution within this world. God creates things in their structure of mutual dependence.

But the human spirit is a separate case. As spirit, man cannot be reduced to a structure within this world. As spirit, he is an absolutely new beginning. Otherwise, he would not be free, but the result of a natural event, which, by its very nature, implies the absence of freedom. God's creation of man in a special manner simply means, then, that he has created a being who, in his spiritual nature, cannot be an effect of ancestors or of nature, but a being who, on the contrary, confronts this nature as an *I*. The transition from the biological to the human cannot be understood on the model of the transition from the mineral to the vegetable and to the living body. Ultimately, the biological or living body is simply a specific complexity of physical chemical elements, even though the new structure is more than the sum of its parts— it is not an aggregate, but rather an 'integrate'.[5] In the case of the transition from animal to man, however, the situation is quite different. Here, some philosophers and theologians are frequently dualistic in their thinking.

These philosophers and theologians say that man's body is derived, by virtue of evolution, from a higher species of animal or at least from his human parents and only his soul is infused into him directly by God. By explaining the origin of man in this way, they are inevitably formulating a dualistic view of man. It is not, however, their claim that God directly infused man's soul into him that is wrong. Although we should not regard this infusion of the soul as a separate 'intervention' on God's part, but as a divinely transcendent act which does not take place from without, but which from the very essence of all things holds them creatively in its hand, we cannot avoid speaking, in human terms, of an infusion of the soul, if we are to safeguard man's freedom. No, what is wrong in this dualistic view of man is that those who maintain it forget that the *humanity* of the body is something of the soul itself, the soul's communication of itself to the body, by means of which man is man. In this way, the human body is the spirit appearing in our world. A corpse is not a human body and really has nothing more to do with the deceased person. (This is despite the fact that our conduct with regard to this corpse is reverent. For higher motives, however, such as the furtherance of medical science, it is permissible to treat this corpse as what it is, namely a piece of nature.) From the moment that man's body, for biological reasons, is funda-

[5] E. W. Sinnott, *The Biology of the Spirit*, London 1956.

mentally and radically no longer receptive to the communication of the soul, we say that this man is dead.

Unlike a corpse, the human body is the visible appearance
of an I. The humanisation of the body is synonymous with
man's being as spirit. Insofar as it is human, our body cannot
be explained by means of evolution, phylogenesis or onto-
genesis. This seems to me to be one of the basic errors of
Teilhard de Chardin's otherwise impressive synthesis. As a
unity of soul and body, man can only come directly from the
hands of God without horizontal bonds with the biological
world, though not, of course, without being conditioned biologically. Living nature, after all, bears within itself the
power, created by God, to grow and feed, in each distinctive
organism, new cells which, alone or together with others, are
the beginning of new life. We have no need to speak, in this
instance, of a divine intervention in rather childish terms—
the whole of this process is, after all, part of God's creation.
But, in the case of man, it is quite different.

From the very moment that the conditions are present for
a new human life—the fusion of two cells—we are confronted
with a new life and thus, concretely, with the beginning of a
new man. At that moment, spirit is present. We can hardly
form any idea of this association of human and divine activity
and so we say that, at that moment, the soul is infused. This
expression is correct because man's creation is the beginning
of a relationship of dialogue between God and the human
person. This creation is unique, an absolutely new beginning
which calls into being a direct relationship with God. This
absolutely new beginning also concerns, via the soul, the
human body. We must be guided by the positive sciences as
to whether there is any question of evolution in this case and
scientists have become increasingly sceptical about this in
recent years. But if there is scientific proof of evolution in
this instance, only the philosopher and the theologian can
reveal its significance—that the *human* body cannot have
come about as the result of evolution and what did possibly
come about as a result of evolution must, in any case, have
undergone a true 'transubstantiation' from the human soul

in order to become a *human* body. It is only in this way that we are able to avoid all forms of dualism and materialism and at the same time avoid falling into a one-sided spiritualism.

There is therefore a discontinuity between the nature of animal and human bodies, even though there may be, from the biological point of view, no hiatus and even though continuity can be established at this level even as far as the mineral world. As a body, the human body may well be the inward culminating point of materiality, but, as a *human* body, this body is completely discontinuous with any other evolutionary form, since it is an aspect of the spirit.

It is only in this way that the distinctive quality of the 'phenomenon of man' in this world can be maintained and that human freedom can at the same time be safeguarded. The more human the body is, the more it is the eccentric mode of existence of the spirit itself, the spirit in its manifestation in this world. An interiority that manifests itself—which is, after all, what the human body is—is very different from any determination by evolution from ancestors! Because of the unique quality of the human, it is possible for the philosopher and the theologian to ask the biologist whether evolution and descent from parents are identical! The distinctive reality of man is not accessible to the exact sciences. It is therefore characteristic of the problem that, while evolution is, generally speaking, becoming more and more certain, the origin of man seems, according to what specialists say, to be less and less clear and more and more problematical. Integral evolutionism can, at present, only be regarded as a visionary idea which goes beyond what can be established by critical data.

C. *Death*

Light is thrown, from the perspective of experience and faith, on the distinctive mode of being that man is not only by man's origin in this world, but also by his disappearance from the world.[6] If we regard death as a biological event, it

[6] For death as a biological phenomenon, see M. d'Halluin, *La mort, cette inconnue*, Paris 1952²; for death from the philosophical point of view, D. de

appears to us as something normal. Death simply points to the fact that man, in his body, is a piece of nature. If, however, we take the *humanity* of this body into account and thus regard death as an event in man himself, human experience can scarcely be reconciled with this fact. This is clear in the case of the death of someone with whom we have had a personal relationship. The death of a person who is dear to us is something that we regard as impossible and absurd. The fact that we are allowing our personal relationships with the dying person to be related to the experience of his death does not mean that our experience of the absurdity of his death is therefore subjective. On the contrary—in this experience, we are reflecting about the death of a person precisely as a person, because it is only in a personal relationship with a fellow-man that someone is encountered as a person, as more than an 'abstract case'. This experience of the death of a person precisely as a person makes clear that there is a disproportion between the biological event and its consequences, which are on an entirely different plane, of the end of personal relationships with this particular dead person.

The experience of the death of a fellow-man, then, causes us to protest against the absurdity of the fact that personal relationships, and thus the person himself, should have ceased to exist simply and solely because of a chance or a necessary biological event, such as the breaking of a muscle in the heart or a diseased stomach, liver or kidneys. But to the evident experience of this disproportion can be added a certainty of a different kind which seems to contradict the first—the undeniable reality of man's essential incarnation. In the case of a person's death, we are also confronted with the evident fact that cannot be denied—that this person has been taken away from us, that, for us at least, he is no longer there, and this

---

Petter, 'De onsterfelijkheid', *Kultuurleven* 23 (1956), pp 11–22, later included in *Begrip en werkelijkheid*, 217–33; for death from the philosophical and theological point of view, E. Schillebeeckx, 'The death of a Christian', *Vatican II, a Struggle of Minds and Other Essays*, Dublin 1963 (published in the USA as *The Layman in the Church*, Staten Island, N.Y., 1963), pp 61–91; see also P. L. Landsberg, *Essai sur l'expérience de la mort*, Paris (1951).

arouses in us the fear that he is no longer there at all. It is clear that we cannot escape from the experience that personal contact and human intercourse, although these are of quite a different kind from those of purely bodily and organic activities, are only possible through the body. The affection that the deceased person had for us existed only insofar as it appeared before us and addressed us in that person's bodily presence and appearance. We may go even farther and say that the body is not simply the medium through which our fellow-man orientates himself towards us—the human person also gives his own inner life form only in his body, in the expressions and effects which bodily activity bestows on personal activity. But death eliminates this body and the result of this is that personal contacts with the deceased person are cut off and new contacts are impossible, so that we live only on memories of the dead person. The human spirit is, in life, essentially directed, in and through its own bodiliness, towards the bodily world and towards other persons; death, rather than, as Platonic and Cartesian dualism claims, the body is its 'prison'. In death it is really as if the soul went to sleep. Even though we are bound to affirm man's continued existence as a person, we can, because of man's essential incarnation, only regard the continued existence of the dead person *naturally*, that is, without the help of the light of revelation, as a continued existence in a state of spiritual lethargy, isolation and non-activity, as a pale, helpless, reduced and inferior kind of existence. This was indeed the way in which death was spontaneously regarded by all primitive peoples and even the way in which it was originally regarded within the pagan religious view of the Greeks and the Romans. Sheol, Hades or the underworld—these were universally regarded as a twilight realm of the departed spirits in which only a shadowy existence was possible. The despair that is present in the experience of the death of a beloved fellow-man is attributable to the contradiction between these two evident facts—on the one hand, that we cannot accept the fact that a purely biological event should cause the person to cease to exist and, on the other hand, the experience of the fact that he no longer exists for us in any case because of the cessation of bodily life.

If we analyse the implicit content of this experience of despair, the result has two elements. In the first place, the person—and let me say here, the soul, although this is inaccurate—must continue to exist because this continued existence is simply another name for the person's transcendence of bodily life. Once it has been called into existence, with and in a body, the spirit can no longer be affected, *in its existence*, by the fortunes of the body and cannot even be affected by death. On the other hand, however, we cannot, naturally, form any positive idea as to how the spirit continues to exist after death. This leads consequently to our feeling that the so-called 'departed soul' cannot be comprehended or grasped, that it is not essential, to our experience of emptiness with regard to it.

It is, of course, this feeling that makes it difficult for us to be certain that the dead person still continues to live outside our terrestrial world. But, if a truth presents itself to us in conditions that are less satisfactory from the psychological point of view, we have the moral and intellectual duty to accept that truth precisely as it presents itself, in other words, with all these difficulties. Insights into living realities are never mathematically or physically certain. They call for moral openness. Man's possession of the truth is always delicate and precarious. It is completely the opposite to rationalism, which is convinced that we have the truth in our grasp. But, for us, truth is no more than a small light in the darkness. This idea that we have of the dead person leading a helpless, reduced and isolated existence, insofar as we can form any judgement of this existence from our human experience, in other words, the absurd end of human life, is confirmed in the light of faith and revelation. According to the view of life provided by revealed religion, death, although it is in itself normal and natural, is in fact a punishment for sin. The dead person's being dead is thus no more than an extension of this punishment, its inner consequence—the state of the so-called 'departed soul' thus shares in the absurdity of sin itself. This state can be understood in the light of mankind's situation in the absence of salvation.

The death of the person who nonetheless continues to exist and its consequence, his state of disintegration, thus essentially merges into a religious problem. Something is happening to man. The problem presents itself naturally, but it is only revelation that can throw light on it. The natural immortality of the soul is certainly a victory of the spirit over matter, but at the same time it is also a fatal failure of the human person. Revelation gives us insight into the religious backgrounds of this datum. It confirms the absurdity of death and of the undesirable state of disintegration of the 'departed soul'. In contrast with Platonic dualism, this means that the natural immortality of the soul does not imply any promise or expectation of salvation. This immortality is the ultimate failure of human life. The absurdity of the 'departed soul' is the freely caused absurdity of sin itself in its anthropological consequences. In itself, the 'departed soul' is, of its very nature, an *unredeemed* soul—a situation of hell. Under the influence of Greek dualism, scholasticism completely overlooked this. The 'departed soul' is not a pure spirit, but an absurd situation of essentially incarnate man, a genuine 'imprisonment', a complete 'de-situation' of the human person—at least without redemption, since redemption makes everything quite different for the departed soul. There is, then, a radical difference between the wretched *natural* immortality of the human soul and its *christian* immortality. Natural immortality is the implication of the human person and, as such, it is a guarantee of the transcendence of the human spirit. But, because this transcendence is essentially incarnate, the natural immortality of the human spirit is a state of disintegration for the dead person. Christian immortality, on the other hand, is the implication of man's community of grace with the living God. Whereas the only idea that we can form naturally of the continued existence of the soul after death is that of a wretched, inferior existence that is thrown back on itself, we know, in the light of revelation, that the post-terrestrial life of the person who has died in the community of grace with the living God is above all a redemption of the soul of the dead person. This redemption does not consist of a redemption *from* the body—this would be non-christian, platonic dualism—but of the human soul's participation in the life of God. Through grace—and only by grace, not naturally—the departed soul is taken into the arms of God the Father and is thus capable of personal activity in grace. The growth of the naturally immortal soul beyond death towards true life and indeed towards life in abundance is therefore attributable only to God's redeeming grace. It cannot be traced back to a dualistic view of man. The tragic aspect of 'being dead' and thus of the 'departed soul' no longer applies to the soul that is justified by redemption. It is, however, true that this divine life of the departed soul is still not fully human until the resurrection has taken place. Direct relationships between human persons and with the world are still not present for the saints. Perfect redemption at the end of time will not take place until the general resurrection, when all these truly human relationships will once again come about and the deified soul communicates its divine mode of being to the body which is thereby glorified. The dogma of the direct beatific vision of God that the holy soul enjoys after death thus confirms the primacy and the transcendence of the soul over matter. But the emphasis placed by faith on the 'hope of resurrection' and the coming *parousia* of Christ also stresses man's essential incarnation and therefore strikingly contradicts any dualistic view of man. Both dualism and monism are contradictory to faith.

D. *The body as an expression of the human spirit. The sacramentality of bodily life*

Man's being spirit even in his body means that, outside the supernatural glorification of the body at the general resurrection, a 'natural glorification' of the body also takes place here on earth, by the fact that a certain quantity of matter is included and humanised by the person. The anatomist, physiologist or biologist may be able to discover patterns, for example, in the facial muscles and nerves that are the same in man and in an animal, more refined perhaps in the case of man, but the fact remains that, perhaps not for the scientist, but certainly insofar as man's integral experience is concerned, the animal's face, with its dull seriousness without any sign of interiority, is quite different from the human face. Man's face is the visible appearance of a spiritual interiority. It is, in fact, this interiority itself insofar as this is visible to us and insofar as it realises itself visibly in the world. In the case of both man and of animals, we are confronted with genuine bodiliness. Yet it is clear that 'body' has different meanings, according to whether we are referring to the existence of a stone, a plant, an animal or man. In human bodily life, the human spirit is present in the mode of bodiliness. This body is the soul itself insofar as the soul becomes 'embodied'. This implies therefore a glorification here on earth of matter in and through its being included in human spirituality.[7] This further implies that the human or humanised body is, in everything, a symbol and expression of the human spirit. It is possible to distinguish many different aspects in this symbolic form of the human body, at least in the light of our already accepted acknowledgement that the human person transcends the material world. The distinctively human element is expressed in man's bodily form. The relative absence of specialisation and the multivalence of the human organism, man's upright attitude—about which Erwin Straus has written in such a masterly fashion—his frontal face and his freely developed hands symbolise man as a being who, while transcending this world, is nonetheless essentially within this world and goes forward freely to meet this world in order to realise something in it. These striking characteristics imply the total distinctiveness of man's anatomical structure.[8] Whether this symbolic structure can also be found in the micro-structure of the human body, as our colleague Lammers has suggested as a hypothesis, cannot be ruled out *a priori* and it may even be a distinct possibility, although I am of the opinion that an interpretation of this

[7] H. E. Hengstenberg, *Der Leib und die letzten Dinge*, Regensburg 1955.
[8] H. Frieling, *Was ist der Mensch?*, Wiesentheid 1948.

symbolism can easily lead to subjective or poetic distortion. Against the background of man's bodily form, the expressiveness of the body as the symbol of the spirit tends to be reflected more clearly in the so-called patterns of human behaviour and especially in man's expressive bodily movements. (These have been well analysed by Buytendijk.[9]) The whole of the human body shares in this expressiveness. It is, for example, typical that man's breathing gains a characteristically human meaning in his speech and language—language is the human spiritualisation of a primarily biological function.

This confirms that the human body is the presence of the spirit in this world, that man is spirit even in his body, spirit in the mode of self-communication to the body. Science, and in this case the biological sciences, which constitute man's spiritual grasp of the bodily, is thus at the service of the glorification of human bodiliness—it is a foreshadowing of the possibility of the eschatological glorification of the body.

Can the human spirit humanise matter to such an extent that it will eventually be able to overcome death? As far as science itself is concerned, this does not, at first sight, seem to be impossible in principle—at least as soon as science is able to create living cells artificially. But, viewed from the standpoint of faith, which teaches us that death was overcome by Christ alone, we are bound to say that this probably hypothetical scientific possibility is absolutely unrealisable and that any attempt to make it real must inevitably result in failure, at least as the consequence of original sin. On this basis, then, we are bound to conclude that this hypothesis is false. We have nothing at all to indicate that the spirit has, in principle, an *unlimited* power over matter. And might this hypothesis not ultimately be the outcome of a one-sided spiritualism?

Finally, the whole of christian sacramentality is based on this anthropological datum of the expressiveness of the body. In the sacramental sphere, the body is not only the active

---

[9] See F. J. J. Buytendijk, *Algemene theorie der menselijke houding en beweging*, Utrecht 1948.

presence of a human spirit—it is also the active presence of a supernatural religious reality. The consequence of God's incarnation in Christ is that a body becomes the visible appearance among us of the living reality of God. The Catholic faith thus implies a glorification of matter. The only possible meaning of the much maligned practice of asceticism within the church is an attempt to safeguard the glory of the body—asceticism is only directed against an inhuman degradation of the body. The very first heresy, which the church shed her blood to fight, was basically an exaggerated spiritualism, and this is all the more remarkable since christianity was later powerfully influenced by platonic dualism, especially in the middle ages (the influence of medieval theology is still noticeably present today in many pious writings), and later still, in our own times, perhaps even more strongly influenced by Cartesian dualism. It is, however, possible to say that early christianity saved the spiritual value of the human body for the West which was tending so readily to accept hellenistic thought. In the religious perspective of man's personal encounter with God, the whole of the material world, then, acquires, through the human body, a sacramental significance. The bodily is not only the sacrament of mutual love in this world, but also the sacrament of God's love among us.

It is also possible, in this perspective, to understand that bodily existence can really become, in a special way, a giving of a sign by God, such as occurs in physical miracles. I should like to conclude by saying a few words on this subject.

E. *Physical miracles*

Reacting against the claims of the positive scientists of the nineteenth century, who insisted that the soul was not immortal and that God did not exist, and moreover that they had proved this, theologians tended, without any justification, to lay stress on the miracle as an act of God's power. It could, they maintained, be proved scientifically that this act was an infringement of the natural laws. They believed, in other words, that the miracle, as a divine intervention, could be the subject of scientific experimentation. This seems to me to be wrong. The biologist can never be confronted with the miraculous element of a cure in his capacity as a biologist.

What, then, is the part that the natural sciences can play and what possibilities are open to the scientist in connection with what the believing christian calls a miracle in the physical sphere, such as a cure? In the first place, the scientist can ascertain a definite fact—the cure of this particular person. He can also ascertain the exceptional character of this cure. Finally, he can also ascertain that such exceptional cases, which do occur fairly regularly, have a remarkably constant relationship with the religious element.[10] He can even show, historically or statistically, that this constant relationship between the observed fact—the cure—and the religious context within which this fact repeatedly occurs has a certain *exclusiveness*—such exceptional cases (at least so long as they cannot be explained psychogenetically) never occur outside the religious context.

The scientist cannot go any farther than this. He can shake his head and say, 'I can make nothing of it,' but, as a scientist, he cannot say positively that a miraculous intervention on God's part has taken place. The natural scientist can do no more than simply be a natural scientist and characterise a certain phenomenon that comes within his sphere as scientifically inexplicable. He studies natural phenomena, after all, exclusively insofar as these can be reduced to general laws.

Natural science can only fulfil its task by assuming that all physical phenomena can in fact be reduced to laws. If, in any case whatsoever, it abandons this principle, it at once ceases to be natural science. In its capacity as natural science, then, it can never ascertain any so-called breach of the natural law. This simply implies that the methodological assumptions of natural science have no metaphysical or philosophical value and that the only aim of natural science is to investigate one aspect of reality, formally abstracting this one aspect from all the other aspects. The scientist should therefore not treat this one aspect as though it were the totality of reality. It is only if

[10] See L. Monden, *Signs and Wonders*, New York 1966.

he has to form a judgement about a miraculous cure simply as a man and not as a scientist that he is able to see in the miracle a *sign* of the living God. The miracle is an utterance, in the act itself, on the part of God, who wishes to give us, through the bodily event itself, a sign. In a miracle, God wishes to let something become clear to us. From the technical point of view, a miracle is not an ascertainable *breach* of the laws of nature. Analysis of those miraculous cures that are known to us has revealed that the miracle is really an animation of existing natural laws and thus a heightened realisation of biological possibilities. This is quite clearly revealed in one of the most miraculous of all cures, that of the leg of Pieter de Rudder of Oostakker near Ghent, in which about an inch and a quarter of the patient's shinbone was restored in a matter of seconds. The analysis of the process of depositing calcium phosphate, which can still be examined in the cured bone, shows that the cure took place normally according to the laws governing the deposit of calcium, that is, by means of the formation of a callus or new bone material, which consolidates the pieces of fractured bone and results in the cure of the fracture. In this case, however, the calcium metabolism, which normally takes place very slowly, occurred very rapidly, the callus forming within a few seconds. There was therefore no 'creation from nothing', but a divine application of the natural law governing the deposit of calcium. But this took place at an incredibly rapid rate, in other words, what happened was a *miraculously* forced *natural* process of cure. Moreover, there was also no period of convalescence and the bone showed no symptom of rigidity. In the case of a miracle, then, God makes use of existing natural qualities which he has called into being. In a miraculous cure, no hiatus can be established anywhere in the laws of biology. What is exceptional is that the natural laws come into play in a *very special way*, usually at greatly increased speed. It is, of course, this which attracts attention and which presents the biologist with an insoluble fact. The special quality of the miracle is that, because of the entire context within which an incident of this kind takes place, God himself wishes to communicate something to us in the miracle—in it, he really addresses us. There is an *intention* in the event and this personal intention transcends the normal possibilities of nature. For anyone who is open and listens to it the natural event *expresses more* than it is able to express in itself—it is the visible aspect of a free act of God. This visible quality cannot be discovered by the biologist as such, but only by man as man in a totally human approach to the incident.

The positivist can, of course, always argue that a cure of this kind is certainly exceptional in the theory of physical indeterminism, but that it can ultimately be explained as a chance statistical exception which, because of the indeterminism of nature, in principle also comes within the physical laws and does so as an extremely marginal case. The only answer that the unprejudiced man or the believing christian can make to this is that this is *theoretically* possible in one particular case, but, because of the convergence of so many exceptions of this kind that have taken place within a religious context—and this has been historically and statistically proved in the case of the great miracles—this solution *cannot be used in practice*. As Monden has correctly said, 'to maintain the hypothesis of a chance statistical exception in the face of a series of facts of this kind is a clear demonstration of the very opposite to scientific thinking and impartiality'.[11] After all, what still remains to be explained is how it is that these statistical exceptions always occur within a religious community. This answer probably means nothing to a biologist as such, but, as a datum which is offered to a totally human critical judgement, this fact is a datum that cannot be explained from the physical point of view. Voltaire, who explained miracles naturally, had to admit that 'believers are certainly idiots, but it is curious that these exceptional forces that are revealed by the miracle only ever take place for these idiots'.[12]

Thus we can see that the body is not only an expression of the human spirit, but that it can also become the expression

---

[11] *Het wonder*, 300. For the English translation, see above p 254 n 10.
[12] Quoted in *Nouvelle Revue Théologique* 60 (1933), 134.

of God's Spirit. Let me conclude by saying that the biologist works with holy material—this seems to me to be the most encouraging thing that a theologian can say about the human body as the sphere of work of the biological and medical sciences.

2. The animal in man's world

I have been asked to throw a little light on the problem of man in his relationship with the animal. In theology-minded Holland, we are anxious to let the liberating light of faith penetrate into the darkest corners of the university animal laboratory where, in an otherwise splendid and humane environment, 'evil' men are busy torturing 'innocent' animals in a subtly refined scientific manner. The problem is thus stated quite clearly—does the splendid environment cloak a base activity or is an innocent undertaking forced, by the excessively well cared for environment, to its highest scientific efficiency? I propose to approach the problem first from the human and philosophical point of view and then see if it is still possible to throw some light on it from the religious point of view.

1. The world and everything that lives and moves in it is the realm of the human person. The world is the indispensable soil for the growth of human life and it is from man that it acquires its ultimate meaning. It is in this world that man becomes truly man. In this world, the animal especially is very close to man. The child grows up in close association not only with people, but also with animals. Cats and dogs are his companions, much better to play with than dolls or toys. He learns how to look after chickens, geese and ducks and has fun in the chicken-run or with the rabbit-hutch. As a lad, he looks for birds' nests and becomes familiar with the psychology of birds, with their roguish ways and their stupidity. For a boy, a cat is a self-willed pet and a dog is a faithful friend. In the past, he would, as a young man, go out hunting with hounds and thus become familiar with a world of animals which had, up to then, been completely un-

known to him. The animal thus really forms part of the world of man, but it belongs to man's world in many different senses.

The whole pattern of these relationships has, however, been to some extent changed by the modern rationalisation and increasingly technical nature of man's life. We have heard it said that the cow is no longer an animal, but a machine for the production of milk. The animal is above all regarded as something that is at the service of increased productivity and, to achieve this higher productivity, man has to treat animals in a way that at least offends human sensibility—an example of this is the shutting up of animals so that they cannot move. In fact, our image of man has changed and, as a result, our approach to the animal is different. The problem is to be found not so much in man's treatment of animals as in a certain tendency on the part of human life to become one-sided. This tendency has resulted in the complete loss of some of the more original relationships between man and the animal and, in reaction to this, in the emergence of new relationships of familiarity between man and the animal. The lady with her little lap-dog is an example of this. I believe that the problem also has a socio-philosophical aspect and ought to be investigated from the sociological point of view. Here, however, I will limit myself to a few philosophical reflections.[13]

Respect for the value of every thing as a being forms, as it were, an essential part of man's being, since man is not only *homo faber* and *homo oeconomicus*, but also simply *man*, a man who finds himself situated in a world of things, of plants and flowers, of animals and fellow-men. In this spontaneously thinking and living man there is a respect for the very varied

[13] A great deal has been written in recent years about man in his relationship with the animal. See especially R. Lewinsohn, *Histoire des animaux. Leurs influences dans la civilisation humaine*, Paris 1953; P. Chauchard and others, *Psychisme animal et âme humaine*, Paris 1954; J. J. Buytendijk, *Psychologie der dieren*, Haarlem 1932, especially *Mensch und Tier* and *Over de pijn*, Utrecht 1943, *Mens en dier* (Philosophische Bibliotheek), Amsterdam and Antwerp 1958; G. Siegmund, *Tier und Mensch. Beitrag zur Wesensbestimmung des Menschen*, Frankfurt a. M. 1958.

mystery of the being of things. The very fact that these things —minerals, plants and animals—*are there* and are, to a greater or lesser extent, included in the world of man is a gift of God. The world is man's companion in his relationships with his fellow-man. It is essentially the world in which we live. It has grown together with our human existence which, in a certain sense, as it were loses itself in this world— man flows bodily into the great body of this material, living world. This world thus does something to man and, from his own spiritual sphere of existence, man also does something to this world.

But man is not only a being who approaches each thing metaphysically in its own value and simply *experiences* it, a being who lets things be what they are, enjoying things because they are as they appear to him, experiencing in a special way joy in every form in the manner in which it appears to him. Man is also *homo faber*—he is man the technician who builds the world according to his own taste and man the researcher who is at the service of the humanisation of the world and of mankind. Man therefore penetrates deeply into the things of this world. He is always doing this, even in his most contemplative attitude, in which he invests things with humanity, even when he is merely looking at a landscape. He sees in a *human* manner and ultimately he sees nothing but a humanised world. By man's seeing gaze, the world is transformed into a human world. In this way, man himself gives *meaning* to things, a meaning which these things do not have in themselves and which they can only receive from man.

If we speak, then, about the metaphysical awe which man has for the special value or the distinctive mystery of things, we should not forget that, without man, these things have no distinctive value *of their own* in the strict sense of the word— they are elements in a continuous cosmic development. This even applies to the animal, although it is in the animal that the supreme, though necessarily always failing, attempt to break away from the purely relative sphere of things within this world and to reach out towards a truly distinctive mode of existence manifests itself. If we look more closely at man's metaphysical awe for created things that are not personal in this light, we see that this respect can only be meaningful when it is for *creative love*, for the creative, personal God of whom we become conscious in these relative things and whose mystery we sense through these things. It is, in fact, not a question of awe for the distinctive value, the *esse proprium*, of these things, for the simple reason that these things do not represent any independent, subsisting value in themselves. As soon as plants and animals are seen to have no personal value in themselves, they can no longer claim any right to absolute evaluation—they are purely relative, subordinate to the value of the human person. They cannot claim any right with regard to man. The world with all that is in it was given by God to man, so that he should give meaning to it. It is a reality which has no distinct meaning without man in it. It is he who, by his seeing, hearing and feeling and by his civilisation and techniques, makes the world human, meaningful and spiritual and transforms it from being something that is uncanny to something that is familiar to man. The only mystery that, apart from a theistic perspective, is present in nature is the fact that it still eludes man's grasp, in other words, its non-humanity. This provisional mystery of sub-humanity requires man to give a human meaning to it and man's task in this world is precisely to humanise, spiritualise and give meaning to nature.

The protection of animals is therefore really a question of protecting human values and not directly of protecting animals, just as the laws governing urban growth are not really intended to preserve the distinctive value of a certain material combination, but to preserve the natural beauty of the countryside, that is, a *human* value. Without man, natural beauty is an empty word. But there are differences here.

The general indignation that we feel about the plan to fill in the canals of Utrecht is different from our reaction against wanton and senseless torture inflicted on an animal, and this again is different from our feelings about the extermination of harmful animals or reaction to the killing of millions of creatures when we boil water or breathe. Although, therefore, the protection of animals is to some extent connected with the laws governing urban development, insofar as it is a protection of *human* values, there is nonetheless a new factor present here. Animals—and especially those animals which we human beings can spontaneously understand—have a certain inward quality and a certain power of expression which enables them to be admitted, more than plants, into the human world, with the result that a very special bond of 'comradeship' can even come about between man and the animal. This means that the animal becomes a *human* value and, what is more, a human value in a very special manner. Furthermore, the forms in which animals express themselves reveal the presence of pain and pleasure. And, even though we men interpret this pain and pleasure wrongly in a human, anthropomorphic manner, an animal's experience of pain is nonetheless, biologically speaking, a reality. It is very difficult indeed for man to try to understand the real meaning of the animal's psychical experience of pain as an animal and our distinctively human experience of pain always plays an interpretative part in any assessment. Precisely because of this, we may say that it is meaningless for man, and unworthy of him, wantonly and without reason to torture an animal. Ultimately, it is a question of protecting a human value, a question therefore of humanism. Similarly, we are also bound to say that it is unworthy of man wantonly and senselessly to damage a plant or a flower or to disfigure a scene of natural beauty. We attach greater importance to senseless cruelty to an animal because the animal, although it does not attain the value of a person, is certainly growing towards a certain form of individuality, so that it is in many respects a foreshadowing of human life. But if man uses these animals so as to make human life more human he is respecting these beings for what they are—a relative value for the good of man. From the philosophical point of view, then, there can be no possible objection to laboratory tests, in which man has deliberately to cause pain to animals in order to test various reactions to pain for the benefit of human medical science. On the other hand, however, there are very many experiments in which reactions to pain are, from the scientific point of view, not necessary. In such cases, human value, confronted with the unnecessary pain of the animal, demands that these experiments should be conducted under an anaesthetic. Human feelings are often opposed to philosophical analyses of this kind. A man knows what pain, even biological pain, is and finds all pain too much in this world. Yet the meaning of pain and of the experience of pain is quite different in the case of purely biological life from what it is in the case of a man who experiences this pain as a person. Nonetheless, there is a certain form of pain and unnecessary pain can never be defended. We must, on the other hand, guard against projecting our human experiences into the animal. The fact that, in the world of animals, one animal lives at the expense of others, animals prey upon and devour each other and that in some cases bringing to life also implies death, makes us, humanly but wrongly, talk of the 'cruelty' of the world of animals. But this is, in fact, simply the plan of God's good creation and it would be going too far and, what is more, it would be philosophically and theologically unjustifiable to give credence to the fantasies of the American writer, D. Runes,[14] who claimed that the so-called cruelty of the animal world was a consequence of original sin or of the intrigues of demons. I am not of the opinion that we should or even can be more sensitive in this matter than God the creator. The pain of animals is made worse by their contact with man and, quite apart from man's aggressiveness, which has its origins in his psychology, his sinfulness also undoubtedly plays a part in this. What is more, those who are closely acquainted with animals insist that the legend of St Francis' friendship with all animals is confirmed by experience—the ferocity shown by animals towards man is partly the result of man's inhuman attitude towards the animal. Now, for example, animal trainers apparently make much greater use of the 'theory of trust' in their work and even though it takes longer to

[14] D. Runes, *Of God, the Devil and the Jews*, New York 1952, 52ff; see also J. Heard, *Is God in History?*, London 1951.

achieve results, it seems to be more persistent and lasting in its effects than the older method of training by inflicting pain. But, quite apart from these aspects of the problem, it is clear from many scientifically established facts that what we call, in human terms, the 'cruelty' of animals forms an essential part of their nature. The immorality of causing wanton, senseless pain to animals can therefore only be based on the value of the human person.

It is man's *spirit* that entitles him to rule over things and animals, but it is this same spirit, in other words, his value as a human person, and not his aggressive instinct or a sentimentality which is very difficult to define, that has to act as the norm in his position of power over animals.

2. It therefore seems to me that it is wholly beside the point to look in the bible for arguments for and against man's association with animals.[15] Not only does the word of God come to us in scripture—it also comes to us via the expressions of an ancient Semitic cultural environment. What comes to us as the word of God is often no more than a passing social phenomenon. Thus, the bible tells us that the Semites had control of animals for their own use, for their own amusement and for observation. Man used animals for food (see Gen 9:3; Neh 5:18; Deut 14:1–20), for sacrifice, as beasts of burden and as mounts. He profited from their products, such as milk, butter, wool and ivory and made their products into material for clothing, tents or water containers. He went hunting, played with birds (Job 41:5) and observed the movements of birds (Jer 8:7).

All that we gain from this is an image of a society, that of a people which was originally nomadic and then became settled, a peasant people with a primitive technique. Since it

---

[15] A great deal has been written, both scientifically and unscientifically, about the animal world of the bible and the so-called biblical view of the animal. See, among others, H. Hilger, *Biblischer Tiergarten*, Freiburg 1954; M. L. Henry, *Das Tier im religiösen Bewusstsein des alttestamentlichen Menschen*, Tübingen 1958; A. Gelin, 'Het dier in de H. Schrift' in the Dutch translation of P. Chauchard's work, *Psychisch leven bij mens en dier*, Bilthoven 1958, 169–78.

was the land animals which were included in man's immediate environment that were closest to man, the author of the
account of creation understandably placed the creation of
these animals on the same day as man's creation (Gen 1:24).
In all this, a factual situation is depicted. Deuteronomy contains a number of laws on the protection of animals, similar
to those prescribed by all peoples. An analysis of these laws
shows that some simply aim to safeguard human values and
to prevent the unreasonable treatment of animals and that
others have an anthropomorphic inspiration—animals too
were to rest on the sabbath (Deut 5:14), a commandment
which prevented man himself from working by depriving
him of the instrument with which he could work. Because
there was such a close association between man and cattle,
the Mosaic law also applied, through man who believed in
Yahweh, to the animal. This 'humanism' is summarised in
the proverbs of Israel: 'A righteous man has regard for the life
of his beast, but the mercy of the wicked is cruel' (Prov
12:10). It is clear from the fact that animals were also subject
to Israel's penal code that a primitive anthropomorphism
sometimes played a part in this—for example, an ox that
killed a man or a woman with its horns incurred the penalty
of death (Ex 21:28). In this connection, too, we should not
forget that no clear distinction was made, in Israel's early
period, between what may be called the animal's 'soul' and
that of man. This primitive view of the world also emerges
from other facts—as in fables, so too in the bible, animals are
made to speak. These fables were intended to be moral
lessons for man (see, for example, Prov 6:6–8; 30:24–28; see
especially Num 23). They are also to be found in the myths
of Babylon.

We do not, however, find the word of God in these elements
of the bible. If we wish to penetrate to the real word of God
in the bible, that is, God's word, not concerning the animal,
but concerning man in his relationship with the animal, then
we come to the following scanty, sober, but fundamental
insights.

Everything that lives and moves in the world is God's

creation, God's *good* creation. Man, however, is God's creation in a very special sense. The account of creation is constructed in such a way that it shows that the whole of the material world is directed towards man. It is for this reason that only he is called God's image. He is, in other words, God's governor on earth, the representative of God's kingdom. Just as, in the ancient world, the king, who could not be present in every part of his territory, had an image of himself set up in recently conquered territories as a sign of his ruling presence, so too did God set up in the world, which he created as his territory, as a clear sign of his rule on earth. This image, however, was not a wooden statue, but living man—man and woman (Gen 1:27). Man is God's governor in the management of creation. To enable him to fulfil this function, God blessed him and his task in this world: 'And God blessed them, and God said to them, "Be fruitful and multiply, and fill the earth and subdue it"' (Gen 1:28). It is, then, man's task to lead the material world and everything that is in it to God. In its turn, this world also leads man to God.

It is explicitly stated in the account of creation that it is only man and woman and not man and the animal who form man's mode of existence in dialogue—the animal is not man's equal partner (Gen 2:18-24). The world and animals are at the service of man (Gen 1:26-30; 2:20). This truth is, of course, expressed in ancient Near Eastern terms, but it is no less strikingly expressed because of this—man himself gives every animal a name. His giving of names to the animals is the expression of his right to control them. The animal's service of man should not, however, be thought of as purely utilitarian. The bible contains many examples of how religious man, believing in God the creator, saw the expression of God's will to create in the behaviour of animals. Sometimes animals are used to provide an example for man (see Job 38-40). The roaring of the lion (Ps 104:21) and the birds' spreading their wings are interpreted by man as praise of God. Religious man is in a sense jealous of the birds that build their nests in God's temple (Ps 84:4). This is, of course, anthropomorphism—the irrational behaviour of animals was seen by biblical man in the light of his faith in creation. In the psalms animals were called upon, together with man, the sun, the moon and the stars, to praise God's glory, in other words, through man, animals also praised God (see, for example, Ps 148: 7-10). The so-called 'objective glory' of corporeal creatures was a divine *doxa* or glory which ascended to God via man. It was precisely for this reason that Israel made the whole world share in man's salvation or absence of salvation. This points to the fact that, as Aquinas suggested, the animal's relationship with God should not be viewed in the abstract—it is a relationship which the animal has with God through its involvement with man in the world.[16] That is why the believer in the bible was able to recognise God's miraculous power in the violence of some animals—for man in the ancient Near East, the mighty hippopotamus especially reflected God's saving power (Job 40: 10ff), just as, for the ancient Hebrews, the storm and the lightning reflected this power.

Finally, the bible also places animals in an eschatological perspective. Here too, however, we must distinguish between the bible's affirmation of eschatological faith and the way in which this faith was expressed. The future is presented as a 'new creation' in which animals also have a place. The author of the book of Genesis, who could not accept that the 'cruelty' of animals was traceable to God the creator, made all the animals inhabiting paradise on earth eat only plants (Gen 1: 30). The same idea can be found among Israel's neighbours and it also persists in the legends of all peoples, sagas which begin with the set formula, 'in the days when animals spoke'. Man's calling the animals by their names in Genesis 2: 19-20 was regarded as an exercise of his authority, as though the animals were really 'tamed' by man's giving them a name. The biblical authors believed that the same situation would prevail at the end of time: 'The wolf shall dwell with the

16 See Thomas, *In II Sent.*, d. 1, q. 1, a. 3, ad 3, for example. See also the following more modern works: V. Rüfner, *Die Natur und der Mensch in ihr*, in the series *Die Philosophie. Ihre Geschichte und ihre Systematik*, ed. T. Steinbückel, Bonn 1934; A. Gehlen, *Der Mensch*, Berlin 1940; B. Brandenstein, *Der Mensch und seine Stellung im All*, Einsiedeln and Cologne 1947.

lamb, and the leopard shall lie down with the kid... The sucking child shall play over the hole of the asp...' (Is 11: 6–8). The fact that there would be no more infants in the eschatological kingdom need not count as an objection here, because what we have here is clearly a *mode of expression*— a human description of the eschatological realm of peace, visualised in the tradition of the national legends of the paradise on earth, in which a state of grace is depicted in a popular manner.[17] In my opinion, Aquinas made a clearer distinction between content and form of expression when he stated calmly that he did not believe that there would be any animals in the eschatological kingdom.[18] Quite correctly, he regarded the animal world as a form of existence which was necessary in order ultimately to produce the body that was, in man, the 'end' of the evolution of the material world[19] and which could only be understood within this totality of living nature.

It should therefore be sufficiently clear from what I have said already that a distinction has to be made in the bible between those elements dealing with the animal world which are theologically significant and those which simply have a social and historical significance, that is, as the form of expression in which God's word came to us in the ancient Near East. All that the bible shows us is the depths of faith in God's creation—of the animal world as well—and, in the bible, everything is regarded as coming from the gentle hand of God who also cares for animals (see Mt 10:29–33; 6:26; Lk 12:6–9). What we call 'nature' was, for biblical man, a 'miracle of God'. But God directed these 'miracles' towards man's salvation. In the spirit of the book of Genesis, Psalm 8 outlines this biblical vision of the animal world in a most striking way:

---

[17] It is, in any case, not entirely clear whether Isaiah had a transcendental and eschatological kingdom or a historical messianic kingdom in mind here.

[18] *In IV Sent.*, d. 48, q. 2, a. 5. The framework within which Thomas made this statement was, however, one of medieval cosmology.

[19] 'Homo est finis totius generationis', *Contra Gent.* III, 22: 'Man is the end of everything that is born.'

What is man that thou art mindful of him?...
Thou dost crown him with glory and honour.
Thou hast given him dominion over the works of thy hands;
thou hast put all things under his feet,
all sheep and oxen,
and also the beasts of the field,
the birds of the air, and the fish of the sea,
whatever passes along the paths of the sea.

This is man's true religious attitude towards the animal. Religious man knows that what the world offers him as coming from God not only furthers his worthy existence as man, but also his salvation. It is precisely in this furtherance of man's existence and salvation that the animal is a relative value.

I do not think that anything more can be said, at least from the philosophical and theological point of view, about the animal without indulging in unphilosophical or pious fantasies. Creation is fine and good. It is also good for man who, serving the salvation of his fellow-men, experiments with animals in an animal laboratory.

12

THE INTELLECTUAL'S
RESPONSIBILITY FOR THE FUTURE

There must also be a place for the subject of faith under the heading of our responsibility for the future, since it would be impossible to give a satisfactory answer to the vital question of our expectation of the future without reference to faith. The personal meaning of man's life is, after all, more than human. It transcends the human element and cannot be realised by purely human and mundane powers. It is only in an act that transcends himself that man can, in faith, receive the personal meaning of his life as grace from God's hands. It is only within man's recognition of his mode of existence as a believer that light can be thrown on his expectation of the future.

Theological reflection about our responsibility for the future attempts to test and assimilate contemporary human experience in the light of God's word heard in a community in touch with the reality of salvation. Theology tries to situate this human experience, as illuminated especially in modern philosophical anthropology, within the sphere of the message of faith.

1. From the philosophical point of view, man is a being who has to define himself by exercising his freedom in the world and in community with his fellow-men. Man's having a future simply means that he is a being of possibility who himself gives content, direction and definition to his being, from the zero of initial freedom. Freedom and expectation of the future are one and the same. An animal is impelled by its natural determinism and thus has no future. By freely giving meaning to his existence, man is always making the future, on the basis of the past, a today. Man's being is an open existence and therefore expects a future. In his book,

La découverte de soi, the phenomenologist G. Gusdorf said, 'We are only free insofar as all personal eschatology remains a risk.'[1] In other words, man is free insofar as his future is still an open question. Anxiety and hope are therefore fundamental existentials of man's being. The fact that this existential conviction is strongly emphasised in our modern society, in contrast with the prevailing conviction of self-assurance in the past, seems to me to be more of a gain than a loss. Modern man has rejected all forms of self-assurance. We failed in the past by thinking that we possessed a certainty which was, in fact, not there. Now the circumstances of the world and the age in which we live have forced us to give up this substitute certainty. But this means that our hands are empty. We are now sufficiently empty to be able humbly to take hold of the truth that will make us free. We are looking for clarity, but we are looking for it within the mystery—we are not looking for a clarity which is as evident as a life assurance with legal guarantees. In the past, we forgot that God is a mystery which overflows on to everything that is created and especially on to man, because man is so close to God. We lost sight of the fact that human freedom, which makes history and looks forward to the future, essentially merges into the mystery. In so doing, we drew down the reproach of a man like Merleau-Ponty on our heads: 'If God is, perfection is already realised here in this world and cannot be increased. There is literally nothing to be done.'[2] Not so much as a doctrine, but rather as the expression of our contemporary feeling about life, existentialism has cured us of our shortsighted sense of self-assurance. But it has also deprived us at the same time of the living God. We are left with the feelings of a Mary Magdalen whose Lord had been stolen away from her. Our image of the future has been distorted by this. We are groping in the dark because we have rediscovered freedom, but it is a freedom to which we have attributed divine prerogatives. This gift is too heavy for us, as men, to carry.

1 Paris 1948, 506.
2 *Sens et non-sens*, Paris 1948, 356.

2. Faced with the problem of our expectation of the future, we have to be bold enough once again to assert that the risk of human freedom implies an intimate security in the mystery of God and that, because of this, freedom is not itself creative, but a creative trust in the mystery of the reality which we do not possess, but which takes possession of us. Human uncertainty is essentially the other side of the coin of the situation of faith, which is an encounter with the transcendent and incalculable God. It is an adventure. The certainty which it gives us is the certainty of a merciful love which transcends all human understanding and therefore always deprives us of false human assurance. In this perspective, then, what does our responsibility for the future consist of, or, to express the same question in different words, what does our responsibility for the use of human freedom consist of?

From the theological point of view, man is a being who has to make his own definition by exercising his freedom in the world in community with his fellow-men *in dialogue with God*. Human freedom, in dialogue with God and with the world, makes the future into a present reality in which it is good to live. In the concrete, man's free act is, after all, only possible in personal confrontation with God. We cannot consider now the extent to which this confrontation with God must be explicitly given. Let me say no more here than that human freedom has a context of vocation. We are responsible towards God for the meaning that we give to our personal life and to this world. The expression 'man is responsible', outside an implicit or explicit perspective of God, is not a complete expression in itself. Being responsible means being responsible towards a living person. Responsibility is not a lonely state of mind—regarding oneself in irreducible identity as the personal and exclusive cause of a certain act or attitude. This is only possible in an implicit confrontation with God in positively turning towards him or away from him. Atheistic existentialism may well claim that responsibility is central to its philosophy: 'I am responsible for everything . . . except my responsibility. My loneliness, that is, my facticity, consists simply of my being condemned to be

integrally responsible for myself.'[3] But what can this responsibility mean to someone who experiences himself 'as being
there *for nothing*, as being *superfluous*'?[4] Where God does
not witness us, where he does not address us, there is, on our
side, no question of being 'responsible'. The last word is
arbitrary freedom and Sartre himself had to admit this:
'Dostoievski wrote, "If God does not exist, everything would
be allowed". That is the point of departure of existentialism.'[5] In his novel, *Le diable et le bon Dieu*, he quite consistently made the immoral Goetz, after various experimental
attempts to give direction to his life, suddenly realise, 'God
does not exist ... I tell you that God is dead. *We no longer
have a witness.* I am the only one who can see your hair and
your forehead.'[6] It is indisputable that there is also a dialogue
between man and himself and that, in this sense, man has a
responsibility with regard to himself. But this interiority only
comes about when man becomes aware of himself within the
security of the mystery of God. This interiority is being
addressed by the living God. Man thus learns, through faith,
to penetrate more deeply into the problem of human
responsibility.

3. The kerygma of the creation of man by the God of Israel,
the Father of the Lord Christ Jesus, implies that man, in his
essence as a person, in other words, as freedom, comes directly
from the hands of God. The human person is cast into this
world by God as a completely new beginning without any
horizontal bonds which might explain the origin of his being
a *person*. This abrupt origin from God's love makes him a
being who is able to confront the world in which he is
situated and its history as transcendent, as an *I*, free and
knowing himself to be directly addressed by the living God.
Because of his direct origin from God's love, man is situated

---

3 J.-P. Sartre, *L'Etre et le néant*, Paris 1948, 641–2.
4 ibid., 126.
5 *L'existentialisme est un humanisme*, Paris 1946, 36.
6 Paris 1951, 268 and 271.

in this world as a being who is directly responsible before God. The human person is a being of vocation.

But this freedom called by God is situated in the world and in human history—it is a situated freedom. Because of God's act of creation, the divine origin of human freedom is essentially incarnate in a bodily life which brings man's freedom into contact with the world of men and things. In this way, man does have horizontal bonds with the world and, at the extreme limits of his existence, he so to speak merges into this world. Man is therefore essentially a being who is in a position to introduce an entirely new factor into the solved problem of the world situation into which he is cast. He is able to do this because of his autonomous self-determination or, to express this in theological terms, because of his direct, personal relationship with God. Because his freedom is a freedom that is situated within the world, it is a responsibility of vocation *for* something with regard to God. This is strikingly apparent in the symbolism of man's erect attitude. Man's transcendental spirituality is symbolised in the vertical attitude of his body. Given by God to itself, human freedom appears as giving meaning in this world in a constant attempt to transcend the world. In this way, man makes history, the future becomes a present and human freedom is always at the beginning of a new future.

We have, however, not yet penetrated to the full depths of this situated freedom. On the basis of their constitutive relationship with God, both the situation and man's personal freedom are, because of the personal address by the living God, subject to grace. The outward grace of the situation is the embodiment of the inward grace which seizes hold of man's freedom and invites it to give active meaning. The situation in which man's freedom, addressed by God, is placed is subject to grace firstly in that God himself defines the content of his intimate invitation to give meaning within this situation, thus making it the divine definition of the limits of man's present task and responsibility. Secondly, this situation is also subject to grace in that, within man's personal relationship with God, it becomes the medium through which man's freedom, addressed by God, can make itself felt in this world through its own bodily existence, by responding to God's invitation, by carrying out his task and thus occupying a personal place in the history of the world.

This essentially situational character of human freedom under God's vocation implies that we only possess an inalienable responsibility with regard to God and our fellow-men within a defined area. This view eliminates in advance the unreal tension experienced by those who attempt to claim for themselves a divine and unsituated 'universal providence' or responsibility and are thus made more and more wretched because of their increasing sense of impotence and failure. Within the whole of world history, each of us receives, through our own situation, in other words, through a divine definition, no more than a responsibility which is *shared* by many others. We are not required to do *everything*. We do not simply have a responsibility for the future. This interconnection does not only imply the need to trust the sense of responsibility that our fellow-men have—it also implies our responsibility towards others, precisely in and through the responsibility that is allotted to us within our own sphere of activity. Our personal responsibility for the universal fate of mankind is expressed in and through our effective responsibility within the sphere of activity that is assigned to us. What is more, this situated and therefore limited responsibility is also covered by our direct and explicit dialogue with God, in which we transcend our own limited and situational point of view by talking with the Lord of history in prayer. Far too often we talk to God about the petty difficulties of our lives and never discuss with him the most important development of the modern world—the birth of a new society and mankind's becoming one as an enormous and new possibility for the universality of genuine christian love!

4. We have thus come gradually closer to the real problem of the responsibility to which the Catholic intellectual is called. From the point of view of faith, man's responsibility—and that of the intellectual—is first and foremost a responsi-

bility with regard to the coming *kingdom of God*. Had we perhaps not forgotten this when the subject of our responsibility for the future was first raised? 'Seek first the kingdom of God'—even for the Catholic intellectual, this is not just an old fairy tale. It means that the first responsibility that we have for the future is the community of all persons with the living God. Our expectation of the future is expressed fundamentally in the eschatological tension of the petition 'thy kingdom come'. This future is a grace. It cannot be attained by human acts. It is the coming of God himself, who is called 'He who is coming'. But this coming is a grace that can only be received with open, reaching hands. The coming movement of God must also set mankind itself in motion. 'Thy will be done on earth as it is in heaven' shows us the way along which the petition of the 'thy kingdom come' can reach the heart of the coming God. Our expectation of salvation as the highest point of our expectation of the future is therefore also a free and courageous human commitment—a going out to meet the God who is coming in eschatological involvement and skilful activity.

But, within this transcendent expectation of the future, human freedom also hopes for a future for this world. The christian also expects a future for this world and its history. Man's task here on earth is one aspect of his integral religious attitude. Within his care for the kingdom of God, the christian therefore acknowledges the reality of this world. This reality is a true dimension of his attitude *as a believer*. Being in the world is thus a part of our situation as believers. The world therefore has an ultimate meaning which is more than simply worldly, a meaning which it does not need to have in itself, but which our being called to responsibility must give it. Our ordering of life within this world, our economic, social and political organisation of temporal society, our intense human experience of everything that is fine and splendid and our creation of really human art and beauty in the world—all this is thus a participation in the eschatology of mankind.

This is also the sphere in which the christian lives and works as well as his unbelieving fellow-man, although the believer can experience this world more deeply and authentically than the non-believer. As christians, then, we are also responsible before God and therefore with regard to ourselves and the whole of mankind for our dwelling-place here on earth and for the fate of our fellow-men in the world. Because we freely intervene in history through our being in the world and our secular vocation, we are also responsible in this intervention with regard to God. And because our being in the world is, in the concrete, a *believing* existence, our task of humanising this world is at the same time a mysterious anticipation of the eschatological glorification of everything that comes into contact with redeemed man. Our humanised world is given a definitive consecration by the eschatological grace of Christ's glory, although we are unable to form any positive idea of this. The mystery of God who is, in Christ, man's *eschaton* also shrouds the ultimate meaning of human civilisation and its production.

Within the mystery of our dialogue with the living God, however, *everything*, including our dwelling-place here on earth, is important and will continue to be important for ever. It is only in the eschatological perspective, in which man does not aim to be simply and solely man, that he can also be fully man. The believer, more than anyone else, takes the profane reality seriously. Because of this, the christian layman is responsible, not only for the heaven that is to come, but also for the world of today and tomorrow. He may not relinquish the task of setting temporal society in order, as though this were merely a useful activity for mere profane mankind. It is rather the true task of the christian layman within the kingdom of God, a task in which he cooperates with all those who are sensitive to human values. In this work, he is autonomous and makes his authoritative voice heard. All that authority in the church has to do here is to take care that the coming of the kingdom of God is not prejudiced by what the layman does in this world.

5. The situation within which the Catholic layman is responsible both for the kingdom of God and for man's dwelling-place here on earth differs, in context and extent, from person to person according to his position in this world. The worker who has to turn screws at a bench has, for example, a responsibility for the future of mankind which is different from that of the intellectual whose sphere of work is wider in extent. Furthermore, everyone's personal situation includes several different sectors. For example, the situation of a woman who has begun academic studies, but who is fully aware that she will soon have to carry out the duties of a wife and mother is wider than that of other women and her responsibility is consequently greater in extent. She will have to try to harmonise her responsibility towards her family with the higher task which woman has in human society, even though this task of woman in society will not always cross the frontiers of her care for her own family. Let us now try to place the responsibility to which the Catholic intellectual is called against the background of the wide sphere within which he is situated.

Intellectual activity is only one specialised function within the human community. A scholar is first and foremost simply a man. The attainment and application of knowledge is a task which forms part of a much wider task in life. As a function performed *by* man *for* man, science and scholarship are ultimately only human within their functional connection with the total development of human life in this world. Truly human intellectual life is not possible without the education of the whole man. Within the academic system, specialised study only acquires its distinctively human value when it is geared to a total structure which makes man more human.

Let us look at the sober reality. If we consider universities throughout the whole world, we are bound to conclude that the number of scholars and scientists trained by the universities is only a very small percentage of the total number of those who have attended university. In the concrete, the real contribution that the universities make to society is to be found in the education of those who later take up leading positions in many different spheres of public life. In the concrete, then, the university has what may be called a twofold fruitfulness. If we want to be realistic, we could just as well call this a twofold aim. In its whole structure and organisation, then, the university must therefore be directed towards this twofold fruitfulness. If the training of pure scholars or scientists were the only aim of the university, we are bound to admit that every university fails completely as far as ninety per cent of its graduates is concerned. It is precisely this conclusion that causes us to presume that the premisses of the argument are unrealistic. But we may then ask whether the whole structure and organisation and the entire work of the various universities are directed, in the concrete, towards the optimum realisation of the factual fruitfulness of the university for ninety per cent of its graduates who leave the strictly academic sphere soon after they have completed their studies and take up leading positions in society. It is certainly not possible to maintain that this overwhelming majority represents a failure and a loss. In that case, the question may well be asked—how can the university, which, in the literal sense of the word, lives from the community, justify its existence to the generous patron who cannot make this liberal gesture simply because of an abundance of wealth, but only through hard work and care. The strict practice of science and learning has, of course, an urgent contribution to make to the humanisation of the world. But it is a special vocation, even though the university must also provide the opportunity for its exercise. The task of the university within the social structure, however, is wider than this specialised aim.

If, then, the aim of the university is to form intellectuals who will later take up leading positions in society, it seems to me that this task is impossible without an ideological background, in the broadest sense of the word. We are bound to recognise that the individual academic subjects only have a relative place in the whole of man's knowledge of reality and in the whole of his activity in life. If we did not recognise this, the university would simply produce people who would view everything purely psychologically, medically, biologically, juridically, physically or sociologically and would be blind to all other, deeper aspects of reality and thus diminish sound human originality. This would be a violation of true humanity. It would result in the unconscious building up of an ideology based on the human nervous system, man's psychical complexes, legal texts or sociological findings, in other words, in making absolute the formal and relative subject matter of each individual discipline. Such a process clearly attacks the foundations of human society and makes it impossible for those who will later have a decisive part to play in the history of the world to succeed. If this were to happen, further education would simply become a kind of technical school for professional skill and not the dynamic centre from which the humanisation of the world receives its impulse. And it is precisely this task which gives the university its right to exist. It is only in its loyal carrying out of this task that the university can justify its existence to the working sections of the nation and the community which, by their support, enable it to live. The so-called 'humanities', precisely because they are maintained by the community, thus impose an even greater responsibility on those who teach them and on those who study them at university. They stress the *serving* function of academic professional skill as the tangent along which the intellectual can exercise his leading function in this world.

The Catholic university teacher carries out exactly the same intellectual activity as his colleague who does not believe and he does so in accordance with the same inner laws which govern every science. In this sense, science or learning is simply and solely scientific, not christian or Catholic. But the christian's practice of it forms part of a higher totality— it is experienced as God's gift to man through man's service of charity in science and living thought. It thus becomes an expression of God's love of man in the historical, tangible form which our intellectual service to mankind gives to this divine gift. From the christian point of view, it is an apostolate of the intellect. As J. H. Walgrave has rightly said, 'The most important task of the university is to form perspicacious, discerning, clear-thinking and critical leaders of the human community in its present stage of existence.'[7] In a really vital university, then, the so-called Studium Generale, in which, against an ideological background, e.g. the Catholic view of life, illuminated by theological study, is brought face to face at the academic level with the contemporary problems of society, has to be the living heart of the academic world, so that the specialised studies of the different faculties can be given their fully human form. This should not be regarded as something that places too heavy a burden on the shoulders of the students or as a necessary evil, but as an urgent necessity that has to be carried out even at the expense of reducing the burden of certain aspects of the specialised subjects. In this context, it is perhaps significant that several social philosophers have, for some years past, been making an impassioned plea for a 'judicious pruning' of the amount of material to be studied as a condition for the urgent task of the truly humanistic aim of the university system.

This wider perspective of academic training will enable the university student who has completed his studies to look forward more confidently to his future. The synthesis which he will later have to make between his task in his family, his professional activity and his responsibility towards the world, can only benefit the nation and the church. The really christian intellectual will, through the creativity of his mature, personal conscience, be able to assess things according to their individual value and merit—this is, after all, his task and prerogative. It is only in this way that he, as someone who has received an academic education, will be able to accept his personal responsibility in the course of human history. Human freedom, that decisive factor in the development of human history, will thus become even more free and will, moreover, not become merely arbitrary, as man comes to regard the world not only from the more limited viewpoint

[7] Humanus, 'Vrijheid en universiteit', *Kultuurleven* 25 (1958), 650.

of his specialised study, but, presupposing this specialised point of view, is also able to raise himself vertically above the unsettled problems in which he is involved together with the world and to regard the world with a wider and more objective gaze and thus deal freely with these problems in truly human wisdom.

6. Although the principles to which I have referred here are rather general, it does at least seem to me that they may form the christian and humanist framework within which a consideration of our responsibility for the future may succeed.

In conclusion, I should like to say a word about the atmosphere of our expectation of the future. Our responsibility for the future is no more than a transposition to the human register of what is heard in the register of the *vox coelestis*—grace. We do not simply possess the future. Expectation of the future is only a human name for *hoping*, man's religious attitude to life. The more clearly our free commitment here and now to the future expresses a religious confidence, the more effectively will we, by our human activity, fashion the definitive future. Our courageous, free and competent movement towards the future is basically a question of being borne by God towards a kingdom of peace, love and joy. We work together with God at the future. Our responsibility can therefore only be borne insofar as we have sincere trust in the guidance that the Lord of history gives to us within the sphere which is assigned to us and in the activity that we undertake in this sphere, doing all that we can in good faith. Here too, intellectuals have a leading part to play, since what J. H. van den Berg has said concerning the responsibility of older people towards the younger generation, 'If adults are invisible, young people live in a mist,'[8] also applies, in a very special way, to the responsibility of intellectuals for the future of the world.

[8] *Metabletica*, Nijkerk 1956, 53.

13

THE SIGNIFICANCE OF A CATHOLIC UNIVERSITY FOR THE WORLD AND THE CHURCH

Introduction: uncertainty about the university system

When we consider how every country has been trying, since the end of the second world war, to frame a new statute for university, academic and scientific education, and read all that has been published in recent years—much of it written almost in a mood of panic—about the 'idea of the university',[1] it is clear that the situation in which the university finds itself today is critical. Indeed, the question is even asked—has the university not lost its fundamental significance as a humanising factor? Has it not become a heterogeneous composition of specialised studies and laboratories in which everyone goes his own way, while the great problems confronting man in the world of today and thus the fate of mankind in the situation in which we live—a situation that is full of promise, yet at the same time in a critical stage—are really settled outside the university? For at least half a century, the view prevailed that 'committed' science inevitably lost its scientific character. Then the 'dehumanisation' and, in that sense, the 'objectivisation' of learning and science, which had gone furthest in the natural sciences, suffered a severe blow when very many atomic scientists found that their consciences were disturbed and began to question the *human meaning* of their discoveries. They realised to their dismay that their 'pure' science was simply a function in military policy. In spite of everything, their science was in fact engaged, not in a grand

---

[1] In the case of Germany, I am reminded here of the monumental symposium, *Universität und moderne Welt. Ein internationales Symposion,* ed. R. Schwartz, Berlin 1962 and, in the case of the Netherlands, of the journal *Universiteit en Hogeschool,* which is edited in collaboration by members of all the Dutch universities and was, in 1962, in its eleventh year of publication.

project for the humanisation of life, but in a military strategy. The 'Oppenheimer affair' was the shock that led to reflection. This was just one factor among many which made men question the human meaning of science and which made it clear that man cannot live by science alone, that science is only one factor in the large-scale plan to create a world more worthy of man. However much learning and science are objectivised, man still remains their *subject*. Our being man is always involved in them—it is ultimately always a question of man in his knowing being in the world and in his control of the world. It is said that a representative of the 'civilised' world once landed by aeroplane among sceptical primitive people and boasted to them that he covered a distance in one day that would take them at least a month to cover. One wise native replied to this, 'What do you do with the other thirty days, then?' That is what it ultimately amounts to.

1. The idea of the university

Every science points beyond itself to man's being and philosophical anthropology is itself based, like all other sciences, on a metaphysical prior datum, namely that reality exists and can, in principle, be understood. A pre-scientific view of the world precedes all science and indeed science is impossible without this view. After all, man experiences his existence in this world even before he reflects about it or thinks scientifically about it. This spontaneous being with oneself in the world is the only access to the various branches of learning and scientific thought. We *understand* reality in a pre-reflective manner in this spontaneous lived encounter with that reality. Thoughts and ideas arise and through these ideas we interpret reality and our life in this world in the mode of living experience. What is more, we always find ourselves in a world which is already full of meanings given to it by man— a *human* world. No single scholar of any kind is able to avoid this 'historical prior datum'.[2] In this way, our immediate experience of the world is included within an interpretation of

[2] See Karl Rahner, 'Science as a "Confession"?', *Theological Investigations* 3, London and Baltimore (Md) 1967, 385–400.

the world, man's consciousness of the world. We may therefore say that our consciousness of the world, which precedes
all science, is an ideology, since human existence is always an
existence which thinks about itself. The pure fact (and this *is*
at the same time something capable of being understood) of
my living as man in a world is already living within a certain
vision of reality. Pre-reflective experience, however confused
this may be, is always an understanding perception. The
driving force behind our seeking being in this world is therefore an *existential need*—'We must conceive the world *in
thought*, since it is otherwise impossible for us to live in it.'[3]
The fundamental existential question—how man can sustain
himself in the material, natural world—is at the origin of
man's exact knowledge of his environment, of the natural
sciences and of technology. But then other questions arise.
What is the purpose of living? What is the meaning of reality
and of human existence within that reality? Man's un-
solicited being in a world that is equally unasked for is a
problem that he is unable to avoid except by rejecting the
problem as meaningless. It is possible to distinguish three
closely interconnected aspects in man's *conscious* pre-
reflective existence in the world, that is, in his pre-scientific
view of the world. These are a physical image of the world,
a metaphysical view of the world and finally an ethical view
of man.

Both philosophy and positive scientific research into the
natural world and the humanities thus have a pre-scientific
presupposition, that of pre-reflective *human* experience. As
human experience, this pre-reflective experience is, however
confused it may be, always a conscious experience and therefore a 'view of the world'. This experience is also the wide
horizon or background against which all our detailed reflection, whatever it may be, stands out. It is only when one
aspect of this pre-reflective experience, for example, that of
social relationships, attracts man's concentrated attention
(and this is partly dependent on the social and economic
situation) that a new science and a new specialised study is

[3] J. H. Walgrave, *Person and Society*, Pittsburgh Pa. 1965, 17.

born. It is precisely because man's pre-scientific experience has ontological, ethical and anthropological implications that a systematised concentration of man's attention on one special aspect of his pre-reflective experience means a *formalisation*. This formalisation, however, continues to stand out against the wider background which will ignore the new, specialised field of study as such and, despite its abstract quality, to *point*, within the whole of man's understanding being in the world, *towards* the original totality and ultimately towards the metaphysical prior datum.

The consequence of this formalisation is that a science, as a *human* science, will not be complete when it reaches a result and even a certain *synthesis* purely within its own formalised approach. The intelligibility of this formalised science and its achievement of practical results for man's life will undoubtedly be of great value, but the partial datum on which light has been thrown from within has ultimately to be *integrated* into the totality from which it was originally derived by means of formalisation. Because the content of pre-reflective experience gave rise to many formalised sciences, the so-called 'interdisciplinary approach' is bound to play an indispensable part in this re-integration. But no reliable reflective insight into an original totality can be gained simply by dialogue between those who practise the various positive sciences and who now claim a monopoly of scientific thought for themselves or by reconstructing this totality by combining the partial aspects on which light has been thrown by means of formalisation.

This is the task of philosophy which, as a science, has spontaneous, pre-reflective consciousness as its sole object and attempts to throw light on this totality as such. It takes as its point of departure a phenomenological ascertainment of the facts on which it proposes to throw light according to their intelligibility. In so doing, it does not ignore the results of research in the field of the positive sciences, since these results point to an authentic aspect of the original datum and do so in spite of formalisation, which philosophy has to some extent to 'do away with' by means of a transposition, if the scientific insight is to be really relevant to philosophy.

Original pre-reflective experience thus requires two complementary studies. On the one hand, because of the confused character of this experience of totality, there is a need for the specialised study of the positive sciences. On the other hand, its original totality itself also demands an inter-disciplinary approach and philosophical reflection.

Leaving the question of theology aside for the time being, it is possible to say that the idea and the ideal of the university as the *universitas scientiarum* grew from this situation. The main reason for combining the various independent branches of learning and science in one common university centre is therefore not purely utilitarian, in other words, simply, for example, for the purpose of accommodation. On the contrary, the university is an *intrinsic* demand of the intelligibility of reality and, within this, of human existence. The university is required because every partial reality is interconnected within the totality of reality and because every branch of learning and science, however 'dehumanised' it may be, has a *human* significance. As a *human* science, every science needs to listen to what the other sciences have to say about reality and all sciences need to be illuminated by philosophy. The factors which bind the *universitas scientiarum* together, then, are philosophy and the idea of humanity. (I shall consider the central importance of religion at a later stage.)

If philosophy and the idea of humanity do not constitute the basic principle of the structure of the university, then the university, as *universitas*, no longer has any reason to exist. It renounces its task and its vocation and becomes, from the totally human point of view, no more than a torso—a hetero-geneous collection of scholars and not an ordered *polis* of wise, learned men, from whom mankind may expect an important and indeed irreplaceable contribution to the humanisation of the world and of man himself. It will not play its part in periods of crisis and into whose hands will the fate of the world fall then? Of course, the university is not a parliament, a UNO, a world government or an organisation to help underdeveloped countries. It does not bring salvation to mankind. On the other hand, however, it does not only provide a professional training, 'producing' lawyers, doctors, social workers, politicians and so on.

The universities are the brains of the world. They place conscious human existence on the level of reflection. Scientific thought is, of course, only one of the factors which promote man's progress towards increasingly more praiseworthy humanity. Certainly, the sciences and philosophy have *human* value and significance only in *relation* to other sectors which are of value to human life—there are also ways of making the free, simple experience of human existence in the world explicit that lie outside the realm of scholarship. But scientific thought in the university—as the *universitas scientiarum* and not simply as a collection of different sciences—has a distinctive and inalienable function which cannot be renounced without bringing disaster on mankind. As the 'university of the sciences', the university takes the pre-scientific view of the world which is inherent to man's consciousness of being in the world as its point of departure and ends with a critically justified idea of the world. Precisely because of its scientific thought and its academic freedom, which is bound only to the truth in order to set it free, the university points in every direction towards a view of the world without which it is not good for man to live in this world. We have come to realise, as a result of the present crisis in the university system, that any reaction against a connection between the 'university' and a view of the world, even though, in the past, this connection was frequently unscientific and therefore alien to the university, must be regarded, on purely scientific grounds, as superseded. Any division between the university and a view of the world is moreover a fiction, since the rejection of any world-view cannot be justified by positive science as such and is therefore an option which lies outside the realm of science and this implies, at least negatively, a view of the world.

2. The Catholic university

1. Seen against this background, the idea of the Catholic university will cause less *a priori* surprise. All the same, we should not ignore the real problems that it presents. In the first place, we must try to clear the field in advance by dispelling various prejudices. The most persistent of these is undoubtedly that academic freedom and adherence to religious dogma are contradictory,[4] as though freedom and being bound had to be contradictory and freedom had to be identified with arbitrariness! The sense of knowing itself to be bound to truth and only to truth is the very charter of the university. It is from this adherence to truth that the university derives the whole of its academic freedom, even its freedom with regard to political powers.[5] Now, by definition, faith offers itself to us as a being bound to divine *truth*. This being bound to divine truth is certainly accomplished in surrender to faith, but its ethically meaningful content is nonetheless critically justified in advance.[6] Despite their completely different character, faith and science are fundamentally very similar to each other in that they are both bound to truth and only to truth.

We may go farther and say that the conviction that the world of human experience is man's *only* access to all truth is shared by both faith and science. Outside human experience, there is no other mysterious source of knowledge. How could a divine revelation which took place outside our experience be heard? How could it, in other words, be a revelation to man? There can be no knowledge of realities

---

[4] See N. Luyten, 'Idee und Aufgabe einer katholischen Universität', *Universität und moderne Welt*, 593–609; see also *Theology and the University. An Ecumenical Investigation*, ed. J. Coulson, London 1964.

[5] We may even ask whether—and to what extent—state intervention in university teaching, however necessary this may be because of subsidies and their just distribution among the various universities within the state, does not infringe this academic freedom and is therefore, to the same extent, a disservice to the population. In the medieval *universitas doctorum et studentium*, exemption from all authority apart from that of the university itself was a *conditio sine qua non*.

[6] See E. Schillebeeckx, *God and Man* (Theological Soundings 2), London and New York 1969, 162–79.

of which no human experience of any kind is given. Human perception, as the basis of all man's knowledge, means that the *world* is, for us, the only access to explicit knowledge here and now of all other possible spheres of reality, in other words, of total reality. In this sense, we know primarily only the material world and *thus* everything that is connected with this material world and insofar as it has any connection with it—in the first place, me and my fellow-man, precisely *as* a being in the world, then God, *as* the creator of this world or, possibly, *as* manifesting himself in grace *in this world*. It is precisely because of this that divine revelation, according to the christian view, takes place in human history, which thereby becomes salvation-history. Man's conscious being in the world is thus the basis and the matrix of science and of faith.

In certain scientific circles, there is, on the one hand, a tendency to limit truth to what is directly verifiable or, on the other hand, not to regard the 'world' as man's only access to all other realities, but rather to see it as the *enclosing horizon* of all human knowledge.[7] This is, however, a non-verifiable *postulate* which lies outside the realm of science and thus goes back to a pre-scientific interpretation of the world. Not only is this particular previously given view of the world open to criticism—the idea that faith or the religious view of the world cannot justifiably be accorded a place within the university system is also not scientific, but ideological. Why, then, should the acceptance of the transcendence of being and consequently of the transcendental range of the human spirit not have a place in the university when the denial of this transcendence does have a place, if both the affirmation and the negation of this concept lie outside the sphere of scientific thought—if, in other words, they both transcend positive science? The acceptance of the absolute openness of the human spirit to the totality of reality seems to me to be the real reason for the very existence of a *universitas scientiarum*, just as it is also the condition of the

[7] M. Merleau-Ponty, 'La métaphysique dans l'homme', *Sens et non-sens*, Paris 1948, 165–95.

possibility of every branch of learning and science. This is precisely why I insisted, in the first part of this argument, on the central place of philosophy in the university—a position recently accorded to it in the Dutch law on higher education, in which philosophy was raised to the level of a separate faculty with the significant name of 'central interfaculty'.

Religious faith—and christianity in particular—maintains that man in his absolute openness is always confronted by the absolute person of God who, because he is a person, can manifest himself in grace and has in fact done so. Indeed, it is even possible to say that this divine revelation is *necessary*, that it is the very essence of God himself in comparison with us. Either God speaks or he is silent. But in view of the transcendental openness of the human spirit, God's silence, his non-revelation of himself, would acquire for man the significance of a revelation, because even God's possible silence would signify something for the absolute openness of the human spirit[8] and indicate something about an ultimate meaning—or in that case rather a non-sense—of human life. That is why, by virtue of the transcendental openness of his spirit—and thus on a *human* basis, not on the basis of a mysterious, unique and irrational source of knowledge—man must *a priori* take a possible speaking on God's part into account. If God positively speaks, this speaking is, on the basis of the transcendental openness of man's spirit, the highest fulfilment of man's being. This fulfilment is certainly transcendent, but it is nonetheless *inward* and through it man is at the same time *revealed to himself*. Faith thus discloses a very special perspective, that of man who fully realises himself only in a situation of salvation which God offers to him in the sovereign freedom of his grace.

Only then can man realise that without this grace, which he cannot claim for himself, he is not so completely self-evident and that his deepest questions about human life and especially about his ultimate fate cannot be solved even by the *universitas scientiarum*, if faith and therefore theology

[8] See, among others, Karl Rahner, *Hearers of the Word*, London and New York 1969, 94.

are banished from it. The ultimate consistency of man's being would then be undermined. The *universitas scientiarum*, with its interdisciplinary approach and philosophy, therefore calls for a theological faculty, precisely because of the idea of totality and of humanity which dominates the university. The idea of humanity thus forms the inward link between religion and scientific thought in the university. This attitude is, in any case, just as scientifically justified as the attitude which accords no place in the university to faith. In other words, it is possible, if need be, to reject all religion and christianity, but it is impossible ever to say that the integration of faith into the university system implies the destruction or violation of the idea of the university.

We can go even farther. I have already referred to lived, simple experience as the prior datum for all scientific thought. If, according to the religious view, man is always confronted in the transcendental openness of his spirit by the God of grace, this implies that revelation in acceptance or refusal is present in every simple experience, either implicitly or anonymously, and that man's concrete attitude of acceptance and affirmation of this mystery of life is already true faith, the unspoken primordial form of religious faith. Religion is the making public of the true form of a way of life which diffidently and reverently approaches the mystery of objective reality and allows itself to be directed by it. Faith thus takes hold of man in that transcendental openness of his spirit which is also the condition of the possibility of every branch of learning and science. Faith can therefore, in principle, not be violated in its existence and in its confession by any science. Just as science or learning cannot give me faith, so they cannot take my faith away either. If, then, science in one form or another is the critical explicitation of the lived experience in which I, as a man, associate with the world of things and other men, then this inexpressible reality which is the prior datum for all scientific thought also requires that scientific explicitation which we call *theology*.

This demonstrates, then, from the point of view of the presupposition of all sciences, that theology, as man's reflection about faith and the reality of this world in the light of that faith, can occupy a meaningful and indeed a central place in the *universitas scientiarum*. Indeed, it also shows that, for the believer, theology, in addition to philosophy, must really be given the name of 'central interfaculty', since the theologian aims to penetrate to the deepest ground of all reality and humanity, although he does this by reflecting about *faith*. The theologian also needs to live in contact with the other faculties, because it is from these that the 'problems' which he has to consider come. A theological institute outside the university suffers from being placed in a predicament which is essentially precarious for theology itself. If theology is to be practised under the most favourable conditions, it essentially requires to be geared to and to form part of a *universitas scientiarum*, in which cross-fertilisation can also take place within the structure of the system itself. It is precisely this which is lacking in a separate theological institute since what is brought to light by scientific research is also of importance to our understanding of revelation, and the profane sciences in turn also need the light that can be thrown on them by the ultimate meaning of reality. If the theologian loses touch with the other, evolving branches of learning or science, he will inevitably fail in his christian interpretation, for example, of the modern process of secularisation and of the new dimension in which man has come to live because of the increasing influence of science on human society.

2. In what I have said so far, I have done no more than simply indicate, on the basis of the idea of humanity and the need for the various sciences to live in contact with each other at the university, on the one hand, the scientific necessity of a theological faculty in the university and, on the other, the necessity of a university if theology is to be carried out to the best advantage. So far, however, I have said nothing about the right to existence that a specifically 'Catholic university' might claim, even admitted that a faculty of *Catholic* theology is vital for a university. The idea of a general 'secular university' is perfectly meaningful and such a university could

have, for example, not only a faculty of Catholic theology, but also faculties of Protestant theology, buddhist theology or even a mixed christian 'ecumenical' faculty. In our present pluralistic society, which is so dependent on dialogue, this type of arrangement clearly offers great advantages. No case for a Catholic—or Protestant—university ought, in my opinion, to be based on a plea for any solely right or exclusively justified possibility—it should only be a plea for one possibility among many. The danger of narrowness and prejudice is, after all, always real in any 'confessional' university, even though this is in contradiction to the academic spirit. But the confessional university undoubtedly has its own special advantages, at least insofar as it remains open to the free interchange of ideas with universities with a differently orientated view of life. The right of a Catholic university to exist must now be examined.

My fundamental concern here is to define the place of the Catholic university in *contemporary* society. This does not exclude the possibility that a Catholic university may have been established in the past for different reasons, which we now perhaps tend to regard as superseded.

The dispute between faith and science, for which the churches themselves were partly to blame, led to the historical development of the universities into bastions of anti-religious opinion. Views which were hostile to religion and the church predominated in many 'secular' universities and many Catholic universities went in for 'concordism' to an almost ridiculous degree. From the historical point of view, it is clear that the Catholic universities established since the nineteenth century were founded in order to make it quite manifest that christians were also able to practise science properly and without prejudice—although it often became obvious at that time how much leeway still had to be made up. Other reasons also played a part in the establishment of these Catholic universities, as was also the case in the setting up of all kinds of Catholic—and Protestant—organisations at that time, the main intention being to provide a 'germ-free' environment for christian students and to protect them from the 'dangers of the public universities'. We must respect the practical 'truth' and the ethical imperatives of those days. What I am concerned with here is to define the *contemporary* place of the Catholic university.

It should, of course, be stressed that this is quite different from a faculty of Catholic theology in a non-Catholic university. The idea of unity which characterises a scientifically pluriform university, the universality of the spirit which is the distinctive feature of the university system, is in a Catholic university the catholicity of the Catholic view of life which presupposes philosophically the transcendental openness of the human spirit as the necessary *praeambulum fidei*. This idea of unity applies to the whole of such a university. In other words, every university teacher or student, even if he is not a Catholic, knows that this idea is structurally the 'inspiration' of this university system as a whole and not only of the theological faculty.

I should like to add at once that this situation does not in any sense imply that the non-theological sciences are subject to a certain guardianship, as though 'Catholic' biology or 'Catholic' astronomy could ever become a meaningful possibility. The catholicity of the Catholic view of life requires that every individual science should be carried out freely and impartially while being bound in freedom to truth within its own formalised sector. In this, all guardianship is pernicious, whether it is exercised by other sciences, by philosophy, by faith or by the churches. On the other hand, we have seen that each formalised sphere of truth stands out against a total horizon, a wider background which ignores the specialised field of learning or science as such, but towards which the content of truth of each science always continues to point. It is within this totality that the Catholic view of life has an essential part to play. It is not in the individual sciences as such, but in the idea of totality on which the concept of the *universitas* of the sciences is based and from which the university as such derives its right to exist that the Catholic view of life has an essential function. The individual, specialised sciences cannot be 'Catholic' sciences, but the *universitas scientiarum* as such is certainly Catholic. This means that it is not only among the philosophers and the theologians teaching at a Catholic university that there must be a lively concern to integrate the achievements of science into thought about faith. This concern is a *scientific task* to be undertaken by *all* members of the academic staff, a task which gives the Catholic university its true right to exist only when it is seen and practised as an *equally original* task as the practice of science itself. Even though the philosophers and the theologians have a distinctive and irreplaceable part to play in throwing light on the totality of the *universitas scientiarum* (because their own 'special' subject, unlike that of the other, specialised scientists, is directly related to this totality), the Catholic university would not be able to justify its right to exist if the other faculties were to delegate this consideration of the totality, and thereby the philosophical and theological concern, to the philosophers and theologians alone. In that case it could equally well take place in the theological faculty of a non-Catholic university. The idea of a specifically Catholic university would thus be superfluous. That is why, in my opinion, some grounding in philosophy and theology is an essential requirement even for those who do not teach philosophy and theology at a Catholic university, if such a university, precisely as a university, is to justify its title of 'Catholic' and to make it both true and effective. If, for example, specialists in the natural sciences are to achieve a total view which will unite both faith and the scientific image of the world, they must also be able to think theologically. The theologian who is not himself a physicist cannot do this separately or even in cooperation with the members of the theological faculty alone. However valuable it may be, it is not enough for him simply to receive a few fundamental data, for example, from the science faculty. The physicist, on the other hand, is not as such a philosopher or a theologian, but because, as a human being, he has a spirit which, of its very nature, seeks meaning and is directed towards a total view, he is bound, as a man, to think spontaneously about the meaning of his scientific truth in the totality of reality and of human existence. A biologist, for example, cannot as such make any statement about man. All that he can do as a biologist is to make a biological statement about man. If, for example, his observation of the atrophy of man's ethical and religious sense after leucotomy leads him to conclude that man's sense of religion is no more than an accompanying phenomenon or a function of a certain configuration of the nervous system, he is in fact stepping outside his own scientific sphere and acting as a philosopher (and perhaps not always as a good philosopher with sufficient understanding of the method and principles of philosophy). It is, of course, because man is, of his very nature, bound to ask questions about the totality of reality that there is always a danger that the scientist will uncritically overstep the boundaries of his own science and make non-scientific, but philosophical and theological statements resulting from his own scientific insights. The believer too may similarly 'integrate' his faith and his scientific findings uncritically, with the consequence that he will do a disservice both to his faith and to his own science. Man's spontaneous inclination to make statements about the totality of reality—a tendency which has its origin in the transcendental openness of the human spirit—must be countered, both ascetically and methodically, within each science, in order to safeguard the scientific principles of each department of science. On the other hand, however, justice must also be done to this spontaneous tendency, and especially at the university level, but this must take place in a scientific and reflective manner. This means that *all* members of the academic staff have to some degree to be involved in philosophical and theological reflection, approaching it from their own special point of view. All those teaching at the Catholic university must be anxious and ready to make their own contribution to a critically justified, unified view of the totality of reality and thus to the ultimate meaning of man's existence in the light of the Catholic faith. They must not, in other words, be exclusively concerned with the specialised scientific problems (and freedom) of their own particular branch of learning within their own faculty. It is only then that the specifically Catholic university, both as Catholic and as a university, can justify its claim to exist and make its title both true and effective in contemporary society.

It is, of course, true that the development of science and—especially as far as the natural sciences are concerned—the purity of the scientific method are not checked or impeded by the absence of a religious view of life. But if man's need to give meaning to his existence and the *integration* of the findings of science into the total view of life are regarded as important, then we are bound to conclude that science must suffer from this lack in its deepest, human significance, even if it is only that scientists will, in the absence of a religious view of life, put forward their own insights (and their philosophical insights) into the totality of reality as valid ultimate and definitive statements. This would have very far-reaching consequences for the ultimate meaning of man's existence. We can, after all, only ascertain this ultimate meaning as God's grace. If we do not allow this to play a part in the discussion, then an authentic, but nonetheless purely partial task of our being man may be regarded as man's total task and to allow something that is not the whole of our concrete state of being man to be accepted as the last word could have a depersonalising influence on our being.

On the other hand, the decisive words that God has spoken about human life in word and deed do not make man's seeking superfluous—revelation gives a perspective to his seeking. The God of creation and salvation, in whom the believer places his trust, is not a direct *criterion* of truth for man. He is rather the ultimate *guarantee* that our seeking for the truth is not meaningless. 'God is not a ready-made solution, but the demand to find a solution and at the same time the guarantee that it is, after all, not absurd to seek for a meaning and to realise a task.'[9] The Catholic university teacher finds that his christian view of life, firstly practised in all that he does as a believer and secondly serving as a factor that throws light on the ultimate meaning of his life as a scientist in this world,

[9] See J. Lacroix, *Le sens de l'athéisme moderne*, Tournai and Paris 1958, 58–64.

does not act as an impediment to his free and impartial seeking for truth and its ultimate basis, but rather that it offers him a liberating perspective which will lead him, through the darkness, into the ultimate truth which is finally revealed to us in grace. The scientific integration of the achievements of science and religious thought takes place in the Catholic *universitas scientiarum*. As a *scientific* integration in a balanced, unified view of life (which is progressive and can be considered again and again), this integration is, of its very nature, the task of a *universitas* of teachers and students within the framework of a *universitas* of the sciences. That is why specifically Catholic universities are required by the Catholic faith of thinking men. Since the Catholic faith is, in the concrete, only one faith among many in a world which seems to be becoming more and more secular in its view of life, the Catholic university can only make its idea of the university true in constant dialogue with other, not specifically Catholic universities. This means that the academic task of the individual Catholic teacher or student does not in itself have to be accomplished within a Catholic university. The Catholic university, however, is—or should be—a very special visible sign, to the world of men and to the other universities, of an ordered, collective christian love, which will make it known that the scientific studies of a Catholic *universitas scientiarum* also contributes to the salvation of man, both in his expectations for the future of mankind here on earth and in his eschatological expectations.

TABLE OF ORIGINAL PUBLICATION

World and Church is a translation of *Wereld en Kerk* (Theologische Peilingen III), published by Uitgeverij H. Nelissen, Bilthoven, Netherlands, 1966, with the omission of §1 (pp 11–58) of the original, which dealt with the situation in the decade immediately following the second world war. The remaining material was originally published as indicated below.

1 **Religion and the world: renewing the face of the earth**
First published as 'Godsdienst en wereld: het aanschijn der aarde vernieuwen' in *Het geestelijk leven van de leek* (Drakenburgh-conferenties 1951), Tilburg 1951, 7–27.

2 **Humble humanism**
First published as 'Nederig humanisme' in *Kultuurleven* 16–1 (1949), 12–21.

3 **Priest and layman in a secular world**
This chapter is based on talks given to young Dominicans in 1952 and 1953, and was previously printed in a magazine circulating among Dominican candidates for the priesthood. The Dutch title was 'Het kerkelijk apostolaat in verband met de situatie 1945–1954'. The original article has been slightly shortened.

4 **The sorrow of the experience of God's concealment**
This chapter was originally a lecture to the congress of the joint student unions of the theology faculties of the Dutch-speaking world and was first published under the title 'Het leed der ervaring van Gods verborgenheid' in *Kerugma* 9 (1966) no 4.

5 **Church and world**
This chapter is based on a lecture given at the opening of the new building of the Dutch Documentation Centre for the Council (DOC) in Rome in September 1964. This version first appeared as 'Kerk en wereld' in *Tijdschrift voor Theologie* 4 (1964), 386–99.

6 The church and mankind

First published as 'Kerk en mensdom' in *Concilium* 1 (1965)1, 63–83.

7 The ecclesial life of religious man

First published as 'De kerkelijkheid van de godsdienstige mens' in *Tijdschrift voor Geestelijk Leven* XV–1 (1959), 108–31.

8 Supranaturalism, unchristian and christian expectations of the future

First published as 'De plaag van onchristelijke toekomstverwachtingen' in *Kultuurleven* 26 (1959), 504–13.

9 Christians and non-christians: 1. The theory of toleration

'The dialogue' first appeared as 'Het gesprek' in *Nederlands Gespreks Centrum*, Publ. 1 (n.s.), Kampen-Utrecht 1960, 11–16.

'Toleration' first appeared as 'Tolerantie' in the DOC Papers, Rome 1962. An earlier English translation by H. J. J. Vaughan appeared in A. von Geusau (ed.), *Ecumenism and the Roman Catholic Church*, London 1969, 169–86.

10 Christians and non-christians 2. Practical cooperation

'Social structures, social work and charity' was prepared in 1962 as a paper for the Dutch National Centre for Catholic Social and Charitable Work and later revised for the International Congress for Social Work, Santiago (Spain), 1965. The Dutch title was 'Sociale structuren, matchappelijk werk en charitas'.

'The Catholic hospital and health service' first appeared as 'Het katholieke ziekenhuis en de katholieke gezondheidszorg' in *Ons Ziekenhuis* 20 (1958), 317–25 and *Hospitalia* 4 (1959), 29–35.

11 Man and his bodily world

'The christian approach to human bodiliness' was originally a contribution to a symposium organised by the medical faculty of the University of Nijmegen and was published under the title 'Christelijke benadering van de menselijke lichamelijkheid' in the proceedings of the symposium, *Symposion. Het centrale zenuwstelsel. Zijn relatie tot de psychische activiteit.*

'The animal in man's world' was originally a lecture given at the opening of the University of Nijmegen Animal Laboratory and was first published as 'Het dier in de "umwelt" van de mens' in *Katholiek Artsenblad* 39 (1960), 58–63.

12 **The intellectual's responsibility for the future**
Originally a lecture given to the Roland Society of Nijmegen University in November 1958 and first published as 'De verantwoordelijkheid van de intellectueel voor de toekomst' in *Roeping* 34 (1958), 390–99.

13 **The significance of a Catholic university for the world and the church**
Written for the *Festschrift* published to mark the seventy-fifth anniversary of the founding of the university of Fribourg (Switzerland), *Recherche et culture. Tâches d'une université catholique/Forschung und Bildung. Aufgaben einer katholischen Universität*, Fribourg 1965, 33–48 (French), 35–51 (German). This translation has been made from the original Dutch text, 'De betekenis van een katholieke universiteit voor wereld en kerk'.

INDEX

ALBERT (the Great), St, 110
 on humility, 19–20
Animal life, 235f, 237, 257–68 *passim*,
  269
 and man, 257–8
 in the bible, 263–8
 morality of laboratory experiments,
  257, 261–3, 268
Anonymous faith
 implicit christianity, 32ff, 93, 101f,
  103ff, 107, 125, 126f, 132
 moves towards church, 127
Apostolate of the church, 32ff, 35,
  153ff
 priestly, 36–66, 67, 74–6
 lay, 66–74, 76
 sacramental, 36, 42, 44–6, 47, 48,
  55–6
Atheism, 32, 78, 83–4, 86, 95, 165,
  181f
Augustine, St, quoted, 19, 29, 36, 37,
  39, 140

BEAUVOIR, SIMONE DE, on existential-
  ism, 3
Bernanos, G., quoted, 14
Bonaventure, St, on humility, 19
Brémond, A., 22n

CAMUS, A., 4
Care of the sick, 213–29 *passim*
 inspired by religious belief, 214,
  219, 220–4
 importance of *caritas*, 223f, 226ff
 duty of both christian and non-
  christian, 217f, 219f
 in a Catholic hospital, 224–9
 see also Hospitals and Health service
Caritas, see Social work and Care of
  the sick
Carrel, A., 239
Catholic Action, 67, 69
Celsus, attacked christian humility,
  22, 29
Christianity, 9, 11f, 99f, 137ff, 184f,
  208, 290
 implies commitment to human
  solidarity, 90, 94, 97f, 133ff, 138,
  156, 158
 and the church, 146, 161f

and the world, 1f
 implicit christianity, *see* Anonymous faith
 explicit christianity (explicit faith),
  32f, 101f, 104f
 in care of the sick, 218f, 220–4
Chrysostom, John, St, on humility, 22
Church, 29, 53f, 60, 66, 96–114 *passim*, 119
 and salvation, 33, 54, 98, 101, 122,
  132f, 146, 157, 217
 the sacrament of the world, 91–5
 founded by Christ, 119f, 121f, 123f
 as motive for faith, 151–7
 founded in love, 135f, 162
 is Christ's grace on earth, 126, 140,
  145–8, 157, 158
 twofold activity, 34ff, 66–7, 133f,
  147f
 tensions between church and world,
  96–114, 110, 119, 122, 124–36, 137
 tends towards 'sanctifying secularisation', 115, 137
 missionary activity, 54ff, 57, 127,
  133
 social teaching, 103f, 108, 110–14
 views on popular superstition, 174–
  176
 attitude to liberalism, 188ff
 hierarchical, not responsible for
  social ordering, 72f, 96, 217, 226
 more than the hierarchy, 160f
 weaknesses of, 149ff
 needs to be brought up to date,
  84–6, 113
 in pagan world, 140–2
 of Israel, 143–5
 see also Apostolate of the church,
  Social work and Tolerance
'Clericalism', 73
Coccioli, C., 14, 155
Communio
 community of persons, 115–18, *passim*, 120, 123f, 126, 128, 131, 134
 a gift of God, 116
 achieved in the 'church of Christ',
  118, 119, 120, 122, 158
Communism, 3f, 32, 47, 65
Conscience, *see under* Freedom
'Cosmos', 5ff, 13
 replaced by kingdom of God, 8